CHILLED WINE
AND
ASSORTED DESSERTS

An anthology of stories and poems

By

March & Doddington Writers' Circle

Published 2006 by arima publishing

www.arimapublishing.com

ISBN 1 84549 160 2
ISBN 978 1 84549 160 4

© March & Doddington Writers' Circle 2006

All rights reserved

This book is copyright. Subject to statutory exception and to provisions of relevant collective licensing agreements, no part of this publication may be reproduced, stored in a retrieval system, or transmitted in any form or by any means, without the prior written permission of the author.

Printed and bound in the United Kingdom

Typeset in Garamond 11/14

This book is sold subject to the conditions that it shall not, by way of trade or otherwise, be lent, re-sold, hired out, or otherwise circulated without the publisher's prior consent in any form of binding or cover other than that which it is published and without a similar condition including this condition being imposed on the subsequent purchaser.

Swirl is an imprint of arima publishing.

arima publishing
ASK House, Northgate Avenue
Bury St Edmunds, Suffolk IP32 6BB
t: (+44) 01284 700321

www.arimapublishing.com

This anthology is dedicated to the memory of

Jean Miller,

much loved member of the March & Doddington Writers' Circle and treasured friend – sorely missed by members of the Club.

PREFACE

This anthology is a collection of the work of past and present members of the March & Doddington Writers' Circle. The 'Circle was formed 20 years ago by a small group of people who had a common interest, that of the written word and creative writing. This anthology was produced specifically in celebration of those 20 years of friendship, companionship and the furtherance of members' interest in developing their writing skills.

Over the years, members have come and gone, but a nucleus of writers has remained to carry on the traditions evolved by "the club". Some members have, sadly, passed away in the time intervening since the club was established. Their inclusion in this anthology is by way of homage to their memory and their contribution to the work of the club. Other people have retained their membership, but have moved far away from the club's normal meeting venues. Nonetheless, they have continued to contribute to the club and its biannual magazine, "The Quill". Yet other members have left the club for their own reasons and we have lost contact with them. Even so, we have included selections of the work of some of these members, whose membership spanned several years.

"The Quill" came into being relatively soon after the club became established. It has remained as the Circle's main vehicle for the publication of its work. We have established a loyal group of readers and have regular contributors of advertising from local commerce. In addition to "The Quill", over the years the club has read its work to local clubs, societies and support groups, providing a rich source of live feedback. Many of the organisations we have read to have come back year after year to book us again for their entertainment programmes for their own members. Through our writing, we have been able arouse old memories of times past, thrill listeners with stories of murder and intrigue, make them laugh aloud with the reader in the presentation of a comedic piece, or elicited the occasional tear through the high emotion of poetry.

We are sure you will find something to enjoy as you progress from the initial story and it's "Chilled Wine" through the "Assorted Desserts" of short stories and poems to follow. We wish you good reading and above all, the opportunity to share in the joy we experienced in writing the pieces included in this book.

The March & Doddington Writers' Circle, Cambridgeshire, UK

CONTENTS

Title	Author	Page
The Gatherer	Phyllis Gall	1
Bull Run	Anne Melville	6
A Sister's Crime	Danny MacCullough	15
The Irish Men-of-War	Eddie Rose	30
The Men of March & Marcheford	Edna Stacey	34
Time to Deliver	Helen Stevens	40
Where the Heart Is	Herta Davey	45
Siggy	Jack Alster	50
Come Back, Mrs Froggart	Jean Miller	56
Carry Me Home	Joan Barnett	61
Alien Mountain Giants	Louis Barrow	63
Lucy	Mary Wise	67
The Tooth, the Whole Tooth & Nothing But the Tooth	Pamela Joyce	71
The Perfect Murder	Phyllis Gall	76
Just a Thought	Rita Carrol	80
A Real Bargain	Ron Radford	92
A Significant Tumble	John Coyne	95
Nowhere To Go	Dianne Wilson	116
In Loving Memory	Joan Barnett	117
Hands	Edna Stacey	118
Reflections on a February Evening	Joan Barnett	119
Drought	Elizabeth Canmelle	120
Autumn	Anne Melville	121
When We Were Young	Helen Stevens	122
Heard in the Bar at the Agricultural Show	Helen Stevens	123
Beyond the Windowpane	Jean Miller	124
Tranquillity	Louis Barrow	125
Change	Mary Oldham	126
Evening	Mary Oldham	127
The Loch Ness Monster	Mary Wise	128
I Think of You	Phyllis Gall	129
That's Show Business	Sandra Finney	130
Summer's End	Wyn Land	131
When We Were Lovers	Terry Schooling	132

CONTENTS

Flight	Warren Scott-Morrow	134
Fallen Trees	Mary Oldham	139
The Old Apple Tree	Mary Oldham	140
Ode to a Lover	Yani Birt	141
The Waterfall	Mary Oldham	142
The Doorway	Yani Birt	143
Wildlife of the Roadside Verge	Dianne Wilson	144
Take Me Back	Jean Miller	146
Harmony	Jean Miller	147
Spider	Sandra Finney	148
Aberfan	Terry Schooling	149
Nostalgia	Yani Birt	152
Saxophone Summer	Yani Birt	153
Awakening	Jean Miller	154
The Hydra-headed Monster	Jean Miller	155
Skylark Song	Joan Barnett	156
Washday Blues	Yani Birt	157
Inheritance	Marion Megit	158
Shall I Be Mother?	Sandra Finney	181
The Ten Minute Job	Phyllis Gall	182
Say It With Flowers	Sandra Finney	184
Time Wins	Warren Scott-Morrow	191
My Chosen Path	Wyn Land	198
Once We Were Famous	Edna Stacey	205
The White Car	Anne Melville	213
Wincey	Helen Stevens	221
To Love and to Hold	Herta Davey	229
The Market Howard Twenties Club	Jean Miller	232
Voyage to Ceylon	Joan Barnett	238
Down Came the Rain	Mary Wise	241
Frank's Day	Pamela Joyce	245
Heartbeats	Phyllis Gall	251
Lesson for a Libertine	Sandra Finney	256
That Was That	Wyn Land	261
PA845	Terry Schooling	266
I'm Getting Another Dog	Danny MacCullough	280

The Gatherer
By Phyllis Gall

Gold-rimmed white china was reflected in the gleaming patina of the oak table, silver and glassware sparkled in the lamplight as Sebastian glanced at the ormolu clock on the wall, which began to chime eight o'clock. Sebastian nodded with satisfaction. "Perfect", he whispered. Everything was ready. His fingertips lightly touched a glass, a napkin, a plate, as the doorbell rang.

'So', he thought, 'they begin to arrive'. He smiled as he thought of the evening ahead. Malicious concepts of his guests' eventual discomfort and alarm sent a satisfactory glow through him. This evening had taken time to prepare, but now the culmination of his plans had arrived.

A last look in the long hall mirror confirmed his sartorial elegance: the perfectly cut dinner suit, his thick, grey hair meticulously cut and styled, his lean handsome face with slanting eyes and eyebrows which gave his face a Mephistophelian look that he cultivated assiduously.

He opened the door and greeted the two people standing on the step.

"How good of you to come. Please, enter."

He held the door wide and smiled as his first guests slowly walked into the hallway. Inward satisfaction chortled through him as he saw the man and the woman half recoil from their image in the long mirror facing them. The mirror had been made especially for Sebastian, and gave a slightly distorted reflection which always caused people who saw it for the first time to look away hurriedly, not sure of what they had seen. Sebastian knew that the mirror made his visitors feel uncomfortable; he revelled in their discomfort and did nothing to alleviate their feelings.

His guests shivered as they hung their coats on the stand in the hall.

"Isn't it a beautiful evening?" said Sebastian.

"It's very cold out", replied the man. "I think there will be a sharp frost tonight."

"Probably", smiled Sebastian, as he ushered them both into the living room where the temperature was only slightly warmer.

"I don't think you know each other, do you?" asked Sebastian as he poured the aperitifs.

"Er, no", replied the man, "we met on the doorstep."

"Andrew Baristow, meet Pamela Kershaw. I feel you will know much more about each other before the evening is over."

Andrew and Pamela smiled at each other over their drinks, not really sure if they were allies or not.

The front door bell broke into the small hiatus.

"Ah, our other guest", said Sebastian, and he left the room.

"Have you known our host for long?" asked Pamela.

"I don't know him at all", said Andrew. "I received this strange invitation, silver letters on a black card, from a man named Sebastian Hobb. Do you know him? He is a stranger to me."

"No, I have no idea who he is …"

She stopped talking as Sebastian came back into the room with another lady.

"Allow me to introduce our final guest: Andrew, Pamela, meet Fiona Taylor. There, now we all know each other."

Sebastian smiled to himself as he crossed to the drinks cabinet and poured two more aperitifs, giving one to Fiona. 'I know your names', he mused inwardly, 'but you do not know mine', and he wanted to laugh out loud.

"I have given orders in the kitchen for dinner to be served immediately, so if you will please be seated", he said, ushering them towards the table. Diffidently, his guests did as they were bid. They were all slightly bemused by this strange gathering, as none of the guests knew each other or their host. Each had received an invitation which had been so intriguing that they had been compelled to accept. *A stiff black card with a deckled gold edge and the writing in gold leaf read: You have been especially selected to attend a Dinner Party at the address below on Saturday, 31st October. Dress formal. Punctuality essential. Travel by taxi as transport home will be provided. No need to reply as I am sure you will wish to come and meet your destiny.*

Each of the three had disregarded the invitation at first sight; Andrew had actually thrown his in the waste bin. 'Time Share' was a first reaction or a hoax or a practical joke. But the card was expensive and the address very up market. Fiona had driven past the house and although she had been impressed by the size and grandeur of the place, had shivered and felt suddenly cold, even though the temperature inside the car was pleasantly warm. Curiosity and an unexplained compulsion had finally led all of them to accept the invitation.

The soup was a cold consommé, delicious but not very warming. Fiona and Pamela wished they had chosen clothes for warmth and comfort rather than fashion and vanity. The fish course was salmon mousse, perfectly turned out onto a large silver dish and decorated superbly. The main course was a magnificent ham and cold roast turkey with salad, followed by chilled fruit and ice cream. Each course accompanied by the appropriate chilled wine.

The meal took two hours to serve and eat, by which time Sebastian's guests, although replete, were as chilled as the wine they drank. Sebastian smiled inwardly, enjoying their discomfort.

"We will take tea in the drawing room", he announced, standing up. "I abhor coffee, a thoroughly uncivilised drink. Please, follow me."

Conversation during the meal had been general chit chat about politics, the latest books, the theatre and an art exhibition. As Pamela, Fiona and Andrew followed their host, they still had no idea why they had been invited to this very strange dinner party.

The temperature in the drawing room was no higher than that of the dining room and the décor did not suggest warmth. The walls were pale grey and hung with pictures by Klimt and Klee. The settee and armchairs were upholstered in ice blue and navy blue. Curtains of a shiny material hung at the window but did not cover the darkness outside. They sat down and accepted gratefully the cups handed to each of them, which were filled with iced tea.

Sebastian settled himself into a large armchair and surveyed each of them as they sipped delicately at the cold liquid.

"I expect you are wondering why I have asked you here", he said, his gaze travelling over them in turn.

"Well, yes", said Andrew timidly, placing his cup, still half full, on a small table. "I mean, I don't know you and I have never before met these ladies."

"Quite", said Sebastian. "More tea, anyone?" They all quickly declined. "The truth is", he continued, "that although you are strangers to each other, you all have one thing in common." He paused and half smiled as they looked at each other then back, to him expectantly. "You are all murders", he said, softly.

Shock, disbelief, fear, astonishment and finally anger swept across their faces.

"Now look here ..."

"This is preposterous ..."

"You can't say things like that ..."

They all spoke at once.

"You have read too many Agatha Christie novels", laughed Andrew. "My, you really had us going there, didn't you? Quite a joke, old chap, quite a joke." Do you consider yourself to be Hercule Poirot, Hmm?"

"I don't think he's joking", said Pamela.

"You are right", said Sebastian coldly, "I am not." He gazed at them, his face as cold as the atmosphere.

"But wait a minute." Andrew's voice was belligerent. "What gives you the right to bring three people to this ... this mausoleum of a house and then proceed to insult us with these accusations?" He stood up. "I've had enough. I'm going home."

"No, you are not. Sit down." Sebastian's tone was not loud, but it was very forceful. "You will hear what I have to say." He re-crossed his legs, settled further into his chair, and tweaked at his trousers to straighten the crease. Andrew sat down slowly, unable to take his eyes from his host's face.

"You, Andrew", Sebastian pointed at him and Pamela whimpered, "you killed two people with your car. You were drunk."

"It was an accident. Everyone said it was an accident", Andrew whispered.

"Oh, you had a clever lawyer, I admit, but you knew you should not have been driving. Two people died because of your selfishness and arrogance." Sebastian's condemnation was cold and admonitory.

"It was an accident. An accident!" Andrew's face was ashen, "I didn't mean it to happen.

"All right, Mr ... whatever-your-name-is", said Fiona, trying to draw attention from Andrew, to give him time to compose himself. This arrogant, bombastic man needed putting in his place.

"What do you have to say about me? I know that I have killed nobody, so whatever you say I shall treat with the contempt it deserves."

"Ha!" laughed Sebastian. "I like your spirit, Fiona. I thought you would have the most fight in you." He leaned forward and looked her straight in the eye. His eyes appeared to have no iris, so dark was the colouring around his pupils. "You had an abortion. You killed your unborn child."

Fiona paled. "How do you know that? Nobody knows about that."

"It was a social decision, wasn't it? A baby would have hindered your career. The great Miss Taylor, the advertising whiz kid." He looked at her with disdain. "You chose to push margarine and washing-up liquid, rather than have your baby."

"It was my baby", said Fiona defiantly, raising her chin. "My baby, my body, my life."

"No", barked Sebastian, "it was the baby's life."

"How dare you sit there in judgement on us? I'm not the only person to ever have had an abortion. Why pick on me?" Fiona was not going to let this man upset her. She had battled for her opinions to be heard in the boardroom and had taken on far tougher men than this. "Who are you to comment on our lives?"

"Oh, you'll find out who I am", smiled Sebastian, "and as for 'picking on you' as you put it, I feel that advertising is a useless profession. Persuading silly people to spend their money on things they neither want nor need. To nurture a child, to see it grow and blossom is a far greater achievement than becoming Businesswoman of the Year. Your kind of work disgusts me."

His face as he spoke was cold and hard, and Fiona found herself tongue-tied under such vituperation. He turned to Pamela, who sat shivering, pressed back into the sofa cushions in search of warmth and finding none.

"So, Pamela, did you think I had forgotten you?"

Pamela shook her head. "No", she whispered.

"Of course not." Sebastian's tone was silky smooth.

'Much like a snake, if it could talk', thought Andrew.

"You killed your mother."

"No, no", said Pamela, wildly shaking her head, "I didn't. She died; she was ill … in so much pain."

"Oh, I agree she was ill", Sebastian said, "but you hastened her end."

"No! No!" sobbed Pamela, her head in her hands.

"This is enough." Andrew stood up and pulled Pamela to her feet. "We are going home. You are a sadist, do you know that? You are cruel for cruelty's sake. Okay, I killed two people in my car, Fiona had an abortion and Pamela's mother died. What gives you the right to torture us with your knowledge?"

"But none of you paid for your sins", said Sebastian calmly, "and I am here to see that you do." He smiled and for an instant his eyes glowed red and then were dark once more.

"Oh, my God!" Andrew's voice was hoarse with fear.

"Yes, I rather think I am", Sebastian said quietly. "However, the evening is over. I promised you would know more about each other, and you do. Come; let me arrange your transport home."

He smiled as he opened the door and the three visitors hurried to the hall, anxious to be away. They collected their coats and looked at their host.

"Don't expect us to say we've enjoyed it, because we haven't", snarled Andrew. "I hope I never see you again."

"Well said, Andrew! Well said: but I rather think you will", laughed Sebastian. "But here is your car. The driver will see you all to your destination."

He stood and watched as his three guests scrambled into the car, anxious to be away from this cold, damnable place.

"Very satisfactory", he smiled, rubbing his hands together as the car drew away. He looked up at the clear, starry sky and the sparkle of hoar-frost on the trees. "Beautiful", he whispered, "beautiful. Three more souls sent to hell." He laughed out loud.

The morning papers reported the car accident in which three people died. It is thought the car skidded on a patch of frosty road, but the strangest thing was that although the car was crushed beyond recognition, the police and rescue services could find no sign of the driver.

*

Bull Run
By Anne Melville

John Buddle stirred in his narrow cot and huddled into himself, reluctant to leave the warm centre he had finally succeeded in making under the inadequate blanket. It had been a cold night and for hours he had been kept awake by his aching limbs.

He became aware of sounds; creaking wheels, clashing hooves, footfalls and a voice, shouting.

"Put that one across the alley, Joe!"

John listened. There were other voices outside. How strange. Monday morning was not usually like this. There was a knock at the door, and his friend, Tom Grundy, came in, leaning heavily on his white stick.

"Are you awake, John?"

"Can't help it", grumbled John. "What's all the noise?"

"Have you forgotten the day? They're running the bull."

John blinked his rheumy eyes, peering up at Tom blearily, still not wanting to move, because the pain would begin again.

"Bull run", he muttered. "They've got no bull like they had in our day, Tom."

"Come on, John, Move yourself", said Tom. "I want you to see it for me." He banged his stick on the floor excitedly, then against the bed legs.

"Come on, old John", he said again. "Up you get. There'll be something to talk about tonight."

John uncoiled his legs reluctantly, wincing. It was always bad at first, until he got them moving. He struggled slowly out of bed and into some clothes. They were clean today. Every Sunday evening the two women handed them out and took last week's for washing. It was too cold for baths, even if such a luxury had been available.

He fished two sticks out from behind the bed-head and hauled himself slowly towards the door, his knees stiff and unyielding.

Tom tapped out ahead of him.

"It's seven o'clock", he said. "Two hours afore prayers."

They breakfasted off thin gruel and bread, with mugs of small beer to wash it down. While they ate, they exchanged grumbles with the eight other old men of the Beadhouse. The two old women who served them shuffled around, banging bowls and mugs and complaining bitterly of the cold, the draughts, the miserable meals and the pittance they lived on.

"There'll be noise and mess all day", said one. "No peace today."

"You women enjoy nothing", said Tom. "Come out and watch with us."

"We got our work to do", said the other old woman. "Not like you lazy pigs. But then, Tom Grundy, you always was vicious. You like to see people hurt. I remember when you was running with them ...."

"Those was the days", said Tom, "when we had bulls that was bulls. These young fellers now, they wouldn't know what to do with 'un."

The Warden, who was almost as old as the Beadsmen himself, appeared in the doorway.

"You misremember, Tom", he said. "Those bulls were lambs. How could old Sarah here have led them in otherwise? You were a good bull woman, Sarah. That golden hair you had then got the shillings rolling in for the bull all right."

Sarah sniffed, but looked a little pleased. "That was a long time ago, Reverend", she said, "a long time ago. Why, my Bill first see me when he paid his shillun in. Lucky for me that day", she added, and began stacking bowls, still reminiscing.

"We'll have prayers early, I think", said the Warden, "then you can see what's going on."

The old men got up, some more spryly that others, and made their way from the dining room to the chapel. Time for their daily devotions and to pray for the Founder's soul.

* * *

Outside, there were many more voices now, feet shuffling and trampling, shouting and swearing and cries of children. As last, Tom and John were able to make their way out to the porch and steps of the hospital that overlooked the wide marketplace in front of them.

It was filled with a great press of people. Most of the men were armed with sticks and there were dogs weaving and pushing in and out of their legs. John described the scene to Tom.

"They've got all the streets and alleys barricaded up", he said. "The wagons are all set round. They should be starting soon."

The milling crowd was getting impatient and arguments were breaking out, men shaking their fists and swearing with indignation at the long wait.

A bell began to toll. A hush spread through the crowd until all were silent and nervous. Then, there was a stir at the west end of the street. Something was happening at the barrier. Suddenly, people pressed back, spreading and running, pushing others aside. The ripples of movement were going through the crowd like a nest of spiders, until the main mass of people was pushed up against the wagons and carts that made up the barricade.

"There he is", shouted John, waving a stick. "There he is! Big black fellow. Look at his horns! They've got a good one there."

Tom strained his ears, hearing the scuffle of feet, gasps and cries, dogs snarling and yelping; and somewhere, he fancied he heard a clatter of hooves and fierce snorts. He had a picture in his mind of the crowd forming a ring around the creature, warily edging away, their sticks held ready in defence. He heard a sharp barking and saw in his mind a hound dog at the bull's heels, snapping and dodging. Then there was a loud squalling yell as the bull caught the dog squarely.

"There", gasped John, "he went right up and over, Tom."

The bull had cleared a space around himself and was absorbed in defending it. Wheeling and snorting, ducking his head, stamping and pawing at the ground, daring the men to attack.

A bolder spirit than the rest advanced, holding his stick like a broadsword. He feinted at the bull's head and leaped back, expecting a rush. The bull braced himself on stiff legs, his head low, swaying like a snake. His eyes began to turn red with his mounting anger. The youth, stocky with reddish hair curling in his neck, made another lunge and sprang back as the bull baulked malevolently. For a moment all movement was suspended, as bull and boy faced it out, then the animal came on thunderously, savagely, and the boy leaped aside, barely escaping the weapons on the black curly head. The bull carried on, seeking another target among the watching crowd. Men scattered wildly, fighting to escape his charge. The beast stopped again, whirling, stamping and snorting his displeasure. Dogs snarled and yapped around him, but not daring to come too close.

"He nearly got young Harry Elwes there", exulted John. "He's a bold lad that one – here he come again", as the bull made another rush at his tormentors, scooping up a couple of dogs this time and pitching them over his shoulders.

John was dancing with excitement, his stiff knees forgotten, and rattled on to Tom beside him, who stood stock-still, listening hard, building his mental images from the sounds and words that reached him.

"You're a bloodthirsty old heathen, John." Sarah's quiet voice came from behind them. "You'd not care if young Harry got himself killed."

"Ay", said John in reply. "He's your sister's grandson, isn't he?"

"Yes", she said and fell silent, fearfully watching for the boy in the press. She had never seen so many people in this small space.

For a time there was less activity. No-one else yet fancied teasing the bull into a rush and the space spread out around him. Moving slowly from one end of the market to the other, a boiling scuffle full of the sordid cruelty that wanted, yet feared, to see someone spitted on those menacing horns.

"All gone quiet", said Tom in disgust, "haven't they got no guts?"

"Please God, Harry, don't try it again", said Sarah. "he's the very last one left after the sickness."

"He won't get in no trouble", said Tom, "he's a good boy!"

"Ay, but daft", muttered Sarah. "Daft when he's with that lot."

"He's got more sense", insisted Tom.

The crowd was pushing little amoebic fingers out towards the bull, with the men being pushed out continually sliding away again out of the head, letting another take their place. The bull, recovering his wind, swung his head, watching them, ready for the stick that would come poking out towards him to catch his ribs or his nose. He prepared for the toss, practising the movement as he watched, making the foolhardy quake and the strong become wary, but not wary enough? He swept forward, too suddenly for one huge fellow and for about twenty yards the man rode his horns, until he lost his grip and fell off, under the feet of the fleeing crowd. The bull rushed on and now men could not get out of his way quickly enough. None were more than bruised by the glancing blow of a horn, or by falling on the ground. Maddened by the success of striking back, the animal charged on until he struck a wagon full tilt. He vented his rage on it, beating savagely at the sides, then spinning again to face the men around him. Snorting heavily, he gathered himself for a real onslaught.

The crowd fled!

Many climbed over wagons to get out of his way as he galloped at them. He became more and more frantic as they escaped from him, dragging women and children out of his way as they lingered with the crowd. Not many were in the arena now. Perhaps fifty or so, too foolish or too proud to retreat; amongst them, to Sarah's horror, was Harry.

"John", she cried, "John, call him up, he'll listen to you."

"He'll be alright", John answered. "Quick on his feet and sharp. He'll not get hurt", and he shouted loudly, cheering on the remaining men. Tom listened, alarmed now, hearing the note of the bull's breathing that told him it had become highly dangerous.

"That's a killer, John", he said urgently. "I heard one like it once before. Call the boy up!"

John stopped shouting, surprised.

"How can you tell?"

"I know it", he said, "call the boy up, John!"

It was too late. Harry had moved away from the front of the hospital towards the west end of the marketplace, where the bull was racing round the edge after men leaping up onto whatever they could get hold of. Others pulled them to safety. He believed, perhaps, that he would reach the nearest wagon, or that the beast would not turn, or if it did, it would not charge him. A big black dog leaped out from under a cart, barking savagely, and as the bull slammed at him, so it turned and saw Harry running towards the wagon.

Sarah screamed as the beast accelerated. Harry saw the gap diminishing too quickly and turned to run the other way, hoping to reach the terrace of the hospital. The bull, seeing a real chance for revenge, came on like a juggernaut. Harry might still have escaped, but with one eye on the pursuing bull, he did not see the stick left lying on the street and sprawled full length as he tripped over it.

Even as he scrambled to his feet, the animal was upon him, using the tearing sideways and backward thrust he had been practising. Harry was flung over his left shoulder and across his back to fall and roll on the ground. Too dazed to get up quickly as the creature turned in its own length and lunged again. Dropping to its knees, using its horns to slash and slash again. Horrified now, men leapt from the wagons to strike and tease the bull away from its victim. Two of the men advanced with a net strung between them. While they manoeuvred to trap the bull, four men picked up Harry and carried him up the steps and quickly into the hospital. Sarah ran in front to fetch water and bandages, for he was bleeding badly. A thick, dark, slightly shiny train followed the group into the porch.

The bull, driven to frenzy and unseeing, had run into the net and entangled itself. Before it could tear free, more ropes were brought and flung around the thrashing form. Men hung onto the horns, made bold now the creature's movements were restricted. Several men dragged it away and shut it up in the butcher's stable, from where it had been brought some three hours before. The animal slashed at the walls in vain, for they were unyielding. Eventually it gave up.

* * *

John was stunned. He had not really believed the bull would hurt anyone seriously. It had not happened before like this. He leaned on his two sticks, shivering, watching the defeat of the bull. He watched more through fear of going in to see how badly Harry was hurt, than to be sure the bull was safely caught. Tom had gone, following after the voices and shuffling steps of the men, listening to Sarah's commands as they stripped the clothing away from the gashes in Harry's body. Some tried to staunch the flow that was draining the life from him.

There was a ragged tear right across his stomach. It seemed to Sarah that the more linen she packed in, the faster it stained with red, while Harry's face became as white as paper and bluish around the lips, like a dead man. The doctor was there now, working with her, and between them they stitched and tied him up like a mummy. Nothing could stop those crimson patches from slowly spreading, joining up like some hideous shadow of disease, threatening and lethal.

They could do no more. Sarah knelt beside him with her face hidden and Tom could hear her murmuring prayers between the sobs. He knelt beside her, putting a comforting arm around her.

"I'll pray with 'ee, lass", he said, "he's a strong lad, happen he'll pull through."

They watched beside him, late into the night. His breathing was slow and feeble and every now and then it stopped. Then they worked feverishly, making his lungs work, calling to him to fight back, until the laborious, snoring sound escaping his lips told then that he had not yet let go.

News of the bull was brought as they watched. It had been released again, about three o'clock, once people had got over their shock at the goring. The animal was not inclined to respond to the teasing now, as though its attack on Harry had been enough of a gesture of defiance. In the meantime, someone had decided to go home and in driving away his cart, had left a small gap in the barricade. The bull chased a couple of young boys through and crashing into the barrier, bursting through it.

It raced through the streets less concerned with attacking than escaping. Turning and doubling back when it was confronted at corners, it was finally driven onto the meadow between the mill stream and the river. There, small boys and dogs were allowed to throw stones and chase it, for it was exhausted and there was no fight left in it. Then it fell into the river, retreating from the same black dog that had turned it on Harry. It fell in opposite the Burghley almshouses just above the bridge and half submerged in mud, could not get out. It bellowed miserably while the butcher and his helpers, exasperated, fetched poles and ropes. After half an hour of pushing and pulling, swearing and falling into the water themselves, they succeeded in getting the animal out.

The day was over. The children were sent home and the dogs were caught and tied up. The men were tired and rather disgusted with the whole affair. The women had gone some hours ago and most of them sat thinking about Harry. Some thanked God it was he who had been caught and not one of their men folk.

* * *

Sarah's sister and niece had joined her in watching over Harry. Joanna, Harry's mother, sat stony-faced and still. She had had nine children. Eight had died, one by one, of sickness, disease or accident. Her husband was gone too, with a cough that had taken all his size and strength before it took him too. Now, she was convinced that Harry was dying and she would have nothing left. Her mother, Mary, watched her sadly and thought idly how Jo's red hair was showing traces of grey. It had been such pretty red hair, similar to Harry's, now damp on the pillow.

Incredibly, he survived through the long night and all through the next day. Many people came quietly to the door of the hospital to ask about him, and went away more quietly when they heard he was failing. Many said the bull should be slaughtered, but the beast was valuable, so nothing was done. Gradually, however, a feeling grew that it was wrong, both for the bull and for the man it had injured. To have done what they did that day, tormenting the creature to killing madness was, itself, wrong. Also, it had cost a lot of money in expense and working time, and damage to wagons and carts.

Evening prayers in the chapel on Tuesday were all for Harry. Then the family settled down to another long night's vigil; anxious, too, about Joanna, who had not eaten or had anything to drink or spoken a word since the incident.

* * *

Sarah had gone out quietly and now she came back with some small beer and bread.

"John, Tom", she said, "you must eat. Perhaps if we do we can persuade Joanna."

"Thank you, Aunt Sarah", whispered the girl, "I'll not take any, though."

"Well, you're speaking, at least", said Sarah. "Come now, Jo, you'll not do Harry any good by being too weak to take care of him. Have sense, now."

The Warden came in with the doctor, returned to resume his vigil with them. The doctor spent some time over Harry and shook his head sadly as he moved away from the cot.

"His life is on the ebb", he said. "You can only pray, now." He sat down wearily on the nearest chair.

The Warden said, "We will all pray tonight", and left the room. Presently, the watchers could hear voices, muffled by stone walls and murmuring gently. They knelt and prayed, too, or bowed their heads as they sat and joined in as well as their troubled minds would allow.

Joanna sat beside her son, holding his hand and she began to talk to him.

"Listen, Harry. Listen to them. They're all praying for you Harry. Try and come back to us. You're my last chick; don't leave your poor grandmother and me alone altogether." She began to cry softly and Mary moved to put an arm around her and say, "Let me sit, child. You're tired now. Rest on old John's bed a while. I'll call you if need be."

Joanna, exhausted, got up and went to John's cubby-hole, where she laid down, pulling the blanket tight around her. It was good to rest her throbbing head and the voices from the chapel soothed her. It was very quiet except for those voices and Harry's laboured breathing. She could still hear him from across the passageway.

Tom was listening, too. His hearing, most acute, was strained to catch the least change in the heavy, slow snoring that was Harry's one sign of life.

Mary was holding his hands now. She had talked to him quietly for a long time, but now she, too, was weary. She looked at Sarah, slumped in a corner, her grey head on one side, her mouth hanging open in sleep. She looked at John, sat quite still and upright, his hands on his sticks. He was hurting inside, knowing that he had cheered Harry on as he had. He felt that the boy might not have stayed in the arena if he had behaved differently. He whispered over and over, "God give him strength!"

Mary looked at Tom, his head resting on his hands clasped on the head of his white stick. She knew that he was listening. Listening for the slightest change that might tell them of crisis.

She looked at the doctor. He, too, was asleep, his hands clasped across the podgy middle under his watch chain, his legs planted firmly apart and his three chins dropped onto his chest. She sighed, her mind going back to when he was as slim as Harry, his dark hair abundant and a twinkle in his eye for all 'his ladies', whoever they were. He would not have dozed then. He would have been counting every breath and every heartbeat. She felt comforted. He would not doze were Harry really dying. She wanted to tell Joanna, but did not like to leave go of the boy's hands, and besides, Joanna was asleep too.

Somewhere a clock began to chime. It was a thick, damp night and the sound came muffled by fog. One by one the different town clocks joined in, but they all added up to one time. It was four 0'clock in the morning.

The chanting from the chapel had died away in a sleepy mumble. The Warden alone still kept vigil, kneeling before the great slab of stone that formed the altar, silently praying. He raised his head as he heard the clocks chiming and slowly he got up off his knees. He shuffled painfully along the corridor to the little room where Harry lay. The rays of the lamp showed him five people crammed in the small room with the sick boy.

"Tom; John", he said, his voice thick with weariness, "do you not think …" He got no further. Tom held up a peremptory hand.

"Listen", he said. As he did so, Harry's breathing caught in a snort and a choke. Mary, nodding off, came awake abruptly and tightened her grip on his hands. The doctor awoke instantly, got up and bent to listen, his fingers seeking a pulse. Only Sarah slept on. John sat unmoving. He felt hope beyond him and could no longer pray, but his eyes glittered as he watched the doctor bent close to Harry's ear.

"Boy", he roared, "boy, it's time you woke up!"

His reward was a grunt, so he tried again, bullying Harry into more grunts and snorts and, miraculously, movement. Harry jerked his head and turned it away from the worrying voice.

"He'll do", said the doctor. "Told you so." He'd done nothing of the kind, of course. Mary smiled to herself.

"Sarah", she called, "Sarah!"

John raised a stick and poked Sarah in the side, not as gently as he might. She awoke, squawking.

"Who jabbed me?"

"Sarah, call Jo", said Mary. "He's going to be alright."

Sarah blinked. She got up and went quickly out of the room to Joanna.

"I hear he's breathing right now", said Tom. "He'll be a long time mending, though."

"He's alive is all", said Mary. "He'll live."

Joanna came in and knelt by the bed. She didn't speak. She just stroked back Harry's red curls from his flushed and sweating forehead that had been so pale before. John dragged himself to his feet.

"Here, Jo, take my chair. I'm off to bed now, for what's left of the night; won't be fit for morning else." His knees complained bitterly as they heaved his weight reluctantly across the corridor, but he ignored them. He felt reprieved now Harry seemed likely to survive.

"He's a game young'un", he muttered, as he crawled into his bed. "Right game. Bulls and all. Can't beat an Elwes." After a while, uneasily, he slept, too tired to dream.

Sarah did not go to bed. She went and heated a pan of thick bone and potato broth. The fire was low and she fed it gently to waken it. When the soup was hot, she thinned it a little from the stock pot. On counting up, she found only Joanna, Tom and herself to feed. The doctor had pronounced Harry strong enough for him to go home, and Mary was asleep in Sarah's chair.

"I'll be back with morning", said the doctor, "but I think he'll do."

Sarah carried the bowls of thick soup in and the heat of it warmed them through. Joanna, released from fear, chattered without stopping. She chattered about the day, the people who had asked about Harry and about the coming Christmas. "He'll be well and strong then. We'll have such a Christmas."

Harry slept between them, pale again now, but not livid, his breathing steadier.

"We'll have a job tomorrow", said Sarah. "We'll have to change all those bandages."

"Ye'd not disturb him", exclaimed Joanna fearfully.

"You want him to be comfortable, girl", chided Sarah. "They'll dry hard as can be and hurt where the doctor sewed him. He'll be alright now the bleeding's stopped."

Joanna looked at her son's face.

"Thought he'd go", she said quietly.

"Aye", said Tom, "but I told ye, lass, he's a strong lad."

Joanna smiled, then hopefully she said, "Maybe – he'd not run – again – next year?"

"No", said Tom roughly, "never fear that! Boy's got more sense." He was silent for some time, and then said, "They shouldn't do it. Bring in a wild one like that, I mean really savage, that bull was. Look at all the damage to them carts, too. Billy Robins'll cost him a mint to mend that side."

"It was that dog", Sarah said. "That great brute of George Edwards'." It was him as turned it on to Harry! Should be shot, that brute. He bit a boy last week; he should be sued.

"It was that dog chased it in the river", said Tom. "Dratted nuisance, that dog."

Tom yawned, desperately tired now.

"Go and take my bed, Tom. I had a sleep a while ago. So did Jo."

"Think I will", said Tom. He got up awkwardly and tapped for the door. "You call me, mind, if anything happens."

"I'll do that", said Sarah.

"Goodnight, Uncle Tom", said Joanna.

Tom tapped out of the room and away along the stone passage outside the old men's dormitory towards Sarah's empty bed. He knew that old Millie, who shared her room, would never hear him. The roof could fall in and she'd not shift. Anyway, he'd only lie on top and dose.

His thoughts ran on. The boy'll wake up and he'll get stronger through the day. Won't be strong by Christmas, though. Still be here, Christmas. That ugly gash in his belly will see to that. Lucky it were no deeper. Come Spring, his strength'll build, but never like it was, poor lad. Can't bleed like that and forget it. Those runs should be stopped.

Tom felt his way to the cot and lay down, falling straight into a deep sleep. Throughout the old stone building, sleep ruled; over the Beadsmen, the Warden, Mary and the sick boy. Only Joanna and Sarah, whispering mutual hope to each other, remained awake to mark the slow, cold hours to dawn.

*

A Sister's Crime
By Danny MacCullough

Michelle Nash was not a morning person – she had never been, even as a child. To get her up and ready for school had been, for her mother, a daily chore. Now it was no different. Aged thirty, Michelle still relied on her mother for that morning push-start.

"Honey, you'll be late for work …." Michelle sighed and stretched her naked body to its full 5'5" length. "OK mum", she yawned, "I'll be down in a minute". Five minutes later her mother called her again. This time the tone of the voice was different, it sounded nervous, excitable. "Honey, quickly! They've found the body of that missing girl; it's on the telly now". Michelle slipped on a white silk bathrobe and hurried down the stairs. Her mother was in the kitchen watching the news on TV. Michelle bent down and kissed her on top of the head. On the TV the reporter was well into his story.

"Police are yet to confirm that the body found in Epping Forest is that of the missing 22 year old nurse, Carol Ellington …."

Michelle's mother's face was etched with concern as she turned to her daughter. "I knew it – I knew they wouldn't find her alive. That's the second black girl murdered this month". Michelle put her arm around her mother's shoulders.

"Mum, you're jumping to conclusions, she could have committed suicide, we don't know yet". Michelle's words did nothing to reassure her mother and she knew that.

"Honey, I do worry about you", her mother continued. "Please be careful".

Michelle held her mother close. "So, it's another black girl – that doesn't mean I'm going to be a victim too, if that's what you're thinking. I can take care of myself – my police training you know". She laughed and her mother smiled an uncertain smile. Michelle flicked the remote and changed to a channel showing *Friends*. "There, that's better, something light to watch, mum". She kissed her mother on the forehead, a soft, light, daughter's kiss. "Right, work beckons", Michelle said at last and hurried back upstairs to the bathroom.

Michelle's mother listened to the sound of bath water running and smiled. It was moments like these she wished she could put the clock back. Back to when Michelle and her twin sister, Tracy, shared the same bath and splashed her as she tried to wash them. Wonderful, wonderful days. But the march of time is unstoppable and so much had happened to the Nash family in the intervening years. Her husband had died and Tracy was married with a child of her own. She loved the twins equally but it was Michelle who had stayed. Now it was just her and Michelle. They were so close and the bond between them was very special. She couldn't explain it and neither could Michelle. Tracy, aware of it, didn't even try. She was content with the occasional contact with her mum and sister – it didn't diminish the love all three shared.

* * *

Michelle walked into an Incident Room abuzz with activity. People were talking animatedly into their mobiles or office phones. Others were checking computer screens. Groups were huddled together in serious conversation. She was looking for DC Mike Waller, her co-investigating officer on the missing girls' enquiry and he wasn't difficult to find. She spotted him talking with her boss, Chief Superintendent Charles Tanner. Tanner was a big man with a voice to match, never speaking in a normal tone but as if he were trying to break a decibel record. Michelle used to think he had a hearing disability but soon realised that the Chief simply liked the sound of his own voice.

"Ah, Michelle", he boomed as she made her way towards him. "We wondered where you were – down at the crime scene, perhaps?" He winked at Mike but Mike had too much respect for Michelle to play Tanner's game. Tanner put an unwanted arm round Michelle's shoulders. "Only teasing – you know me". She did. She also knew his wandering hands, never missing an opportunity to run them over her tight little bottom. She moved away out of his reach.

"Sir", she said, "Mike and I need to talk to the team".

"OK, go ahead; just keep me informed won't you?"

Michelle and Mike watched Tanner return to his office, barging past subordinates en route. Mike vowed then that he would never become a "Tanner".

Michelle hated press conferences, the prying cameras, the probing questions, they unnerved her. How the famous coped she could never understand. She was simply grateful she was just a normal working girl, a girl who, after the questions, could return to a world of anonymity.

"Ladies and Gentlemen", she began. "I can confirm that the body found in Epping Forest at 6:15 this morning is that of Carol Ellington. The next of kin have been informed and a post mortem is being held as we speak. That is all I can tell you". The assembled media were like a pack of wolves, scavenging for any morsel to satisfy their hunger. They pounced on her, questions coming fast and from all directions.

"Was she murdered?" Was it a sex-motivated crime?" Was it drugs?" "Is there a link to the Jolene Annobi murder?"

Mike, sensing Michelle's discomfort, quickly took control.

"OK, guys", he said in his soft Edinburgh accent, "the Inspector has told you all she can. "Now, if you hurry, you'll be at the Crown and Anchor by opening time – I can assure you the beer is good there." "Thanks Mike," said Michelle as he escorted her back into the station. "No problem. I just don't know what you would do without me", he replied with a cheeky grin on his face.

* * *

Michelle drove her unmarked police car into an empty space in front of Livingstone Towers, carefully avoiding broken glass strewn on the ground. Opening her notebook she checked the address – Flat 32, a flat in this high-rise complex that had seen better days. She guessed that number 32 was on the third floor, not too many stairs if the lifts weren't working.

She locked her car under the watchful eyes of a small group of hooded youths who whistled at her as she made her way past them. In her experience cars left unattended in such areas were prime targets for idle hands and those young men seemed to fit the bill. As suspected, the lifts were out of order so Michelle took to the stairs, glancing round once to check on her car – it was still there, complete with wheels and wing mirrors!   Sidestepping the condoms and syringes littering the ground as she reached the third floor, Michelle did not at first notice the little old cockney woman confronting her.

"Look at this place – bleedin' mess – not like when me and me old man came 'ere in '62, spotless then it was". Michelle smiled and attempted to continue on her way but the old woman wasn't finished. She held Michelle's arm in a surprisingly tight grip. It was clear she needed to talk. "I've 'ad me windows smashed, yobs urinating on the front door but no-one does sweet Fanny Adams about the buggers. Councilors. All they want is your vote at elections then afterwards it's 'sod-off' time. You're not from the Council are you luv?" Michelle released the old biddy's tight grip. "No, sorry, I'm not." "That's aw'right then, what are you doing in this piss-'ole then? Just visiting! Oops, sorry, none of my business". With that the old woman went on her way, muttering to herself.

Michelle thanked God she didn't live in this concrete hell. She rang the bell of No. 32 and waited. No answer. She rang again and eventually the door opened. Standing in front of her was a woman of similar age. Michelle showed her ID card. The woman didn't speak but moved aside to let the detective enter. The living room was a throwback to the 60s – and obviously hadn't been decorated since then.

"Dad will be back in a moment", said the girl – "he's gone out for some pipe tobacco. Oh", she added, "I'm, Rene Ellington".

The front door opened and a small middle-aged man entered. "Dad", Rene Ellington began, "this is – "

"I know; it's the police. You can sit down, you know, we don't charge for our chairs". Michelle waited for him to sit first then she selected one of the armchairs. "Mr. Ellington, I just want to ask you a few questions about Carol …."

"Waste of time".

Michelle was taken aback by his abrupt words. "I'm sorry?"

"Waste of time – that's what she was, thought we wasn't good enough for her. All that education, she wanted that too. Ended up being a nurse, when she could have been a doctor. She never fitted in 'ere with me or her mum or Rene". Michelle ought to have asked questions, ought to have recorded the conversation but it was pointless, so very pointless. "How did she die?" Mr. Ellington finally asked.

"Asphyxiation, that's what the post-mortem revealed".

"Same as the other girl then?"

"Same. Look, Mr. Ellington, I'll call back another time". Michelle got out of the chair and made her way to the front door, Rene following close behind.

"My dad, I'm sorry", Rene began.

"It's OK".

"No, it isn't, it isn't OK", Rene Ellington countered. "I was fond of my sister but dad just couldn't accept her being 'different' from us". She opened the door. "Carol's funeral is next Thursday, will you come? Mum would appreciate that".

"I will".

"It's at the Baptist Church in the High Road at 11 o' clock, do you know it?"

"Yeah, I do, I'll be there".

Making her way down, Michelle glanced over the balcony to see if her car was still there – it was. The windows appeared intact and it had all four wheels. The hooded youths had disappeared, that must have been a first for Livingstone Towers.

* * *

Mike Waller was busy studying the case notes on his computer when he was suddenly aware of someone standing behind him. It was Tanner. "Mike, I'm taking you off the case". Tanner's words hit Mike like a ton of bricks. He swiveled round in his chair to face his Chief. "You can't", was all he could manage to say. "Sorry Mike but I have to, I'm short of bods on the Bank Robbery case so I'm not only taking you but I'm also scaling down the enquiry team here". "Does Michelle know Sir?" "Not yet but I'll tell her when she returns". Mike knew it was no use protesting. Once Tanner made a decision, that was that. "So, Mike, shut the computer down and get over to DS Fuller, he'll bring you up to date". Mike wanted to call Michelle but there wasn't time. Anyway, she'd find out soon enough.

The Annobie residence was in stark contrast to Livingstone Towers being situated in a tree-lined close, an expensive area of woodland where house prices were akin to monopoly money. Michelle parked her car opposite the house. No hooded youths hanging around here. She walked across the road and rang the bell of number 22. When the door opened she was greeted by a tall, bespectacled man – Mr. Annobie, the murdered girl's father. "No need to show your ID", he said in a cultured voice. "DS Nash, isn't it? You said you would be here at 3 o' clock and 3 o' clock it is, precisely. Please come in". Mrs. Annobie was waiting in the tastefully decorated sitting room.

Michelle was struck by her elegance and classic good looks. She must have been a model in her younger days, she said to herself. A slender hand was placed in Michelle's own. "My wife is a concert pianist, she plays with the LPO", Mr. Annobie said by way of introduction. "Oh, he loves to tell everyone that", said his wife. "He must be proud of you", responded Michelle. Mr. Annobie was indeed proud of his wife and, as it turned out, he was just as proud of Jolene, his murdered daughter.

Michelle asked all the questions she needed to ask and with a brief "thank you" left the Annobies to their grief. In her car she glanced at her notebook. She had hardly written anything down.

* * *

Mike found it hard to concentrate on the Bank Robbery case, his mind was still focused on the deaths of those two girls. The similarity bugged him. The cause of death – asphyxiation – the location, the apparent lack of motive and, more importantly, no identifying clues. Could it be, in both cases, a perfect murder? He decided to phone Michelle once he got home, safe from the listening ears of colleagues and Tanner who had the uncanny knack of turning up when you least expected him.

His children, Thomas who was four and two year old Oona were delighted to see him home and he helped his wife put them in the bath, staying to play with them for a few minutes before calling Michelle on her mobile. He got no response so he sent her text:-

"Michelle, its Mike. Please call me at home tonight – urgent". He spent a restless evening waiting but she didn't respond. "Where was she? Why didn't she call?"

The following morning Mike sat through seemingly endless CCTV footage searching for a glimmer of hope of a breakthrough in the Bank Robbery case. He was watching footage of the area close to the Bank at 2 o' clock in the morning - about the time the crime was committed. The screen was showing a quiet street, just a few cars driving along it.

"There's nothing here," Mike muttered to himself and asked a probationary PC to take over from him. "Just having a coffee", he lied, intending to take himself off to *The Crown and Anchor*. The young PC, anxious to impress, readily obliged and slid into Mike's chair. "OK Guv", he said. "OK, Guv", Mike smiled to himself. The youngster had obviously been watching too many TV Cop programmes - he had once been as wet behind the ears.

The topic of conversation at *The Crown and Anchor* was, of course, the murders of the two girls. Everyone had a view, everyone was an expert. Mike listened courteously as the regulars mulled over the events. What seemed to puzzle them – and indeed it still puzzled Mike – was the motive behind the killings. One said that only Freud would have the answer and maybe that was right, Mike just didn't know; not that it was his case any more. If only Tanner had set him to continue working with Michelle, he was sure a "result" would have followed.

* * *

Michelle sat at the back of packed chapel and waited along with the other mourners for the coffin to arrive. It was carried up the aisle by four men whom Michelle assumed to be relatives of the dead girl. Following closely behind came the parents and her sister, Rene. Michelle noticed Mrs. Ellington's face. She looked serene, no sign of tears. Maybe, thought Michelle, her tears were locked in her heart. The family took its place in the front pew, first Rene then her mother, then Mr. Ellington whose eyes were transfixed on the coffin in front of the altar. Michelle wondered if he was now touched with thoughts of remorse at Carol's death. When she had interviewed him at Livingstone Towers he had shown little feeling of fatherly love for his daughter, hurt by her desire to live her life away from the bosom of her family. Michelle watched as the pastor embraced Mrs. Ellington and shook Mr. Ellington's hand. Returning to the altar, he began the service.

"Listen to that singing", exclaimed a middle-aged woman sitting next to Michelle as the congregation, spurred on by the Gospel Choir found its glorious voice. "God is here, right here", she added, her shrill voice joining in the singing. Michelle decided it was time to leave the chapel and she slipped unnoticed outside. If she hadn't given up smoking she would have lit up, it was that sort of moment. Lost, alone, nothing to occupy her mind – or so she thought.

"Excuse me". Startled, Michelle turned round to see a smartly dressed man on the chapel steps. "I saw you inside. You are Detective Inspector Nash, aren't you?" "Yes, yes, I am", responded Michelle. "Do I know you?" "You do – unless your memory is playing tricks. I'm Wayne Francis".

The name and the voice were beginning to sound familiar. Suddenly she remembered. It was three years ago and he was one of three men she had arrested for causing an affray outside *The Tropicana*, the gay and lesbian club in town. "How long have you been out?" she asked him. "Just last week, that's when I heard about Carol". "Oh, did you know her?" Michelle's curiosity was aroused. "Yes, we were both members of the club. I'm surprised that more of her friends aren't here", he continued, "but then, things move on in three years don't they? Did you know Carol too or you here in your professional capacity?" Michelle was not used to answering questions. It made her feel inadequate, not in control. It was an uncomfortable feeling. "Rene asked me to come", was all she could say.

"Look", he said in a serious tone. "I know I shouldn't ask but have you any idea who murdered Carol and the other girl?" "The enquiries are still ongoing". He could tell Michelle wasn't going to take him into her confidence but that didn't stop him pursuing the matter. "I can check out the gay community for you – someone would have known Carol's movements". "Thanks for the offer but I'm sure my colleagues are capable of solving the murders", Michelle said in a dismissive tone. But Wayne Francis wasn't finished; he had one surprising observation to make. "The word is that the other girl, Jolene Annobie, was a lesbian too. Anyway, Ms. Nash, if you need me you know where to find me". He lifted up a trouser leg to reveal an electronic tag. See you". Michelle watched him walk to his people carrier, hoping that would be the last she would see of him.

Sitting on the low wall in front of the building, she watched the Ellingtons follow the coffin out of the chapel and into a waiting black limousine. The driver pulled slowly away from the kerb, a sign for a procession of cars to follow, including Michelle in her soft-top MG.

At the cemetery, the rain that had threatened all morning began to pour down, soaking the mourners and giving an even more sombre feel to the day. She watched as Mrs. Ellington and Rene each threw a single rose into the open grave, standing there for a while, thoughts of Carol filling their minds. Michelle let all the mourners take their leave till she stood alone, reading the tributes on the many wreaths. One in particular caught her attention. It read: "Love hurts and I am hurting now". It was from Rene. Not knowing why she did it, Michele bent down and kissed the rain-soaked card. Suddenly, she felt a hand on her shoulder, it was Rene. "Lovely words, Rene", she said. Rene held out her hand. "You are coming back to the flat, aren't you?" she asked. "Mum would appreciate that". "Yes, yes I am, I'll be right with you".

32, Livingstone Towers clearly had undergone a transformation. It was like one of those TV makeovers where you see the before and after. "What do you think", asked a smiling Rene. "My uncle's cousins did it for us. They paid for everything, furniture, carpet, the lot - got finished at 2 o'clock this morning". Michelle thought about the closeness of the Jamaican community and how tragedy brought them together in dignified solidarity. Rene's dad appeared beside them "Inspector Nash", he said, "thank you for coming. I'm sorry for the way I behaved the other day and the things I said about Carol – just a father's disappointment you know that our dreams are blown away like dust. Just dreams, that's all they are. Reality is harsh for people like us". There was nothing Michelle could say. She just half smiled, an inadequate response but it was all she had to offer. She stayed long enough to have a cup of tea and decided to leave, making her apologies to Rene. Outside in the cool air she stood for a while trying to get her thoughts into some sort of order. She turned to look at the Ellington's flat. Part of her wanted to go back in, part of her felt tormented at her sense of indecision.

* * *

Chief Inspector Tanner was becoming impatient with the progress of the murder cases while not accepting that it was his decisions that had resulted in the slow pace of the investigation. He called Michelle into his office. Michelle knew what to expect as she knocked on his office door but what she did not expect was to see another woman sitting alongside him. "Ah, Michelle", he boomed. "This is Doctor Lewis; I've brought her in to help you. You know each other already I believe". Doctor Lewis smiled at Michelle. "Yes, yes, we do sir", she said in what Michelle deduced was a public school accent, the clear and precise diction a world away from her own estuary English.. Doctor Lewis was well known to the Murder Investigation Team, her psychological expertise and profiling skills had already helped in solving several murder cases.

"Inspector Nash", Dr. Lewis began. "I don't have to lecture you on the mind of a killer; you are far too experienced an officer for that. It's clear to me that the killer is suffering from a rare type of mental disorder. I mean, both crimes were identical, no sign of sexual motive. Both women were of similar age and both were black ...." Dr. Lewis' words were lost on Michelle, she'd been over that ground already, and there was nothing in what the Professor said that Michelle didn't know. The next words jolted Michelle.

"It is clear", Dr. Lewis said with authority, "the killer has a special agenda. He – the chances of the killer being a woman is remote - kills for a specific purpose. The victim is not necessarily known to the killer, it could be anyone – even you Michelle.

What we have to find out is, as I said, the killer's agenda. Once we know that we can narrow down the field. I'm convinced we'll find this murderer is local with knowledge of the area".

Dr. Lewis propounded her theory. "This killer is going to strike again soon", she went on. Tanner was impressed. With the expert witness on board, he was confident that Michelle and her team would soon bring the two cases to a closure. Doctor Lewis turned to Michelle. "As we'll be working closely together, can we be on first name terms – Michelle? The first thing I need to know is – when you interviewed the families of these girls did you get any clue to a connection between them? Were they friends, had they been at school together? Did they frequent the same nightclubs, go to the same hairdresser? Anything".

"No, there was nothing to suggest a connection, for a start, their backgrounds were entirely different", volunteered Michelle. "Well, if I could start by looking through your notes", Dr Lewis continued. "My notes!" Michelle began to panic. She remembered the Annobie interview – and how, inexplicably, she had not recorded the conversation. "OK. They're on my desk; you can pick them up later".

"And one other thing, I understand you attended Carol Ellington's funeral, is that right?" 'How did she know', thought Michelle. 'Who told her?' The detective was convinced that she hadn't told anyone about it. Dr Lewis read her thoughts. "Wayne Francis let slip about your being there. I'm guessing you went in the line of duty; a good police officer explores every angle. Maybe you were hoping to meet the killer there?" She laughed at her little joke. "Wayne Francis", said Michelle hesitantly. "What did he tell you?" "Well, he actually said it to Mike Waller because he assumed that Mike was working with you. Wayne said he knew Carol Ellington – they were members of the same gay club, The Tropicana. Maybe that could prove to be the breakthrough for you. Look, Michelle, I'm hoping that my being here will help the investigation, we need to work together".

Tanner broke in. "I'm sure the inspector is grateful to you", he said and Michelle nodded her head thinking at the same time that she must contact Wayne Francis, - quickly.

* * *

Tracy had always taken an interest in her sister's work, the mysteries of criminal investigation held a strange fascination for her. Michelle often joked that Tracy should have been a policewoman rather than her. So when Michelle phoned to see if she could take little Amanda to the zoo, Tracy was delighted. It was an opportunity to quiz her sister on the investigation. Michelle arrived early at Tracy's house and Tracy was still clearing away the breakfast things as Michelle entered the kitchen.

"Your early-bird sister is here", announced Joe who had let Michelle in, "so I'm off now". "Was it something I said, Joe", asked Michelle and all three of them laughed. She liked her brother-in-law, such an easy-going guy and a good husband and father. The husband and wife kissed and Michelle got a peck on the cheek.

"Haven't you forgotten someone?" asked Tracy. "Oh my God! Amanda! Where is she?" "Here I am, daddy", cried the little girl, running into his arms for a bear hug. "Where have you been?"

"I was hiding from Aunty Michelle in your bed". Joe laughed. "Well, that's a good place. Wouldn't expect to find Aunty Michelle looking there!" All three adults laughed.

The two sisters chatted as Tracy got Amanda ready for the trip to the zoo. Just small talk, which Michelle enjoyed. It was a welcome break from the pressure at work. Tracy, sensing it wasn't a good time, didn't ask her sister anything about the murders. At the zoo the child could hardly contain her excitement. Running from one animal enclosure to another, Michelle had a job trying to keep up with her. "God, when would she tire?" she asked herself. But eventually the little girl was ready to go home and on the way she fell asleep.

Tracy carried her daughter upstairs to her room while Michelle busied herself in the kitchen, making tea. She wouldn't be able to escape Tracy's questions now, she knew. She couldn't think why her sister was so curious about the Carol Ellington murder. Perhaps it was because of all the media coverage, seeing Michelle on TV with Mike making the appeal for witnesses. Now Mike was off the case for some unexplained reason. They were a good team, Michelle and Mike and it seemed a senseless thing to do but who knows how Tanner's mind worked? Of course Michelle was competent to handle the case as the SIO and she knew her sister was very proud of her and what she had achieved as a black woman in the police force.

With steaming mugs of tea in their hands, the sisters sat opposite each other at the kitchen table and Michelle told Tracy about the criminal psychologist. This only added to Tracy's curiosity. Would the psychologist pinpoint the reason for the killing? Yes, she probably would but first there needed to be an arrest. As Tracy questioned her sister she became clear in her mind that an arrest wasn't far off.

* * *

Looking through the case notes of Michelle's investigation, Dr. Lewis was puzzled to find that when the bodies of the two girls, Jolene Annobie and Carol Ellington, were discovered, neither had a mobile phone with them. Now, every woman she knew had a mobile – it was as much a part of a woman's essentials as her lipstick. So, where were the mobiles?

Surprisingly this was something Michelle had overlooked. Even Mike, when on the case, missed that one. Dr. Lewis decided to tell Tanner of her concern. Needless to say he was furious – how could an experienced cop like Michelle overlook the obvious?

* * *

Dr. Lewis's working relationship with Michelle began to worry her. She realized that when Tanner brought her onto the murder investigation, Michelle would feel slighted. I was only natural. Michelle was an experienced officer as her record clearly demonstrated. But Dr. Lewis knew it had to work – the solving of two murders was more important than a woman's pride and that was the problem, Michelle obviously felt her handling of the cases was being questioned – and it was. To Dr. Lewis it seemed as if Michelle was holding something back. Was it, she wondered, a race thing, her being white, Michelle and the two girls, black? No, that was silly. She even surprised herself that such an ignorant thought should have entered her head. Whatever it was, for the time being, she had no answer. But answers she had to have.

For Tanner, his patience or lack of it, had cast a cloud over the station. The investigation, Michelle's, and now the one Mike Waller was involved in were, it seemed to him, going nowhere. He wanted results and he wanted them quickly. That's why he decided without consulting Michelle, Dr. Lewis or Mike, to get himself directly involved.

On the Bank robbery he looked at CCTV footage and spotted a sports car close to the Tropicana Night Club just a few doors away from the Bank. Getting into the car were two women, whether they had anything to do with the robbery he didn't know but the timing on the CCTV was close to that of the time of the robbery. He ordered Mike to have the footage enhanced. His positive action was the same with Michelle's investigation. Taking a hands-on role he told uniform to bring in Wayne Francis. It was his gut feeling that Francis could provide the breakthrough. After all, he knew one of the murdered girls and maybe, thought Tanner, Francis knew them both. He was never to find out. The news came that Francis was killed in a freak accident. He was at the time working underneath his car when the jack moved and the whole weight of the car came down on him. Death was instantaneous. Tanner's questioning mind was unhappy. Had Francis secured the jack properly? Perhaps it wasn't an accident? Francis, his main hope for an early resolution of at least one of the murders, was now dead. Tanner had the car brought in for a forensic examination hoping for the answers he needed to bring the investigation to a positive closure. Michelle didn't need telling about the accident, the news of Francis' death swept through the station and everyone had his own idea about what must have happened. Tanner had it in mind to seek Michelle's thoughts on it but decided to wait until after the station Christmas bash at the Crown and Anchor.

* * *

"This one's on me", Tanner's unmistakable voice roared above the noise of the bar. "But", he added, "you've only got five minutes before I withdraw my offer". It was the only time many of his staff had seen him in a jovial mood. The poor barman was besieged in seconds; it was the drinker's equivalent of the siege of The Alamo. The only person not caught up in the rush to the bar was Michelle. She stood near the door where she had entered a few minutes before Tanner made his generous offer and looked round for a seat. She spotted one but as she sat down a voice said, "Excuse me, Michelle". It was Dr. Lewis.

"Oh, I'm sorry, were you sitting here?"

"I was but it doesn't matter, I've been sitting all day at my desk so I'd rather stand. The Chief invited me, that's why I'm here". Michelle felt uncomfortable in her presence. "Ah, here he is now and Mike is with him. Now that's interesting". "Interesting?" Michelle was puzzled. "Oh come on, Michelle, you know Mike has the hots for you – Tanner knows that and I should think everyone at the Station knows too." Michelle felt like throttling her. Just because two people of the opposite sex work together – often during unsocial hours – doesn't mean they are going to jump into bed with each other. The very idea was ludicrous.

"Ah, I see you two beauties are enjoying a girls' night, just like Mike and me, a boys' night out". Tanner roared with laughter at what he considered his witty observation. He laughed so loud, he completely missed Mike's snigger but Dr. Lewis didn't. She gave Mike a look that had a "knife-in-the-back" in it. Not that it worried Mike, he was confident in his relationship with Tanner. He knew the Chief respected him and as long as that respect was there dirty looks were mere irritants – even from Dr. Lewis – or Jean as Tanner insisted on calling her.

"Right, Jean, I want to introduce you to one of my old buddies from the Hendon days and we'll leave these two to chat as long as tonight they don't talk shop". Tanner led Jean away but not before he patted Michelle's bottom. "God", Michelle thought, she was glad she wasn't Jean. For a while the two detectives remained silent. Mike sipped his beer and then noticed that Michelle wasn't drinking.

"Where's your glass?" he said at last. "I'm not bothered Mike, I'm only here just to show my face. Look, you go and enjoy yourself; I'll be slipping away soon". Perhaps the irritating doctor was right and Mike did have the hots for her. "Michelle, to tell you the truth this isn't my scene either. I'll walk you to your car". "That's a hell of a walk Mike; I've left it at home!" They both laughed. It seemed such a long time since they had laughed together and it was something they both missed, those light-hearted moments they had shared to relieve the stress of the job. Mike put his hand on her arm. "I'll get you a taxi".

The night air was cold and Michelle shivered a little as they walked toward the taxi rank. It was then that Mike made a move. "Michelle, I know a small hotel …." She knew what was in his mind and she was surprised she didn't resist his overtures. Somehow she just went along with the flow of the moment. At the hotel, a small, middle-aged man handed Mike a key. He didn't bother to look at Michelle. To him she was just another woman about to have sex in one of his rooms.

In the bedroom Mike and Michelle undressed with no hint of excitement or expectation in either of them. Not that is, until Mike took Michelle's hand and drew her body close to his. In bed, Michelle felt like an actress, playing a part. It wasn't her, the real Michelle, lying next to Mike. It couldn't be. Suddenly, she sat bolt upright and screamed: - "no, Mike, no!" Without looking at her or saying a word, Mike got up and began to dress. For several minutes Michelle remained in the bed, her mind searching for an answer why she had allowed Mike to take her to the hotel. Was it because she wanted to test her sexual leanings? If that was the case, she now had the irrefutable answer. Mike walked towards the door then turned to face her. "You can stay till the morning", he said. "I'll go and settle the bill on my way out".

Michelle didn't respond; she was still in shock. Shock that she had found herself in a situation that had taken on a life of its own. Why did she let him take her to the hotel? Why did she, naked, let him kiss her and caress her body? Why? WHY?

She felt cheap yet Mike was not a cheap guy. So why the feelings of guilt? To all these questions, the answers she sought were not there. It seemed to her at that moment they would never be. She would go on with life a little less sure, a little less confident. But one thing she realized, she now knew her true sexual orientation.

* * *

Tanner was in a foul mood. His voice blasted through the door of his office and seemed to rebound off the corridor walls as Michelle approached. She knocked on the door.

"Come in", he roared barely stopping the tirade he was launching against Mike Waller and Lewis. "Jean" last night, but definitely not "Jean" this morning. Michelle opened the door to find Tanner at his desk and Dr. Lewis standing uncomfortably alongside him. Michelle looked at Mike but he deliberately avoided her gaze; last night still troubled him it was not what he had expected.

"So, Inspector Nash, nice of you to come". Tanner's tone was bitingly sarcastic but that wasn't unusual. Sarcasm was a weapon he employed when asserting his authority. Michelle had seen him use it on countless occasions, humiliating those it was directed against. But Michelle was able to ignore it, Tanner knew that too but, being thick-skinned, he couldn't resist venting his sarcastic bile on her – as he did then.

"You know why I called you in? You, Dr. Lewis and Detective Constable Waller?" His eyes scanned the three of them. Of course Michelle knew, as did the other two but what was the point of responding. No point whatsoever.

"You know that Wayne Francis is dead, the very man who could have helped us to make a breakthrough on the murder investigation". Tanner's voice was now more controlled and noticeably less loud. "Now, I may not appear to be professional about this but I have a gut feeling his death wasn't accidental. Perhaps you share my feeling, Inspector Nash?" Gut feeling or not, Michelle knew Tanner was about to spring a surprise. She was right, absolutely right.

"I want you to look at these pictures, Inspector Nash. Dr. Lewis and Detective Constable Waller have already seen them". Tanner spread the photographs out on his desk; there were three. Three damaging photographs; damaging to Michelle. "The picture shows two women leaving that gay club. Would you say that one of the women bears a marked resemblance to you?" Michelle didn't answer. "The other photograph I believe is one of the murdered girls, Carole Ellington". Tanner knew he had Michelle worried. He pushed on with his case. "And this photograph clearly shows two women in a car and, remarkably, the number plate of that car. A car, Inspector Nash, which is registered in your name". Tanner was like a wild beast devouring its prey. Piece by piece he tore her apart. Michelle was finished, no one could help her. The photograph had condemned her to her fate. Tanner, the "wild beast", gloated over his success. "Detective Constable Waller", he said, "charge her now".

It seemed unreal, the Interview Room; the bare table across which she faced Mike. But unreal it wasn't. The situation in which she found herself was inescapable. Mike looked uncomfortable as did her lawyer, Grahame Pemberton. Mike switched on the recording machine and began his questioning of Michelle. He showed her photographs of the CCTV footage – the ones Tanner had shown her earlier. Yes, that was her car outside the Tropicana…. yes, the woman did look like her ….yes; the other woman was probably Carol Ellington.

"Michelle, is that you in the photograph?" Mike asked. Michelle hesitated before answering: "No, it isn't me".

"So, you're denying you are the woman in this photograph?" It was a question Michelle hadn't wanted to hear – just like all the other questions being put to her.

Michelle looked at Mike's face. It wasn't that of the man she had come to know. The man she considered to be more than a colleague – a man she considered to be her friend. Now he was just another cop and she, another suspect. "Then", he continued. "If not you, who is it? Mother Goose?"

The longer the interview went on she knew it was going to be difficult to extricate herself from this nightmare. She could see herself in Court. See the faces of a disbelieving jury and a sceptical judge. The walk to the cells wasn't far away. Mike desperately wanted Michelle to be innocent of the charges against her. He didn't want to see her condemned to a life in prison.

"I'd like a few words with my lawyer, please". Michelle whispered.

"OK". Mike suspended the interview and left the room to Michelle and her lawyer. Grahame Pemberton was puzzled. "Michelle, I think you are holding something back. If you are, I need to know; otherwise I shan't be able to help you".

"I have to talk to Mike in private", she said.

Mike returned to the room and was about to switch the recording machine on when Michelle grabbed his arm. "Mike, before you do, I have something to say". Mike looked at Pemberton who shook his head in a dismissive way.

"Michelle", said the lawyer. "As you know, this is highly irregular. You have put me in a difficult position – so much so that you'll have to find yourself another lawyer". With that, Pemberton thrust his notes into his briefcase and left the room.

"It's OK to talk now", Mike said at last.

"Mike, the woman in the photo is my sister, twin sister, Tracy. She killed both Carol Ellington and Jolene Annobie".

"I'm going to have to record that, Michelle".

"Mike, please don't! Let me take you to Tracy. I want to talk to her before you make an arrest".

To say Tanner was surprised at Mike Waller's request is, as they say, an understatement but he wasn't as surprised as Mike was when Tanner agreed to let Michelle go with him to Tracy's house. There was no denying that Tanner was an intuitive cop. He knew when to set aside the rule book and this was the time to do it. With Tanner's blessing Mike and Michelle headed for Tracy's house.

* * *

Drawing up alongside the terraced house in his unmarked police car, Mike told Michelle she had just ten minutes to talk to her sister. Michelle rang the doorbell and waited for a few seconds. Behind the door she could hear the voice of her little niece and it brought a lump to her throat. Sweet, sweet Amanda, she loved her as if she were her own.

"Aunty Michelle!" Amanda brushed past her mother and into Michelle's arms. Michelle held her tightly as Tracy watched.

"What are you doing here Michelle? I thought ..." Michelle didn't let her sister finish.

"I know, look, I have to talk to you". Michelle, still carrying Amanda in her arms, followed Tracy into the kitchen.

"I'll put the kettle on Michelle".

"No, no, there isn't time".

"No time – why? What's wrong?"

This was the moment Michelle had dreaded. Tracy instinctively took Amanda from Michelle's arms.

"Amanda why don't you go to your room and get your new doll, I'm sure Aunty Michelle would love to see it".

It was an opportunity for the sisters to talk but Michelle found it hard to speak. She wished that things were different but it was a forlorn wish. Eventually she found the words she dreaded. "Tracy, forgive me, but I've told Mike that you murdered those two girls".

"You what?"

"I'm sorry. There is CCTV footage of my car outside the Gay Club with one of the girls getting into it. I told Mike the other girl was you".

Tracy slapped her sister's face. "Bitch! Bitch!"

Tracy slumped into a chair, her head in her hands. For a few seconds neither girl spoke. Then Tracy looked up at Michelle.

"Michelle, you know I didn't have anything to do with the murders. I can't believe what you did – why, why Michelle? I thought you loved me. I'm your sister for Christ's sake."

The doorbell rang. Michelle left the kitchen and opened the front door. Mike and a uniformed officer stood in the doorway. Mike looked at Michelle.

"OK, where is she", he asked abruptly. For a few minutes Michelle was transfixed. How could she have incriminated her sister? What will happen to little Amanda? Will Tracy ever be able to forgive her?

"Mike", she said at last. "Tracy didn't do it, she didn't murder those girls".

"But …."

"Mike, I know. I'm sorry. Sorry for Tracy".

"Are you telling me you killed those girls?"

"Yes. I don't know why, Mike. Perhaps I did it because of my suppressed lesbian tendencies. Perhaps I was in denial at the time and that denial manifested itself in that horrible and tragic way. Whatever, Mike. I'm sure Dr. Lewis will have the answer".

"Take her to the car". The officer took hold of Michelle's arm.

"Mike, tell Tracy I love her and I'm sorry, so sorry".

*

The Irish Men-of-War
By Eddie Rose

It was the 'phone ringing a little after twelve fifteen that was to awaken Terence O'Hara. He lay there hoping it would stop and he wouldn't have to get up and answer it. Hoped he would not have to cross the cold linoleum floor in his bare feet, nor descend the cold, draughty stairs that would take him down to the bar area where the 'phone was kept.

But the 'phone did not stop and eventually, grumbling to himself, he was forced to get up. He glanced at his wife who was tacked up and snoring for all the world to hear.

More grumbling ensued as he left the bedroom and descended the stairs. Midway down, his bare foot came into contact with something that had earlier been deposited on the threadbare carpet. It was then that O'Hara realised that his wife had forgotten to let the pub mouse-catcher out before coming up to bed, and the cat had crapped on the stairs.

He cursed his wife. Cursed her for being tucked up warm and sound asleep, cursed her for the all-too-familiar smell associated with cat excrement that now invaded his nasal passages. He was behind the bar now, reaching for the receiver with one hand and the bar light with the other, when the ringing suddenly stopped.

Outside it was raining. The yellow glare of the street lamp cast an eerie shadow upon the pub's interior. The headlamps of a passing car pierced the relative darkness for a few moments, enough, it seemed, to illuminate the brandy optic and thus entice O'Hara to partake of a nightcap.

It was the sound of a match being scratched across the sandpapered surface of a box of Swan Vestas that was to cancel O'Hara's thoughts of a second tipple, and to cause him to look in the direction of the noise. The match fizzled, then burst into a pool of light as the figure drew deeply upon the newly-lighted cigarette; then the match was gone, extinguished in the ashtray.

The harshness of the match, though only momentary, offered but a fleeting glimpse as to the identity of the intruder. In that moment, gone was all thought of ever again ascending the stairs to a warm bed and a wife who snored.

Gone, too, was the past memory of stale tobacco smoke and stale sweat from stale people who invariably unburdened their troubles to a sympathetic landlord. A moment's anger that had come with the invasion of the striking match was gone, to be replaced with stark fear of a man under sentence of death.

"Mr Cahill", blurted O'Hara. "It is an unexpected Honour, sir."

The lone figure remained silent as the red glow from the cigarette intensified then faded, intensified then again faded as the smoke hung, blanket-like, to the contours of the silhouetted figure.

"Is a fair terrible night", O'Hara continued, whilst hoping in his heart of hearts that it was all an almighty mistake. If not, then perhaps he'd be able to talk his way out of the inevitability that death was maybe only minutes away.

"Fair terrible, sir, and no mistake."

Silence fell, with just the noise of the wind driving the rain against the panes. Silence that O'Hara was to mistake as a time in which to unburden and plead for his life.

"Look, sir", begged O'Hara, "I didn't tell 'em nothing, honest."

"It's nothing personal", replied the voice, now finishing his cigarette, "but orders are orders."

"But I didn't tell 'em anything, pleaded O'Hara, as a second presence was made known by the cold feel of a pistol barrel touching the side of his head. O'Hara was taken from behind the bar into the pub itself, and there forced to his knees by the butt of the pistol catching him between the shoulder blades. His hands were tied behind his back with masking tape.

"Holy mother of God", begged O'Hara, "Holy Mother, please forgive me. Please forgive me."

Cahill approached and looked down like a sympathetic parent.

"Please, sir, don't do this to me. Please don't kill me."

"You shouldn't have blathered to the Brits. If you hadn't blathered, the court would not have found you guilty, and I wouldn't be here carrying out the court's wishes. But take heart, for the lads back home asked that I convey a message of thanks. That last shipment of arms and semtex, we let it be known to you, knowing all the while that you'd blather to the Brits. We told you it was due on the 15th, when in fact, we took delivery eight days earlier. Now the boys will be looking forward to getting Christmas off with a bang."

Cahill said no more as he proceeded to put on a pair of black gloves. O'Hara began to pray out loud as a warm trickle of urine formed a pool around his knees. The offending smell of excrement became obvious as fear caused him to lose control of his bowels.

O'Hara was executed in the manner prescribed by the Provisional IRA's handbook, by means of a soft-nosed bullet in the back of the head. His lifeless body collapsed onto the carpet as his brains fragmented outwards against the face of the polished wood of the bar.

At the door Cahill paused, looking out into the rain.

"What would you have done if he'd sent his wife down to the 'phone", asked a voice.

"Then we'd have shot the bastard in his own bed", replied Cahill, as he drew his raincoat high about his neck and stepped out into the night. It was still raining when the car dropped Cahill off.

He stood for a while watching it drive away, then turned and walked the one hundred yards along the cut, through onto the council estate. It was still dark when he let himself into his home, shutting out the rain that seemed to fall incessantly. The hall light was on; had been all night. Cahill's youngest had a fear of the dark.

He looked in on his brood, two girls and a boy, the youngest being five, before carefully letting himself into the darkened bedroom. Shelagh breathed deeply as she slept the sleep of an angel.

Cahill felt, as he always did afterwards, the intense surge of adrenaline in which his senses were heightened. The sense of touch, the sense of smell, his intense need to communicate sexually with another was all consuming.

Now, as he lay naked between the sheets, Shelagh felt so deliciously inviting. The scent of her; the warmth from her body; the feel of her skin beneath the thin cotton nightdress. Her body responded as his hands gently ventured beneath the fabric. Her breast felt so firm, so erotic to his touch as she moaned sensuously and moved, allowing him total access to her eager body. His hands explored her taut belly as his mouth nibbled at her flesh, his tongue heightened her pleasure as he searched lower and lower.

Even semi-conscious she was saying take me, penetrate me. Over and over, louder and louder, till she was in danger of waking the whole house with her passion and need for him. Cahill covered her mouth gently with his hand as she went over the edge, as wave after wave of ecstasy washed over her. She drowned in an intense orgasm as her body arched to meet the moment. The rigid form lasted but a moment, and then relaxed as she sank into a sea of calm in the aftermath of her climax.

Her legs came up high to accommodate him as he mounted her, then wrapped themselves around his body as she pulled him into her with gentle thrusting from her hips. Then she eased her motions slightly as he began to thrust in his wanton response, harder and harder, faster and faster, until the very room seem to jar with each penetrating movement.

His intense need to ejaculate was only seconds away, but was held back by an overwhelming desire to have Shelagh join him at his moment of no return. On and on his thrusting into her. He could feel the rising irreversible sensation of wanting to come, but holding back waiting for her. He felt her clawing at his back as she responded to his urging thrusts. His tongue darted in and out of his mouth, as her body gripped his manhood. Then both their writhing bodies held the moment as they erupted in their shared pleasure.

The flood of their love for each other flowed and was accepted as they lay panting, then enclosed in their embrace, subsided into a deep relaxing sleep.

* * *

It was the unexpected RUC road block that was to throw the driver who had chauffeured Cahill that night. The flashing lights that suddenly appeared out of the rain and the bollards filtering any traffic that happened along into a bottleneck. Ahead, the reflections of the lights illuminating the Land Rovers and the armed men who stood in readiness. It was the surprise of the encounter that caused the driver to panic as the wipers fought to clear the slanting rain.

He hesitated, started to slow down, and then remembered the reason he was so far from town. He had not yet disposed of the gun that had been used to dispose of O'Hara. There was no course open to him but to make a run for it.

He gunned the car. The engine protested momentarily at the sudden demand for power, then surged forward. A RUC man narrowly missed being run down as he threw himself out of the path of the oncoming car. Machine guns chattered, bursting the radiator; the windshield shattered in a hail of glass fragments; the front tyres disintegrated as the vehicle slewed towards a gap between the waiting Land Rovers and potential freedom.

The engine was screaming as the car hit the stinger spanning the road, then hurtled into the embankment at the side of the road. It stopped abruptly in a cloud of mud and steam. The driver had died with the car in the deluge of bullets that had entered the car from several directions, engulfing him in its merciless stream.

*

The Men of March and Marcheford
By Edna Stacey

Among the documents relating to the Manor of Doddington is a book which is a copy of two agreements entered into by the lord of the manor, and the commoners of the hamlet of March, the latter being once referred to in the earlier of the two documents as the *'Men of March and Marchford.'*

This earlier document is dated Wednesday 13th November 1612 and the later one August 18th 1669. The date of the book itself is not formally given, but in a schedule which refers to the allotting of certain plots of land in the later document, there appears, in connection with one of the lots, the phrase in brackets- "now 1745," so this undoubtedly fixes the date when the book was written.

Apart from the formal contents of the book, the volume itself appears to have had a history. It contains about three hundred pages, all written by hand, and in size measures six inches by eight inches; it is stoutly bound in leather covered boards, with tooled gilt back, and had several designs, end pieces and other decorative work, all executed in pen and ink. The only printed matter in it is a label pasted on the inner cover, which bears the name in cursive type, *Thomas Shepheard*, the same being surmounted by a coat of arms, or other heraldic device. He was probably the original owner of the book as the name appears as one of the nominal defendants in both of the documents, though this person could not have been the same as the first owner of the book; but it is pretty certain that the name on the label is that of the person who ordered the book to be prepared.

There is a note on one of the flyleaves that the book was left by Thomas Shepheard in his will to Mr. Daniel Barley, attorney at law, of March, who in turn appears to have left it to a relative, Mr. Edward Barley. Another note states that the volume subsequently became the property of the late Mr F.J. Wise, by whom it was given to Mr. King (of King and Sharman), the then lord of the manor. Two pencil notes on one of the pages show that Mr. E. Barley lent the book to someone whose initials were J.J. on December 2nd 1814, and the book was returned on the same day the following year. The only other note is on one of the end fly-leaves, and refers to the *'Bound of the Hamlet of March as by memorandum in the court Rolls of the manor of Doddington, 1642, the limits being at Whittlesey Dike, extending to middle drain at Ransonmoor, then to Studbridge, and thence to Stoney-ditch, and then on to the north part via Stoney Grange to Hamlet Hamps, and lastly to the Chatfor Fen corner.'*

The question at issue arose out of a dispute between the lord of the manor and the men of *"March and Marchford"* as to the liability of certain areas to a payment of rents to the lord of the manor. An agreement of 1612 appears to have set out that formerly the manor was part of the possession of the Bishopric of Ely, and later became the property of the Crown. On March 29th 1602, it was granted to Sir John Peyton by Queen Elizabeth in consideration of the sum of three thousand pounds, and a yearly fee of £74 6s 8d.

The copy of an old map now in possession of March Museum that shows the enclosed lands in the Manor of Doddington, is supposed to date about 1601, and it seems fairly certain that this map must have been prepared in connection with the grant of the manor in 1602. Apparently, after entering into possession of this purchase, Sir John Peyton and his advisers investigated the position of the rights of the lord, and as a result claimed that certain lands which at the time when the Bishop of Ely was the lord had yielded rents, had now ceased to do so; also that other lands, which at that time had been part of the private demesne of the lord, were being treated as common lands by the men of March and Marchford.

A denial of these contentions was made by the alleged culprits, and no doubt during the ten years that elapsed between the purchase of the lordship and the date of the agreement there was a lot of argument, friction, and threatenings between the disputants. Approximately 130 names are mentioned as offenders in the document, beginning with Sir Richard Cox (Bishop of Ely) and Robert Balam, Esquire, but the rest, excepting a Doctor of Civil Law, appear to have been ordinary commoners. It is interesting to note that of John Cowerd de Badgeny this seems to be the only reference to that part of the present town.

By the mediation of friends a conference was held between the parties, which ultimately resulted in an agreement being arrived at, and it was further agreed that the settlement should be *'established, confirmed and agreed in the Honourable Court of Exchequer'*. The agreement provided that, in consideration of the abandonment of his claims, the lord of the manor should hereafter hold as his own absolutely, certain lands in various parts of the manor. Sir Richard Cox and Robert Balam, Esquire were placated by a grant of land to the knight and his lady for their lives, with succession to Robert Balam. The commoners being confirmed in their own existing rights of common in the rest of the area of the manor, and were granted the right to sub-divide the common land, should they think fit, without hindrance from the Lord.

The commoners appear to have received a concession in the matter of fines on admittance to copyhold. These fines had been hitherto *'arbitral'*, but for the future they were to be *'certain'*, and were not to exceed the sum of one year's ancient copyhold or customary rent. The commoners were also allowed to commit *'waste'* upon their holdings, and to *'demise and let'* them for a period of 21 years without leave or license of their lord.

Further, it was decreed that copyholders should be freed from the payment of any *'Heriot's*, which were rights of the lord to the best beast of the copyholder at the time of his death. They were also freed from the obligation from *'doing any days work and carriages for or in respect of their customary messuages, lands, tenements, or hereditaments held of the said manor of Doddington (the fetching of the lord's drifts only excepted)'*.

The second agreement referred to earlier between the lord of the manor of Doddington and the copyholders of March was confirmed by decree of Chancery on Saturday 27th November 1669. Unlike the previous agreement of 1612 it did not originate from a dispute between the parties. It sets out that in nineteen specific areas besides other *'waste grounds, fens, small pingles and small greens'* over which the owners of the ancient houses in March exercised right of *'common of pasture'*, this right had been without stint, the lack of which resulted in an excessive number of cattle being fed thereon to the detriment of the commons generally. Further, that as the commons had very little or no severals or enclosures for mowing hay for their cattle for winter food, the said cattle were almost starved during the winter. In order therefore that the pastures should be fed in an orderly way, it was agreed that they should be stinted for the future, though still being held in common, and that for the effective provision of winter food for cattle, three large areas of land hitherto held in common, should be parcelled out into lots to the different owners of the ancient houses to be enclosed by them and held thereafter as their exclusive copyhold, no rights of common over them continuing.

The lord of the manor, two gentlemen, and twelve commoners were appointed as trustees and empowered to carry out the agreement. The names of all the commoners affected by the agreement some 180 in all, are set out in full detail, some three or four times, and a Book of Rules, Rates, Orders and Agreements was made and agreed upon. It is curious to note that in the agreement the parties thought fit to put on record their opinion that it would be inadvisable to extend further the division into separate severalties the rest of the pastures and commons. They said that such a course *'would very much tend to the impairing of our estates and ruin the hamlet of March'*.

Certain lands in the parish, totalling in area 3,440 acres were to be kept and used as cow pastures, and the grazing of these was regulated, a definite number of animals being allocated to every commonable house. The number of these varied with the seasons, a larger number being allowed from Michaelmas to Lady Day than from May Day to Michaelmas, and no grazing was allowed from Lady Day to May Day, but the numbers might be varied from time to time by the trustees. No difference however was made between one house and another in their respective numbers. On the stinted commons the number of animals allowed to graze was less for each house than was allowed on the pasture; sheep could be grazed on the commons all the year, except between Lady day and May day, but were allowed on the pastures only from Michaelmas to Lady day. There were penalties for trespassing animals, the excessive number grazing and for animals not bearing marks of ownership.

Only animals belonging to the commoners or those hired from commoners were allowed to graze and one or more fen reeves were appointed by the trustees to see that theses arrangements were strictly carried out. They were authorised to impose and collect the appropriate fines and penalties for non-observances of the conditions. A steward or bailiff was to be appointed at a salary not exceeding £10 per annum by the trustees at a meeting held each year on Easter Monday, when that official was to render an account of all monies received and paid out by him in connection with the trust, and at another meeting to be held on the second Tuesday in April each year the trustees could make or vary byelaws and orders for the ensuing year. These were to be entered in a book and a duplicate of these rules was to be provided for the entry upon the Manor Rolls, the registrar or town clerk being paid five pounds per annum for this work. The expenses of measuring and surveying the 180 plots of allotted lands and all other expenses and costs in connection with the preparation and carrying out the agreement were to be met by a rate on every commonable house, and this was not to exceed 30/- per house for each of the first two years and not exceed 5/- per annum afterwards.

All differences or disputes respecting the areas of plots or other matters were to be settled by the trustees and every commoner was to give or find labour for not more than five days in each year for mowing thistles on the pastures and commons and for generally keeping them in good order and condition. The digging of clay, sand or gravel, on the pastures and stinted commons was to be limited by the trustees to the actual necessities of the commoners and to such places as the trustees might select. A list of 20 poor persons without commonable rights was to be furnished to the lord of the manor by the trustees each year, and he was entitled to select from it as many persons as he chose; those so chosen were to be allowed the right to keep no more than two cows each on the pasture and not more than twenty in all. Any names on the list not so selected by the lord, could be nominated by the trustees to exercise a similar right. A license for one year only was issued to all those having this privilege and a fee of 4d charged for each license granted.

Continuing the details of the agreement of 1669 between the lord of the manor of Doddington and the commoners of March there was a provision that 200 acres of fenny ground in Burrowmoor adjoining Hatchwood, were to be set out for the poor of March in order that they might dig turves there for fuel. The trustees granted licenses for this purpose and the number of turves to be cut in any one year by any one person was not to exceed 3,000. The lord of the manor was also allowed to grant licenses to a number of poor persons not exceeding twenty in all, with a similar limitation of 30,000 as a total.

All houses reputed to be ancient at any time since the agreement of 1612 and since that time that had right of pasture in the commons were to be reputed commonable houses. The tenant of the rector of Doddington at Tythe Barn Green, in the town, was to have the liberty of keeping two cows on the adjoining pasture.

Next follows in the agreement about 180 paragraphs each one setting out one plot of land, defining its area and position, and stating the particular ancient house in the town to which the land is appropriated. No house was to be built on any plot under a penalty of 10/- per month as long as the house remained standing. The Courts of the lord of the manor were precluded from altering the agreement in any way, but might confirm it if they elected to do so.

The lord of the manor was to have common rights in respect of the manor of Hatchwood, and Roger Jenyns was allowed two plots in Whitemoor for a roadway in order that he might have access to his 600 acres of land held by him severally in West Fen.

There was only one objection to the confirmation of the agreement when it was before the court. Sir John James asked that Read's Fen House should be regarded as a commonable house and be entitled to a certain plot of land similar to that allocated to each of the other commonable houses. The court agreed this and all parties then confirmed the agreement.

This concluded the lengthy task but it was followed by an appendix, giving details of a meeting of the trustees, at which a perpetual order was made for the fencing of the plots of land allotted by the agreement.

Then follows a double schedule of the houses entitled to participate in the allotment of land.

The first schedule gives the lots in proper numerical order as marked on the maps, and gives the second schedule lot number of the house to which each plot was to belong. The second schedule gives the houses arranged in a proper numerical order and shows the first schedule number of the plot apportioned to each of them.

The second schedule arranged the commonable house in six groups in the following order: -

Norwood Side 38 houses
Whittle End 27 houses
Outward End 38 houses
High Dyke 35 houses
Town End 36 houses
Knights End 6 houses

Whittle End and Outward End are now known as West End and Nene Parade, and High Dyke is the present High Street, Causeway and Avenue. Except for Norwood Side, the township appears to have been fairly compact, developing originally from the Town End area and it is surprising to find so large a number of ancient houses in the isolated district of Norwood Side. The land allotted under this agreement is confined to three districts: -

1. The area in Horsemoor and Binnimoor lying between and on either side of the Hook and Horsemoor drains.
2. The Creek drainage district.
3. The land on both side of Middle Drove as far as Plantwater Drain, and the land on the north side of White-moor Drove as far as Plantwater Drain, and nine plots of land in the present Wisbech Road from the Guide Post to Westry House. The land on the south side of Whitemoor Drove was then held in severalty and was probably the land of Mr Jenyns already referred to.

In all cases the arrangement was based upon the drains, which are practically the same today as they were then.

A map each of the three areas showed every plot, with its area and lot number. These old maps are very interesting. The Binnimoor and Horsemoor map shows that in those days the Hook and the Horsemoor drains were not connected and worked by one pump; each drain had its own windmill pump. The Horsemoor windmill was almost on the same spot as the later Binnimoor engine and the Hook drain windmill was on the riverbank of the field near Read's Fen gate, a brick culvert marked the spot. Upwell Road was then known as Horsemoor Drove and Coleseed Road as Colestead Drove. In the Creek district the windmill pump was nearer Creek Road and close to the site of a cottage.

The present Twenty Foot River was known as Moors Drain, but on the larger museum map the river is marked as Hobbs River. Flaggrass Hill Road was then Low Drove and School House Road was White's Fen Drove. In the Middle Drove and Whitemoor Drove areas there were two windmill engines, one where the present West Fen engine is and another on the riverbank a short distance beyond Middle Drove, but the whole drainage was connected just as it is at present.

The last plot along Wisbech Road bears no lot number and is not in the schedule of plots, being marked on the map as *'Lot to ye Angel'* and the corresponding lot on the other side of the drain at the end of it, which fronts Whitemoor Drove is also without number being marked *'Lot to ye house next to ye Angel'*. In all the areas most of the fields can still now be easily identified, but the coming of the railway affected some of them. As it is more than 300 years since the allotment was made it is not a little surprising to find so little change in the arrangements of the fields from then to today.

*

Time to Deliver
By Helen Stevens

Lucy Sweetacre had been delivering mail in the village of Marshwillow for almost fifteen years, and now she had been "invited to take early retirement", in other words, she thought, they don't want me any more. I can hardly refuse the invitation! Now I am on the scrap heap at forty-five, there are very few local jobs that would be available to me. Mail delivery was being taken over by the local town, Charton, and postmen, or women, would be coming out each day in vans and deliver around the village. They called this rationalisation, but Lucy felt it was a backward step.

By now, she knew almost everyone in the village, and she particularly kept a look out for anything out of the ordinary, especially where the old folk were concerned, and made sure that they received help if they needed it. Sometimes she would call, even if there were no mail to deliver, just to check up on someone or other who had been unwell, or who she had not seen for a day or two.

Lucy took on her job after her husband, Luke, had abandoned her for another woman. Most men leave their wives for a younger model, but Luke had bucked the trend and fallen for someone older. His new wife was seven years older than he was, and twelve years older than Lucy. Lucy and Luke's two children, Anne, who was six, and Paula, five, missed their dad being at home. Lucy did everything that she could to give them a happy home life, and made sure that Luke took them out from time to time, even though his new wife did not appear enthusiastic about it.

Some two months after Luke left, Lucy was in the village post office combined village shop when Mrs Fenton, who ran the business with her husband, told Lucy how difficult it was to recruit a new postman, to replace the one who had retired. "People today don't seem to want this sort of job," she said; "They seem to think that getting up at five each day is a terrible hardship. I suppose it interferes with their social life, as they have to go to bed a bit early."

"Could I apply for the job?" asked Lucy.

"You? Well, I don't see why not. You'll have to make an early start every day, so you'll have to have someone to get your two girls off to school."

"That wouldn't be a problem, Angela Swailes next-door-but-one would help me there, I know. I already look out for her children after school, until she gets home from work. I could carry on doing that, as I would be home every afternoon."

So Lucy had applied, and had been given the job to deliver the mail in Marshwillow village. She had loved the job, and her children had coped well with Lucy leaving early each morning, and with Angela getting them up, breakfasted and ready for school. Lucy found the exercise kept her very fit, and, despite a hearty appetite, she managed to keep slim. Now it was all at an end. She accepted that she would have to retire at some time or other, but not now, at only forty-five. Of course, there was a small pension, in addition to the lump sum she received. It wasn't the money aspect that bothered Lucy. She did not feel like retiring, she liked delivering the mail, and she liked keeping an eye on her customers. She would miss the work, and hoped that people would miss her.

TIME TO DELIVER

Her last day at work came and went, but Lucy found it hard not to still get up at five each morning. The post these days always arrived after lunch, and Lucy wondered how the old people felt about it, especially as she noticed that there always seemed to be different people delivering. The old folks like continuity, she knew. She had thought of visiting some of them, but felt it would be intruding; it was different when she had the excuse of delivering letters. Her days stretched out in front of her, and without the daily contact with people, and with the two girls growing up and leading their own lives away from home, she began to feel a little lonely.

Noticing that she had run out of bread, Lucy put on her coat, and walked to the village shop. She liked going to the shop, rather than driving to the supermarket in Charton, at least she might see someone she could enjoy chatting to. Mrs Fenton was in a bit of a flap on this particular morning. She told Lucy that her husband would have to dismiss the newspaper boy, as he was unreliable, and often late. Today he had called in, saying he had got up too late. "He doesn't seem to understand that we need to depend on him," grumbled Mrs Fenton. "It's hard to get youngsters to deliver the papers these days, they all go to school in town on the bus, and if they are late, they miss it. And now Fred has had to go out and do the job himself, and today we have the weekly free paper to deliver as well."

"Mrs Fenton," said Lucy, "I can help!"

"What do you mean?"

"Well, since I lost my job delivering the post I am at a loose end. I'm used to getting up early, so I could deliver the papers for you. The free ones as well, if you like."

"I would certainly give you the job, but you don't have a bike, do you? Anyway, we can't afford adult wages; we could only pay delivery boys' rates."

"It's not the money I need, it's a job! And I don't need a bike. All the years I delivered mail I used a cart; I could do the same with the newspapers."

"Only problem is, we don't have a cart."

"Mrs Fenton, please leave that to me, I'll organise it."

So Lucy went home, collected her car, and drove to the junk-shop in Charton. "I'm looking for an old pram," she said, "The type with big wheels with inflatable tyres, and springs. It doesn't have to be in good condition, in fact, I only need the chassis."

The owner sucked his teeth for a moment, rolling his eyes in thought. "I think I have something in the shed at the back. Hold on a minute."

He came back with the remains of what once had been a classic, coach-built pram. It looked sad, it was very rusty, and the tyres were flat.

"Perfect!" said Lucy.

They agreed on a very reasonable price, and the pram was put in the back of Lucy's car. Next stop was Peter Jarman's house. Peter had married a school-friend of Lucy. Lucy knew he was a bit of a handy man, and was good at making something out of very little. Also, it was time she visited Maggie, Peter's wife. Lucy felt that she had been neglecting her friends of late, while wallowing in self-pity over losing her job.

Two weeks later, Lucy had her cart. A smart black wooden box had been mounted on the now rust-free pram chassis, there was a handle to pull it with, the tyres had been inflated, and it was, as Peter said, ready to roll. There was even a cover, in case of wet weather. Peter would take nothing for the work, but, when Lucy insisted, agreed on the modest cost of the materials; he said that most of the bits had come out of his shed, anyway.

On the first Monday of her new job, Lucy dressed herself in a comfortable, warm tracksuit, put on her sturdy walking shoes and set off to arrive at the shop by seven o'clock. Mr Fenton had the papers all marked up and waiting.

"The lad used to make three trips," he said, "But with your cart, you need only do the one. At least I don't need to tell you the route!"

Lucy was in her element. The weather was dry, she was working again, and she could keep an eye on the old folks without appearing nosy. As it was her first day, she decided against just stuffing the papers through the letterboxes of the old people, and instead, knocked on each door. Of course, this made the job slower than it should have been, but she wanted to see her old friends again, and let them know she was 'doing the rounds' again, even though in a different guise. They were so pleased to see her. She lost count of the times she was invited in for tea, and had to refuse them all, otherwise the job would have taken all day.

And so she continued for the next year; delivering daily newspapers Monday to Friday (there was a reliable week-end lad for the other two days), and the weekly free paper to every house on Wednesdays, and was also able to keep an eye on the old folks.

One day one of the old ladies, Mrs Freegate, asked Lucy to do her a favour. "My rheumatism is bad, and can't get to the post office to collect my pension," she said, "If I sign it, could you get it for me, and bring it tomorrow?"

"Is there anything you need from the shop?" asked Lucy. "I could fetch it for you at the same time."

"Well, my daughter usually fetches my shopping from the supermarket when she gets hers, but I do like the village shop. It's much more friendly. I'll tell you what I'll do, I'll phone an order through to Mrs Fenton, I won't need much, and you can pay it out of my pension."

As Mrs Freegate told her neighbours about the help she had from Lucy, and so Lucy now found she had started another service for her customers. If the orders that were phoned through were too large for her to carry comfortably in the cart, Mr Fenton would deliver them in his van. The Fentons were delighted with the arrangement.

"All over the country village shops are closing," said Mr Fenton. "More and more people are shopping at the town supermarkets, but our business is increasing, and it's all thanks to you, Lucy. If you hadn't lost your job delivering the mail, and taken on the newspaper round, we would probably have closed by now."

* * *

TIME TO DELIVER

It was five years after she started the newspaper deliveries that the Fentons took Lucy aside and told her that the time had come for them to retire, and that they were selling their business to their nephew, Gerald Parker.

Lucy was concerned about her job, and said so.

"Don't you worry, my dear," said Mrs Fenton. "Gerald knows how important you are to the business, and it is written into our sale agreement that you will be kept on. After all, without you, the shop would not be as successful as it is, and we have made that plain to Gerald."

Gerald Parker was a tall, fair-haired man, about her own age, with pale blue eyes; he seemed to have a smile hovering on his face most of the time, and Lucy often found him staring at her. She liked him very much; he was a considerate boss, despite his stares. He was always polite, and from the beginning had addressed her as "Lucy Sweetacre". She had called him Mr Parker out of politeness, but one day she started calling him "Gerald Parker" instead, and this amused him.

From time to time Lucy and Gerald spent Sundays together; they both enjoyed visiting country houses, and, in the summer months, this became a regular outing. They both delighted in walking in the gardens and grounds. Gerald was amazed that Lucy, despite her on-foot delivery every day, still enjoyed walking. Each seemed to enjoy the other's company, and Lucy began to feel very relaxed when with Gerald.

"Well, Lucy Sweetacre," he said one day; "It's been two years since I took over this shop, and things have got better day by day. Will you join me for a drink to celebrate?"

"Why not?" replied Lucy. "I have something to celebrate myself."

By way of reply, Gerald raised his eyebrows, but Lucy did not enlighten him.

They met at the village pub that evening, and almost the first thing that Gerald said after they had their drinks was "Well, what are you celebrating?"

"I am about to become a grandmother."

"How thrilling! Are you pleased? Is this your first grandchild?"

"So many questions! Yes, I am pleased, and this is my first. My daughter Anna married three years ago, and this is their first child."

"I hope you don't mind me saying so, Lucy Sweetacre, but you look remarkable young for a grandmother. You are slim, and not at all mumsy, or should I say, granny-ish at all!"

"I don't mind, Gerald Parker. I don't feel mumsy or granny-ish. But it is a lovely feeling, expecting a grandchild. It's a great morale-booster, becoming a grandmother; it gives a feeling of continuity."

Gerald sat looking at Lucy; he looked at her for so long that she began to feel a little uncomfortable. "What is it?" she asked.

"I'm just wondering…"

"Yes?"

"We make a good partnership, don't we, with me running the shop and post office and you doing the deliveries?"

"Yes, I agree that it is working."

"Do you know that my uncle made a proviso when I took over the shop?"

"Yes, of course I do. You had to keep me on."

"It went a little further than that. He said that if you stayed at least two years, and you have now, you were to become a partner in the business."

"I don't have the money to buy a partnership!"

"Oh, there's no money involved. My uncle took care of that. It's his gift to you, a quarter share in the business."

Lucy looked at Gerald for a long moment, unable to think of what to say. So, eventually, she held out her hand.

"Shake, partner."

*

Where the Heart Is
By Herta Davey

Tim and I were spending that Saturday morning just lounging about. Recovering from a gruelling week at the office, we got up late and decided to have breakfast on the patio, to take advantage of the all too rare summer sunshine. I had forgotten the last time we had a whole weekend at home together, enjoying the simple things like reading our newspaper in bed, or taking a leisurely stroll around the garden. It was sheer bliss!

Then the 'phone rang. Tim answered it. When he came back his face was ashen.

"It – it was mother", he blurted out. "Father's very ill, she wants us to come right away."

I was stunned. "Poor Harold", I uttered, "what's wrong with him?"

"I don't know Jane. Mother didn't say and I didn't think to ask."

"Mmm", I wondered, could it be another one of their ploys to get Tim to go rushing home at a moment's notice, only to find there's nothing wrong.

"You are coming, aren't you darling?" He asked anxiously.

"Of course I am. Why do you ask?"

"Oh, I just wondered", he muttered, hurrying off to change and pack a few things.

Tim knew I felt uneasy about going back to 'Rooks Farm', that gloomy old house out in the middle of the Fens, ever since that time two years ago when he persuaded me to spend Christmas there with his parents. We weren't married then. His mother, a pleasant but somewhat straight-laced person, insisted we slept in separate rooms. Mine was in the oldest part of the house which was built of stone. No doubt to get me as far away from her beloved son as possible.

When it was time for us all to retire for the night, she escorted me to the guest room, as she so proudly called it. Although, having spent a night in this room once, I was doubtful whether any guests would wish to repeat the experience.

"You'll be quite comfortable in here my dear", she said as she opened the heavy creaking oak door.

"There's no central heating, but Harold made a nice big fire for you. The bathroom's through there", she said, pointing to a door next to a large wardrobe. "Well, goodnight then Jane, I hope you sleep well."

As the heavy door closed behind her, I fervently wished that I was at Siverdale, my bright and beautiful, centrally heated home in Oxford.

I must have been out of my mind to let Tim persuade me to come to this God forsaken place. A shiver ran down my spine. The room felt cold in spite of the huge log fire blazing in the medieval grate. I glanced anxiously around the room fearing something horrible might be lurking in the shadowy recesses.

"Pull yourself together Jane", I told myself, "you're a grown woman for heaven's sake.

I moved closer to the fire to thaw myself out and sat down on this old rocking chair, wishing that Tim was with me, wondering if he ever missed me now that he was at home, surrounded by his doting parents. Suddenly I felt shut out of his life and very lonely.

Gradually, with the gentle rocking of the chair and the warmth of the fire, an overpowering sense of tiredness descended upon me. My eyes fell on the bed a few feet away. I slipped off my shoes and slid beneath the soft downy duvet, too weary to undress. Oddly enough I slept quite well in my gloomy surroundings, although I could have sworn I heard a repetitive squeak penetrating my slumbering senses some time during the night. My heavy eyelids opened for a moment, the embers were still glowing in the grate, faintly illuminating what I perceived in my semi-conscious mind to be a woman dressed in black with a white bonnet on her head, rocking to and fro in the rocking chair.

Next morning, in the cold light of the day I shrugged it off; putting it down to a bad dream. When I mentioned it to Tim, he just laughed.

"You were definitely dreaming darling, there are no ghosts rattling about in this house and I have never seen a lady in a white bonnet."

* * *

"Hurry up Jane." Tim's impatient voice rang out from the car.

"Just locking up darling", I called, and the moment I managed to get into my seat, we were off.

The journey was quite pleasant. As I wasn't driving, I was able to appreciate the ever changing scenery. Tim had lapsed into total silence, lost in his own thoughts. Just managing to answer with a grunt if I spoke to him. I slept for a while. When I opened my eyes the towns and villages had given way to the wide open spaces of the Fens. Sprawling acres of ripening wheat and barley as far as the eye could see. Enhanced by a profusion of red poppies here and there. A lump came to my throat at this awesome sight.

"Nice, isn't it darling?"

Tim had suddenly come to life, his eyes shining.

"The Fens have a beauty of their own, don't you think Jane?"

"Yes, I suppose they do Tim, especially at this time of year."

Secretly recalling a time in mid-winter, when I thought otherwise.

We were both greatly relieved when we drew up outside Rooks Farm. It had been a long, tiring journey. Louise came running out to greet us with open arms.

Well Tim, really! Clasping him to her ample bosom the moment he stepped out of the car. From where I was standing, the parable of the prodigal son sprang fleetingly to mind.

"I'm so glad you came, both of you", acknowledging me at last with a peck on the cheek. "You look a little peaky Jane. A few days spent out here will soon put you right. "But let's go inside", she said, linking her arms through ours, "it's cooler in the house. There's some lemonade in the fridge, you must be thirsty after your long journey in this heat."

She wasn't joking, my throat felt like sawdust.

"Supper will be ready presently, but you might like to freshen up a bit first. I've put you in the guest room for now."

My heart sank on hearing those words. I had hoped never to set foot inside that spooky room again. And what did she mean when she said "for now". I consoled myself with the knowledge that Tim would be with me this time.

"What about father", Tim asked anxiously. Hardly listening to a word Louise was saying. "How is he? What's wrong with him?"

"He's quite ill dear, as I told you over the 'phone. He had a slight heart attack during the night and Dr Fox ordered him to stay in bed. He'll be looking in on him every day."

"Why isn't he in hospital, mother? Surely with a heart attack, that's where he ought to be."

"The doctor didn't think it was life threatening, Tim. I'm sure he knows best dear. You mustn't worry too much, your father's quite strong. I'm sure he'll be up and about in no time. You'll be able to see him in the morning, after the doctor's been; he's probably asleep now."

"We might as well go up and freshen up then Jane."

I could see he was disappointed at not seeing Harold that day as he'd hoped.

The dreaded guest room had undergone a surprising but pleasant transformation. Bright floral curtains had replaced the drab, depressing drapes. A soft rose pink carpet covered the rough, wooden floorboards. The dark, heavy furniture which looked so menacing that night in the dim light, struck no fear in my heart this time. The rocking chair was still there; it had been pushed into the niche next to the chimney breast.

As I stood there staring at it, the memory of that night came flooding back. I couldn't help wondering yet again, whether it was just a dream after all.

Tim's excited voice suddenly broke the spell, grasping my hand and pulling me towards the window.

"Look over there Jane", he cried out. "You won't see anything like this in the city."

Glancing in the direction he was pointing, I had to admit it was the most spectacular sunset I had ever seen. The setting sun had transformed the whole of the western sky into a fiery red phenomenon. Words could not describe this awesome wonder of nature.

* * *

Dr Fox had already left by the time I surfaced from the bedroom next morning. Tim had been up for some hours, unable to sleep over worrying about Harold. He was in the kitchen waiting anxiously for me, handing me a freshly poured and much needed cup of tea as soon as I walked in.

"Father's been asking to see us", he said, "but the doctor warned us not to tire him out."

Harold was propped up in his huge bed, surrounded by countless pillows. Louise was fussing around him, making sure that he was comfortable. His face lit up at the sight of Tim.

"Hallo my boy", he said affectionately. "I'm delighted to see you, and you Jane", he added as an afterthought.

"Hallo Harold", I muttered, bending over to plant a kiss on one of his pale, sunken cheeks. I had a deep sense of remorse at doubting the authenticity of Louise's 'phone call the previous morning.

"Sit down, both of you", he said, indicating feebly some chairs conveniently placed beside his bed. "What I have to say won't come as a complete surprise to either of you. As you can see, I'll have to take it easy from now on and obviously, I won't be able to run the farm anymore as I used to. So it's up to you now Timothy to keep this place going. You must come home now. We need you here."

"But what about our advertising agency in Oxford and our house", I butted in, surprised at my own audacity.

"Sell the lot", came the cold response from Harold. "You'll get used to being a farmer's wife Jane, as Louise did. Have some children. It's about time we had some younguns running around this place. It'll give you something else to think about."

'Oh, what a nerve', I thought, and glared at Tim, hoping for some support, but there was none forthcoming. In fact, he seemed in total agreement with his father. I felt the blood rush to my face. I had to get out of there. I wrenched open the door and fled down the wide staircase out into the open air, determined to get as far away from there as possible, until I found myself at the edge of a deep dyke.

Frustrated by this insurmountable obstacle, I sank down amid the long grass and burst into tears of anger and self-pity. How could I, a city girl, ever get accustomed to life out here in the middle of nowhere. The nearest neighbour is miles away.

Louise found me there, still feeling sorry for myself.

"Didn't get very far then Jane."

"No", I replied dejectedly. She sat down next to me with a deep sigh.

"You know, Jane, I wanted to run away once. It was a long time ago now. I was billeted here when I was a land army girl during the last war. Oh, by the way, I don't come from these parts either. London, that 's where I come from. You look surprised."

I was.

"Well, anyway", she continued, "I was installed in the room you and Tim are in at the moment. One night I awoke with a start for some unknown reason. Perhaps the branches of the laburnum were scraping against the window panes, or the wind whistling through the eaves, I don't know. I was about to close my eyes when I noticed this shadow of a woman standing by the fireplace. It was the white bonnet that attracted my attention. It positively glowed in the dark. Well, I ran screaming out of there and I would have run straight out of the house wearing nothing but my nightdress, if I hadn't run into Harold's arms. He had come out of his bedroom to see what the racket was. Clinging to him like a vine, I told him what I saw. He laughed his head off.

"There's no need to be afraid of her, he said, she appears every now and then in that room to frighten young ladies like you out of their wits, but she's harmless."

"Harmless or not, I'm out of here in the morning Mr Fenton. I'm not spending another night in that room. I protested vigorously, still trembling with fear and reluctant to free myself from his strong, comforting arms. However, I was allocated a different room there and then, so I decided to stay. The truth was that Harold stole my heart that night, and neither the ghostly lady nor the midges at harvest time could induce me to leave here after that."

"It's different for me, Louise", I agonised. "Tim and I have made a good life for ourselves in Oxford. We're happy there."

"I don't doubt it, but are you sure it's what Tim really wants. Have you ever bothered to ask him if he was as happy there as you thought he was?"

"He never said that he wasn't", I replied tartly.

"He probably wouldn't, because he loves you too much. Well, I must get back to the house, see if Harold's alright and get lunch ready. Come back with me, Jane. Think things over. You can still run away later on, after you've had something to eat", she said jokingly. With that, she struggled to her feet and made her way back to the house.

Food was the last thing on my mind right then. I suddenly realised how selfish I had been all those years. There had been occasions in the past when Tim had spoken wistfully about dropping out of the rat race and of going home. I never listened. Never took him seriously. I loved Tim more than anything, yet I failed to see that while he loved me, part of him would forever be rooted in this place. He was a Fen man like his father.

Tim was still in Harold's room when I got back. Sitting in the same chair he was in when I left so angrily earlier that morning, his head buried in his hands. He rose to his feet as I walked towards him. Tears welled up in my eyes at seeing him so miserable.

"I'm so sorry", I said between sobs and suddenly we were in each other's arms.

"We'll go home as soon as father's recovered darling. I love you too much to lose you."

"No Tim, we *are* home. Besides, it wouldn't be fair to deprive our future 'younguns' as Harold likes to call them of their natural right to be spoiled by their grandparents."

A sigh of relief emanated from the (supposedly) sleeping Harold.

"Good on yer, Jane", he said, "welcome to Rooks Farm."

*

Siggy
By Jack Alster

Certain images of people remain sharp in the mind. My ever-present image of Uncle Siggy is of an arm raised awkwardly so that his elbow could get under the shiny brown strap, which went down from his shoulder into that mysterious area somewhere near his legs. I never saw his legs, so buckled and twisted were they and so ashamed was he of them. Perhaps when I was watching, his legs were pushed sideways so I couldn't see them, but I knew he worked his legs by moving his shoulders and somehow got his dead limbs over the ridge of his wheelchair. Having done so, he settled down for the day, never to move his legs again until the shoulders raised them. He was a living marionette.

He'd had polio in the 1910's and it shaped his life, for apart from the completely twisted body and dead legs, he was all bones. His head (except for the marvellous brown eyes) was a skull with tight skin on; he had a high, rather noble forehead and then the head caved backwards as if in retreat. There were virtually no lips and his cheeks were hollowed out; the neck was skinny – an old man's neck (though he could only have been around 30). Then his startling, perpendicular shoulders, which descended like an inverted triangle into the rest of the misshapen body, from which even I, at 8 years old, averted my eyes.

When mother said: "Uncle Siggy will look after you when I'm at work", I almost, but not quite, cried an objection. "You don't mind, do you?" she persisted. I'd turned my head away. It wasn't lack of affection for Uncle Siggy, but the aversion children have of the diseased.

I didn't argue with mother – we were so close after my father left that emotion was transmitted by telepathy. She knew I didn't want to go to that room on the third floor in one of Vienna's poorer districts where Uncle Siggy slept and worked, but she couldn't deal with my reluctance. She had enough to worry about with work and making ends meet, without caring over-much about my feelings: they had to take a back seat.

The odd thing was I did feel a sort of sympathy for Uncle Siggy, because I was often ill myself. But sympathy is one thing, being with him for hours on end is another.

Now I realise he was as reluctant as I. In fact, when I was left by mother in his one large room, he looked nervously at me.

"I've got some books for you", he said eagerly, "I've also got your favourite chocolate balls."

Why didn't I smile at him? Why didn't I have the heart to see an adult making desperate efforts to 'get on' with a child? Because a child (anyway, this child) had a rather priggish honesty. I saw the long day stretching ahead without much talk and within the claustrophobia of one adult and one child. I foresaw only tedium in a hot room and frustration that might well lead to tantrums and temper. Worse, temper that had to be suppressed, for Uncle Siggy was the family victim: the poor soul who had been dealt some lousy cards by life and who, I was constantly warned, must always be treated kindly, even pitied. So, tantrums were out!

The books meant nothing. With few pictures and indecipherable writing, a blur of print I had no intention of even attempting to understand. Much more interesting, at the other end of his large, thick work table, was a glitter of jeweller's instruments. Especially eye-catching was the electric cleaning wheel, the dentist-like cutting drill, the immaculate leather-shiny cloths and a whole range of boxes. All the boxes were cardboard, except one: a black metal box with a lock on it. I guessed that was where he kept *real* gems, the immensely valuable diamonds, rubies, sapphires and emeralds.

I couldn't wait to see those colours in twinkling flashes be worked by him. Impatiently, I waited for him to start. He clicked: here we could be together, here our interests would coincide. So, with a sly grin, he unlocked the box and there were little, light-brown envelopes, all marked. He took one out. His hands were surprisingly steady and, very carefully, he spilled out five diamonds.

He sighed and glowed at me: "These", he pointed, "are absolutely beautiful."

I was disappointed – no colours!

"What about ....?" I pointed to the others.

"Ah! You like the colours, but they are not so valuable."

"Can I see?"

And slowly, like exposing Aladdin's cave, he rolled out a few rubies, a few sapphires, and a few emeralds.

"What if they fall in the holes?" The table was pitted with hundreds of holes made by cutting instruments, holes that were black with dirt and some looking very deep.

"They won't", he said, "because I won't let them."

"But what if they *do*?"

"Then I'd have to cut the table to bits to get them out." And he took from his rack a steel-shiny chisel which, to this day, I can see glinting in the sunlight with its razor sharpness.

"Cut, cut, cut", he said, miming the action. "If I lose one of these …" He stopped, not daring to speculate – it was too horrible to think of. So, as if the event was about to happen, he carefully returned most of the stones to their envelopes, closed the sacred box and locked it. A few stones were left out.

"Now read", he commanded and ignoring me, got to work. He was a transformed man at his job. The bony fingers would flicker like things possessed. The ring was placed delicately into the tiny blue vice, the eye-glass was put into his right eye and then came the rasp of cutting. Light rasps, longer rasps, always followed by a look of judgement. He picked up each stone with a sucking tube and inserted it precisely into the hole in the ring.

"Those are valuable?" I asked.

"Very! But never mind those – here." And he got out one of the other boxes and spilled out an orgy of coloured stones onto the table.

"You can play with those."

"All of them?"

"All of them", he smiled.

"What about your stones – the ones you're working?"

"What about them?"

"They're special?"

"They certainly are."

"Who are they for?"

"A lady."

"Is she pretty?"

"Ah!" His smile turned into a sort of glow. "She's rather", he picked his word carefully, "attractive." But I sensed that this 'attractive lady' was not a wife or a girlfriend and that Uncle Siggy would never have either, nor would he have children. He was the sort of person who made you cry when you thought of him. But, I decided, when dinner came along and he carefully presented me with my ration of one chocolate ball, he was really OK.

The day had presented me with a myriad of images, many to remain forever. But curiously, it was the five diamonds lying innocently on his workbench that stayed with me most vividly.

On March 12th, 1938, we all heard it on the wireless: 'Keep calm, the Chancellor will make an announcement. The German armies are our allies.' Siggy was so pale, his skin a sallow grey, that he couldn't pale any more in response to all this. Mother could, though: she had the Jewess' dramatic black and white colouring and I'd never seen her more ashen.

"What's happening", I asked.

They ignored me. The brown plastic radio was our lifeline. The two adults mumbled. I felt fear without knowing its source. Cocooned by ignorance and bored with what I didn't understand, I began to play with the cheap stones Siggy had given me as toys. I arranged them in two lines: one paste diamonds and the other coloured.

"The German army", I pointed, "and the Austrian army." I moved a coloured (Austrian) one up and shot down one German 'diamond' and then another and then another until the German army was vanquished. Mentally, I raised the red-white-red flag of Austria in triumph. Suddenly, catching me completely unaware, arms were around me and mother's well-known smell engulfed me. Tears dropped on my shoulders, her hair entangled with mine. I couldn't bear these impulsive outbursts of hers. I knew she was upset and trying to take comfort from me. I knew my love had to respond to hers – it was my duty, but I shrank away. She retreated and looked at me – hurt. I turned away and rushed back to my stones. They had become my world, more real than the real world, more amenable to my wishes and much easier to understand. On that day, after my mother left and to my relief, Siggy said nothing. He returned to his work and once there, he was like me, totally engrossed. We were companions in evasion: here in our tiny world, the Nazis could go to the devil and leave us in peace.

It was Siggy's lack of concern about the Nazis that made his large, sunny room so attractive. He was different from my other uncles and aunts, who became so nervous that I shunned them. They rushed back and forth, for documents, in queues, desperately gossiping themselves into safety. 'England will take a few!' 'Switzerland is closed!' France – they'll be there soon!' America, the goal, would take only the healthy and rich. However, Siggy was immune to all this. He worked his rings; he carved stones of immense beauty. He bowed his head, put on his straps and every day he gave me a chocolate ball. Even better, he began to take an interest in my games: 'Nazis and Jews'. I pointed to my army lines that had now changed character.

"And who wins", he asked, smiling.

"The Jews!"

"Of course", he said, and mumbling something to himself went on with his work. I sensed a mutual affection, for we had lost all our self-consciousness. WE were companions, as regular in our habits now as before the Anschluss, the world excluded from the sunny room that was now almost my home.

If Uncle Siggy was calmer than my relations, it was because he had no hope of England, America or anywhere. He knew that no country in the world would take him in his condition and that gave him a sort of peace. But one day, I realised it was a superficial peace for suddenly, we heard strutting troops singing the Horst Wessel song not far from our house. He stopped to listen, as did I. Then I rushed to the window to look.

"Get back", he shouted, and he was surprisingly harsh. I stared at him and his magnificent eyes were filled with hate. It scared me, for he always seemed a person of gentle emotions. I saw his hands trembling and realised he was as frightened as I. When the song faded, he called me to him. He looked straight into me.

"Sorry", he said. "Sorry, but never, *never* watch!"

Then in a more sympathetic voice, "Were you frightened?"

I nodded and then, suddenly and as impulsively as mother, he embraced me. I smelled his smell, different and sweaty. I also found my legs between his dead ones and my body crushed to his bony breast. I felt his straps, his hot shirt and some metal object. He kissed my head, once, twice and when I looked up, he'd turned his head away to hide his tears. The motion was too much for me; I'd never so much as touched him before, or he me. I recoiled and trying desperately to hide my revulsion, went to my stones for sanctuary. He returned to his work and only the rasping of worked stones broke the silence. But then, suddenly, he turned away from the bench and moving his wheelchair very fast, he retreated behind the flimsy, grey curtain that separated his bed from the rest of the room. I heard the clanking of a pail and knew he was about to do his toilet, but had forgotten to tell me to leave the room and wait outside in the corridor. I looked at my stones for distraction, arranging them in familiar lines then noticed that in his hurry, he'd left the real diamond packet out and four of them were lying temptingly near the vice. With the devil in me, I switched one diamond for one of my paste ones; they looked indistinguishable. Just as I was doing this he swished the curtain back and in my confusion, the real diamond dropped into one of the holes and disappeared. As he came back in his chair, I starred in horror at the hole. My vision blurred and I couldn't remember which hole it was. Apparently, he'd noticed none of this. He returned to work and clicked on the cleaning wheel while I tried to force my mind to remember *which* hole, but they seemed like a bizarre pitted landscape, one hole like the other. I comforted myself, thinking no-one will know. Mock diamonds are like real ones; once they're polished only experts can tell.

It was a stifling day and we passed the afternoon in silence and then mother called to take me home. She seemed perversely cheerful; she'd almost got an English visa!

"England, eh!" said Uncle Siggy, waiting for my reaction. "So you'll soon be off!" I made no response and he gave me a strange look as if sensing something was bothering me. England to me, at that time, was unreal, whereas the discovery of my deed was very real indeed.

It took two days for retribution to come and it was the worst kind. I could stand harsh words, even slaps. I could stand mother's not infrequent hysteria, but what happened was two adults looking at me with doleful, puzzled looks of 'How could you!'

"Why?" asked my mother, "In heaven's name, *why?*"

I had no answer, but sensed that Uncle Siggy understood and the understanding made it worse. I think he knew how unwelcome his embrace had been. He knew the toilet bit, but what hurt most was that perhaps he thought I didn't like him and had taken a very nasty revenge.

"Give it here!" Mother held out her hand.

"Haven't got it."

She paled. "Then where ..."

I pointed vaguely to the pitted table.

"It dropped down there."

"Where? Whereabouts?" There was panic. She stroked the table, tried to put her fingers down the holes but couldn't get them in.

"I don't know!" I shouted. "Just about here", and drew a circle that included about fifty holes. Uncle Siggy looked at the spot as though willing the diamond to rise from its grave. He got the chisel and began, with fury, to carve out the table. Cut, cut, cut. Mother and I stared and stared, anxious not to miss the sparkling object amid the curled shavings.

"Don't go so fast!" mother shouted.

He slowed down. I ran over to the rack, got another chisel and wanted to join in, but his harsh voice stopped me.

"Put it back!"

I did. He'd exhausted himself and still no diamond.

"How much – how much is it worth?" Mother's voice was barely more than a whisper. Siggy didn't reply. He was exhausted. His head was on the bench, his breathing came in big gasps and his back heaved. Mother went over, bent down and kissed his cheek and tears came into his eyes. I couldn't stand a man crying and turned away. I'd have given the earth for that diamond to appear and then, as if by some malignant fate, the army came again and the cursed Horst Wessel. We all listened with shivers running down our spines to the brutal, haunting melody.

"*There* it is!" I'd spotted it – dulled and covered by tiny bits of sawdust. It laid there, an innocent symbol of a boy's revenge, of the devil in the soul.

* * *

Yes, we got our visas. Yes, England beckoned and a few English words were learned. Colour came back into mother's cheeks. I swanked to all and sundry about 'getting away'. Then, when we were packing, I asked, "Where will Uncle Siggy go?"

Mother didn't answer. I knew, at least I think I knew, he never would leave Vienna. Much later, I learned that suicide had cheated the Nazis.

The ring remained his one memorial – the ring on mother's finger.

*

Come Back, Mrs Froggart
By Jean P Miller

"Little Varmints", Bill Thrower growled. "If I was ten years younger, I'd show 'em."

He turned away. The next minute he was holding his leg as cramp in his calf made him wince. He cursed softly, annoyed at his weakness. He rubbed it as hard as he could.

"You okay, mister?"

The voice startled him. He'd thought the boys who'd come after his apples had all run off. This one hadn't. He stood there, half defiant, holding two apples in his hand. He had a lively face covered with freckles.

"It's a bit of cramp", said Bill. He paused and then added, "Why didn't you run away with the others?"

The lad looked up at Bill's six foot frame and dark bushy eyebrows. "I was a bit too slow, then I saw you'd hurt yourself."

"Weren't you scared of me?"

"Yeah, a bit."

"Then it was plucky of you to stay. Now, how would you like to pick six good apples off the tree and leave those windfalls?"

Quick as a flash the boy chose six apples and was off, calling, "Thanks, mister."

Bill Thrower, the cramp having eased, walked slowly towards his home; a lovely old house with the evening sun mellowing the bricks on the wall at the back of the building. He went in through the back porch. He put on his slippers and poured himself a whisky before he sat down in his chair.

He could remember when he was fit enough to throw up the morning room window, squeeze through and chase the boys who came scrumping his apples. An odd one would have a clip round the ear or a good telling off. And how Helen used to laugh at him.

"You'll do yourself a mischief getting through that window", she'd say, her eyes laughing at him. "They're only doing what boys always do."

Today, he was too old to squeeze through the window. Something in that boy's manner appealed to him. Normally he'd have hated to be called 'mister'. He sipped his whisky slowly. It was five years now and he still missed Helen. It was selfish, but he wished he'd gone first. He shouldn't grumble, because he could afford a housekeeper. It was better than living with Joanne and her family, or worse still, facing the prospect of a home. He smiled wryly thinking of the names they chose: Sunset Villas – Spend your twilight years with us; Rainbow Valley Retirement Home; Evergreen Homes. It was good that his daughter Joanne came up regularly to see him from Devon.

The youngster's face came to mind. If only James ... he thrust the thought away angrily. Why should a drunk driver have taken away his son's life? The man would be out now and living his life. Bill couldn't forgive. It still made a hard knot in his stomach whenever he thought of it.

Tomorrow was one of Mrs Froggart's days. Mrs Froggart was his housekeeper. She was good at her job, but oh, her sayings irritated him. She'd start off with, "And how are we this morning?" This was punctuated with various remarks during the day. "It's no use looking on the black side. That's what I always tell my Ron." And later, "If it doesn't rain before seven I'll eat me hat."

Those sayings nearly drove him mad. He wanted to put his hands over his ears when he knew she was about to produce one.

As he finished his drink, he thought of his game of golf that morning. He'd played with Alec for years, but for the first time, Alec had suggested they gave up the small bet they had on the game. Bill wondered if it was that he felt sorry for him, as he was so often the loser. He cringed at the thought.

Mrs Froggart arrived promptly at nine thirty the next morning. "And how are we this morning?" she asked brightly, as she hung up her jacket.

"Fine, Mrs Froggart", Bill answered wearily.

She got out the vacuum cleaner. Bill decided to walk down to the orchard while she was busy. He wondered if he'd see the young lad again, but he'd hardly come on his own, or so soon. Bill couldn't shake off his depression. He wandered among the apple trees and then sat for a while on the seat he and Helen had put there years ago. The sun was warm on his back, but inside he felt cold. He sighed. The bluebells last spring, which had bloomed among the apple trees, had been as lovely as ever, but Helen hadn't seen them.

Suddenly he remembered he hadn't given Mrs Froggart any apples yet. He gathered as many as he could from the lower branches, laid them on the seat and returned to the house for a basket. As he opened the back door he was struck by the silence, until he heard a cry. "Mr Thrower, is that you?"

He hurried upstairs to find Mrs Froggart lying on the landing with her leg twisted beneath her.

"Stay where you are. I'll ring for an ambulance." He ran downstairs to 'phone and then fetched a blanket from the bedroom, which he put over her as she was shivering.

"It's my leg, and my hip feels funny, too." Mrs Froggart's usually loud voice was almost a whisper.

"You must keep still till they come." Thank goodness I came back for a basket, he thought.

In five minutes the ambulance arrived and Mrs Froggart was whisked away to hospital. How quiet the house felt. He'd always been irritated by her sayings, but now he wished he could hear her saying, "If it doesn't rain before seven I'll eat me hat."

Next morning he went to buy some flowers to take to the hospital. He was looking in the florist's window when he heard a voice.

"Hello, mister."

He turned to see the lad who had been scrumping apples. "Hello."

"The apples were great."

"What's your name?"

"Sam. Sam Simpson."

"Well Sam, if you go back you'll find some apples on a seat near the trees. Help yourself."

"Gee, thanks." He ran off.

Bill visited Mrs Froggart in the afternoon and found her looking vulnerable, and much smaller in the hospital bed; quite unlike the bustling, cheerful person she normally was.

"It's good of you to come", she said.

"How are you?"

"Well, I've broken my hip. They've fixed it up, but it means I'll be off work for a fair time."

"Don't you worry about that. Just get better again."

"I slipped. It just happened."

Bill stayed as long as he felt he was doing some good, but when he noticed she was looking tired, he left.

Now the house was emptier than ever. He hadn't realised how much she did and how ungrateful he'd been. He visited her regularly and learned that her only daughter lived in Aberdeen and would come to stay with her when she got home.

"That's why I appreciate you coming My Thrower. If no-one visits you, you feel worse."

He thought of all the things he could have said to her over the last five years and hadn't. When had he told her how clean the house looked – he couldn't remember. Or had he ever thanked her for preparing a meal for him to pop into the oven? Probably not! Just because she wasn't Helen, he hadn't really thought of her as a person, just someone who did the work.

The house had become a bit neglected, sadder, as if it missed Mrs Froggart's ministrations. Bill struggled with the vacuum cleaner, did his own washing and ironing, and refused to go and stay with Joanne. He began to have the odd meal out, although he hated eating alone. It was as if he was telling the world he had no-one to cook for him.

One day, as he ate his steak and kidney pie in 'The Coach and Horses', in his usual corner seat, he noticed young Sam coming in with his mother. They sat a few tables away and took a long time studying the menu. Then Bill heard a loud whisper.

"Look, Mam, over there in the corner – that's the man who gave me the apples."

"Don't point, it's rude."

A few minutes later a fresh faced young woman, wearing a smart navy-blue suit cam to his table. She smiled at him. "Sam tells me you are the gentleman who gave him the apples. That was kind of you."

"Not really, I can't eat them all myself", Bill replied.

"Sam has an appointment with the eye specialist at the hospital, so I brought him out to lunch for a treat first.

"I'm going to the hospital later. The lady who helps me has broken her hip and I visit her most days."

A few days later as bill watched the news, he heard the front doorbell. 'Wonder who that is at this time of day. Hope Mrs Froggart is alright.' Standing on the doorstep was Sam's mother.

"If you need any help in the house, I could come on a Friday", she said.

Bill hesitated. "It would only be on the understanding that when Mrs Froggart is better, she comes back."

"Of course, I realise that. I work at the school dinner time, so it would only be for three hours."

"Right. Can you start this week?"

"Yes. See you at eight thirty on Friday, then. I have to be at the school at twelve."

Bill was used to taking his time over his breakfast, and wondered how he would cope with an early start. Mrs Simpson came at eight thirty. Bill had been up since seven, had his breakfast, seen the news and washed his dishes. Mrs Simpson rushed through the whole house at breakneck speed, managing to leave everything in a different place.

"Don't move anything in the study", Bill warned.

"Just a quick dust round and I'm done", Mrs Simpson replied.

The 'quick dust round' dislodged an Aynsley vase, swept October off the calendar altogether, and changed the setting on the central heating. Carefully folded newspapers slumped in an untidy heap, a photograph of James leant drunkenly against the clock, and the coffee jar ended up in a cupboard.

Bill gave up. After she had gone he began rearranging things the way he liked them. It took him half the afternoon.

On Friday he asked Mrs Simpson to prepare a simple meal for him. Before she left at eleven thirty she showed him a pan of minced beef. "Just reheat it and simmer at boiling point for ten minutes and then add a tin of tomatoes. Put some pasta in boiling, salted water for ten minutes. You'll love it."

Bill sat down after she had gone and wished fervently that Mrs Froggart was back again. He heated the mince and made the pasta, but it didn't feel like a real meal to him. He thought longingly of the hotpots that Mrs Froggart had made for him. He'd stopped visiting Mrs Froggart, as her daughter from Aberdeen was with her now she was home again.

After Mrs Simpson had been coming for two months Bill was exhausted. It was as if a mini-tornado tore through his house each Friday morning. He felt as if he was living in America's mid-West.

He began playing more golf to take his mind off things. As he was hitting the ball, he'd suddenly see Mrs Simpson knocking ornaments off the mantelpiece, one after the other.

One night he dreamed that she had come into the house when he was golfing and had made a bonfire of all his papers. He could smell burning. Then he realised something *was* burning. He raced downstairs to find he had left a pan on the hotplate. It had burned away completely. Frightened, he switched off the electricity and poured himself a whisky. 'I could have burned the house down', he thought.

The next morning was Friday. When Mrs Simpson saw what had happened, she promptly gave in her notice. "I can't be responsible, not if you don't know what you're doing. So, I won't be coming anymore."

Thankfully, he paid her wages, although she had not done any work. He shut the door and a huge wave of relief swept over him.

A month later, Mrs Froggart came to the back door. "I can start whenever it suits you", she said.

"I'm so pleased", Bill replied.

Two days later, when she arrived, they both spoke together.

"And how are we this morning?"

Then Bill began to laugh and Mrs Froggart started laughing, too, though she could for the life of her have told you why.

*

Carry Me Home
By Joan Barnett

At the airport in Richmond, Virginia in July 2000 *Old Lady* was hoping to catch the plane home, but no luck. That annoying voice rang out over the fifty or so would-be passengers; "The aircraft at Gate 6 will not leave for thirty minutes due to engine trouble. Thank you for your patience."

The announcement was repeated at thirty-minute intervals during the next three hours and people were muttering dark threats against the airline. Some were marching up to the departure desk demanding alternative flights, all to no avail, until miserable looking *Old Lady* yelled: "I'll miss my connection to Gatwick if you don't do something!"

It appeared that *Old Lady* was the only passenger not booked on a domestic flight.

Everything swung into action.

Blue Jackets seemed to be everywhere. "Okay, okay, ma'am," said a rather pushy lady, wearing a Blue Jacket, "There's a flight at Gate 24 in fifteen minutes. It's to Boston."

"But my connection is at Newark," replied exasperated *Old Lady*.

"Never mind, you were on a flight from Newark to Gatwick, but now its Boston to Gatwick. You'll need to be quick there – you'll only have twenty-five minutes," and Blue Jacket handed *Old Lady* a crumpled slip of paper, saying, "Don't lose this."

On arrival at Boston *Old Lady* was surprised to be met by a pretty young girl wearing a Brown Jacket. She settled *Old Lady* into a wheelchair, which was a completely new experience. However, it seemed sensible to allow Brown Jacket to take charge, and *Old Lady* was pushed quickly to a road where Brown Jacket informed *Old Lady* that a bus was due to carry her to the over-seas section of the airport.

The bus did not arrive! Brown Jacket put the brake on the wheelchair and bade *Old Lady* "Stay here." Then went off to phone some unknown Jacket.

On her return she told *Old Lady* that the bus had gone to the wrong side of the airport, but that it had been re-directed. Finally, it arrived – a whole double-decker just for one old lady, whereupon the driver, who wore a White Jacket, addressed *Old Lady* in amazed tones, saying, "I can't understand why I have to take you to 'A' section; it's the wrong airline. Still, that's Braided Jackets orders."

By this time *Old Lady's* twenty-five minutes had shrunk to fifteen minutes.

White Jacket on reaching 'A' section left *Old Lady* alone in the bus, saying he would look for someone to help. He returned with a jolly man wearing a Green Shirt – No Jacket.

"I'll look after you, darling" announced Green Shirt, as he helped unresisting *Old Lady* into a wheelchair. By this time *Old Lady* thought her only chance of finally boarding a plane to Gatwick was to obey all instructions, including meekly riding in a wheelchair.

Green shirt then hurried with *Old Lady* to a booking-in desk, where two astonished Red Jackets engaged him in an animated conversation in Spanish – incomprehensible to *Old Lady*. Next, in English *Old Lady* was asked to show them her passport and ticket. Fortunately, *Old Lady* understood English, and produced the required documents, together with the crumpled slip of paper given her by Blue Jacket at Richmond. This bore the legend 'Transferred Flight' and it seemed to be a good idea to offer this with the ticket.

By this time *Old Lady* was considering the possibility that she might have to stay in Boston over night, but eventually Red Jackets returned the passport, tickets, and crumpled slip of paper, then one asked, "Can you walk?" *Old Lady*, by this time quite resigned to missing her flight, replied, "Yes but I have no idea of the Flight Number or the Gate and my daughter hopes to meet me at Gatwick!"

"My God!" said one of the Red Jackets, almost shrieking, "They are boarding now!"

Fortunately, Green Shirt – no jacket, had stayed to watch the fun.

"I'll take care of you, darling," he beamed and rushed *Old Lady* in a wheelchair through the crowds until they reached a door marked 'Authorised Personnel Only.' He pressed the coded buttons and *Old Lady* found herself in a small lift (sorry elevator – she was still in the 'Good Ole' USA)

José, (by this time Old Lady had discovered that this was Green Shirt's name) was saying "Don't worry ma'am, I'll get you aboard okay."

The elevator arrived at the corridor leading to a beautiful big 'Virgin' plane, and every one but the last dozen or so passengers had boarded.

"Excuse please," said José and they politely allowed *Old Lady* to board ahead of them, mildly surprised but uncomplaining when she left the wheelchair to walk unaided up the steps where a delightful stewardess (*Old Lady* completely forgets the colour of her jacket) showed her to a comfortable seat for a pleasant, if a little sleepy flight to Gatwick.

Arriving there at about eight am, *Old Lady* was surprised to be met by another wheelchair, but the Navy Blue Jacket with it was so pleasant it seemed churlish to refuse the lift and anyway, the amazed expression on her daughter's face really amused *Old Lady* when they finally met.

By the way, *Old Lady* was booked with a different airline and never expected to travel home with Virgin.

Old Lady arrived at Gatwick less than ten minutes later than the original arrival time. Could our divided up British Railways have done as well? This is the true story of my return journey after a month in America – I expect you guessed *Old Lady* is the author of this piece.

The ultimate miracle was that my luggage arrived on the same flight. The staff at Richmond airport had had only fifteen minutes to trace it among the other passengers baggage and transfer it onto the Boston plane.

Well done! And thank you.

*

Alien Mountain Giants
By Louis Barrow

Out in space, five million light-years from earth, was a planet identical to earth called Speney, heated by a star like our sun.

Life first formed on planet Speney before any water flowed on the surface, before even any solid rocks formed. For Speney was then only a cloud formation. This species slowly developed as gigantic eggs the size of a mountain, to be known as "True Mountainians"! Mountains which eventually formed on planet Speney were the actual eggshells of this first species!

The Mountainian eggs were to take around four thousand years to mould, before hatching out as the largest and most advanced type of life ever known!

Over the recent five hundred million years of Speney's existence, various life forms dwelled in the seas and on land, following a pattern rather like the evolution upon our earth. Speneyian life began in the similar way, from simple sea forms to man. Yes man, and on Speney too, mankind behaved like us with wars between nations, people striving for peace through religion, and Speneyian scientists seeking knowledge.

* * *

Now the first Mountainian was due to hatch. It was early hours in a summer season, where thunderous echoes stirred from within mountains called the Alapees.

A volcanic eruption caused the land here to tremble. Terrorised people, inhabiting a village within a nearby valley, ran and hid under rocks.

A little dome-shaped house, made of marble, stood isolated upon a steep rocky embankment of the valley, opposite the active mountains. Here lived a beautiful lady with her two children.

This lady was called Sha'jar. She stood just two metres, the average height of a Speneyian woman, with snow-white skin and twinkling silvery eyes set deep within her sockets.

Speneyians possessed very fine hair upon their oval heads, with heavy jawbones and high cheekbones. Speneyians had a finger less than earthmen possessed on each hand and webbed feet with three long toes on each.

Speneyian garments were generally shiny robes of a thin elastic-type material.

Sha'jar had a young chubby boy called Cycol, who was recognised with several spiky whiskers upon his brow.

The other child, a girl named Na'waha, had a wide yellow streak down her forehead between deep tawny eyes.

Na'waha suddenly started and glared up at the highest mountain across the valley. For a flicker of lightning had shot from this mountaintop into the blue sky, followed by clusters of spitting black dust from crackling rocks, bringing darkness for a brief moment over the land, making the sun appear temporarily black.

Trees uprooted and several houses tumbled to pieces, as the highest mountain incredibly split in two, in sight of terrified villagers!

The first gigantic Mountainian leapt out from the broken rocks, being almost the size of earth's Mount Everest, to confront the Speneyian highlanders.

The Mountainian hovered above the Speneyian landscape, appearing at first as a white streak, as if made up of billions of glittering crystals. Also, sunlight cast colourful rays upon every speck of the Mountainian body.

Na'waha was comforted by her mother as she stood trembling, with her mouth wide open, as did her brother Cycol. Na'waha was unable to fathom her emotions, for although she thought the Mountainian monstrous, she felt strangely unafraid, with an overwhelming passionate sensation for it.

Surprisingly, every local villager shared an experience like Na'waha had, including inhabitants close by who had not yet witnessed the remarkable sight.

As Na'waha studied the mountainous streak of light, she observed that the Mountainian was shaped like a gigantic eagle, with feathers of ever-changing colours. Many golden eyes shone in the sky like stars over the entire monstrous body, partially dazzling the eyes of every Speneyian witness.

Na'waha planted a hand over her pounding heart, awe inspired, as she observed the Mountainian, for the giant was, to her mind, as a mighty god form heaven.

That was not all Na'waha saw, for the Mountainian was completely surrounded by a dense fog, stretching for miles east to west across the sky. Forceful light waves projected from the Mountainian, casting luminous colours through the fog and upon the Speneyian land, like rainbows in all directions.

These colourful rays contained a mysterious radiation, to cause at least two thirds of the villagers to feel drowsy. Affected people even collapsed in fields, as though drunk through a strong wine.

* * *

The eagle-like monster twisted its neck and ferociously flapped its wings, sending lightning bolts of electricity, striking telephone lines and uprooting trees. Electricity struck people outside too, but no delightful soul was harmed, but just sent into a sound sleep.

Na'waha too, along with her mother and brother, was sent into deep sleep upon grass outside their dome home.

Other villagers sharply took cover upon their knees beneath rocks and inside houses, because the people awake feared the lightning to be dangerous.

Under cover, everybody continued worshipping the many glorious stars, which were the Mountainian's eyes.

Although the Speneyian people saw fellows struck by lightning, they were all entranced by an inspiring magnetism the Mountainian possessed. This unexplained sensation caused Speneyians to devote themselves to the Mountainian as a god, as though hypnotised!

The Mountainian's huge glittering wings swept gently upon the colourful foggy sky. Then the Mountainian lowered to the ground, as silently as a feather falling upon sand, resting with wings outstretched among the people.

The violent lightning then ceased. Many Speneyians emerged warily out from shelters, anxiously hugging their wives and children.

Nobody could resist the gazing upon the charming wide golden eyes covering the Mountainian.

Na'waha awoke, after sleeping soundly enough to recall nothing consciously of what had occurred to her since a mere second before the lightning struck.

Na'waha was awake several moments before Cycol and Sha'jar, her mother, eventually awoke, to see the mighty Mountainian had surprisingly landed in the valley.

Na'waha knew, whatever occurred during her sleep, she actually experienced something wonderful – something which stayed with her after waking – an extra-sensory feeling of a loving oneness with the Almighty Creator, with the Mountainian, and every Speneyian soul. So Na'waha felt a new refreshed Speneyian girl. Na'waha perceived that her mother and brother too shared this fantastic experience.

This feeling was to remain with Na'waha and every other Speneyian soul forever!

* * *

Suddenly another mountain crumbled in the distance. A rhythm of echoing rumbles followed, as rocks bounced one after another.

There above, appeared another sparkling, eagle-like giant, just like the first Mountainian, with many golden eyes searching the countryside beneath.

Within thirteen hours, ten more Mountainians hatched, out of mountains situated in entirely different continents of Speney.

All eleven Mountainians copied the first-born, landing between people. Each Mountainian chose a different country. So a powerful giant dwelt in all locations of the planet Speney.

Therefore, the entire planet was illuminated by colourful rays surrounding these giants. For the radiant bows stretched far enough to make all twelve Mountainians blend as one. From outer space, planet Speney would have seemed on fire by colourful flames.

The whole planet, all of a sudden turned into a peaceful sanctuary, ruled by the superior giants. Because wherever wars existed, the hateful fighters (every one of them) were struck by that powerful lightning and paralysed.

For this mysterious lightning was poisonous to wicked minds, because when these two mixed, a conflict of chemical reactions occurred – yet beyond the knowledge of the cleverest Speneyian scientist.

* * *

By fourteen hours since the Mountainian emerged, everybody among the survivors – those who had no hateful intentions towards other nations – were living in harmony.

The Speneyians, from that famous day, happily worshipped the twelve 'gods' with great devotion.

The Mountainians neither ate nor drank except solar and similar energies, which their skins absorbed for vitality.

This advanced species was to produce offspring in a unique way, because each body possessed both masculine and feminine qualities. Also, the twelve Mountainians were forever bound in oneness by their surrounding magnetic waves, to continuously produce offspring.

The Mountainians were to travel through space, to multiply and fill the universe. Not by the normal way of travelling, for no Mountainian was to leave planet Speney.

They were to travel by expanding in numbers, like a climber plant emerging from earth with just twelve leaves, to grow to a treetop.

Every Mountainian was to remain bound together by their powers of light, till their light would fill the entire universe forever.

*

Lucy
By Mary Wise

It was indeed a Red Letter Day in 1956 when I spotted an advertisement in the Nottingham Evening Post, offering a 1932 Morris Minor for £25! Now I cannot claim to be an expert in the field of the combustion engine, my sole experience being riding pillion on George's various motorcycles, but I always had a yearning for a car of my own and this seemed an excellent opportunity to make my dreams come true. I couldn't get to the telephone quickly enough to dial the given number which was answered by a friendly male voice inviting me to 'Come along and inspect', that evening.

On arrival I found that the owner of the voice was indeed amicable, he was a member of the Fire Service, and as such, knew all about the maintenance of vehicles, in fact he told me that during the war whilst serving in the army he had stored some of the car's vital parts in his front room! Before we go any further I had better tell you what he told me, i.e. that his mechanical masterpiece was entitled 'Lucy' and would not answer to any other moniker, her registration lettering being LCY and his name being Locket! He put Lucy through her paces for me and said that in the usual way she was quite reliable, although if she did have a fit of pique she did the thing properly, for example; she once held up the Lord Mayor of Nottingham's Procession by refusing to budge at a road junction in the busiest part of the city.

However, by this time I was so ensnared by her that little things like that didn't seem to matter very much and I handed over my money saying someone would be collecting Lucy the next day.

Delighted with my bargain I asked a motor mechanic with whom I worked if he would collect the car for me so that I could give George a surprise when he came home.

He duly delivered Lucy outside my front door and gave me a few words of advice.

"Get rid of it," he said simply "It's a load of old junk, whatever made you buy that? I suppose you actually gave good money for it? You did? Well all I can say is I am more than surprised."

A little deflated I began to wonder if my bargain was as much of a Godsend as I had originally thought, but that seemed disloyal to poor old Lucy and I pushed such unworthy thoughts away comforting myself by anticipating George's pleasure when he saw her. All agog I waited anxiously for the sound of his key in the lock and eventually he burst in.

"Whoever has left that old banger outside our front door?" he demanded, "If they don't move it immediately I'll send for the police!!"

"It isn't an Old Banger," I said indignantly, "its Lucy and your birthday present!"

"Heavens above don't tell me you've actually bought that scrap-heap. You just couldn't have done anything as batty as that!"

"I have," I said firmly and what's more she's come to stay. Let's go for a run now, you'll like it once you get used to it."

"Right", stormed George, "We'll go as far as that scrap yard over Trent Bridge, and in all possibility we'll get run in as my licence doesn't cover so called cars!"

Anyway, we boarded Lucy and as she proceeded by leaps and bounds my spouse muttered something about 'Kangaroo Juice' under his breath. After a mile or so, however, George began to succumb to her charms.

"She might possibly be useful for a week or two", he admitted reluctantly, "In the meantime, I'd better get somewhere to park her, she's a proper eyesore."

Now it so happened, that we were due for a holiday, and although George hadn't passed his driving test, owing to the Suez Canal Crisis, driving tests were suspended, and he was able to drive without being accompanied by an experienced driver, so that the next week after Lucy had had a much needed service, we set off for North Wales. We were on our way to that beautiful City of Chester, via Nantwich, when Lucy suddenly decided she had had enough for one day. In the High Street during the rush hour she refused to go any further and stopped dead.

"You'll have to give her a push while I steer," said George.

"Dressed like this?" I demanded, "In my Sunday Best?"

"Well there isn't much option, you can't drive can you?"

"Not yet," I admitted, "but this will certainly make me think about it!"

Luckily some friendly soul told us where there was a garage that might help, and a couple of chivalrous males took over my pushing job, so we pressed on.

When we arrived at the garage (a one man enterprise) The proprietor was enjoying a cuppa whilst watching the test match on TV so he was not overjoyed at the prospect of persuading Lucy to take to the road again.

"It's an electrical fault," he declared. "Whoever wired this thing up? It's more complicated than the Blackpool illuminations!"

After half an hour or so, during which time the air had been blue on several occasions, Lucy was ticking over and we were off again. We stayed at Chester for the night at the Blossoms Hotel (the porter winced when he saw our transport), but he was a man of dignity and self-control so he treated us with the usual courtesy, and we enjoyed our stay. We walked along the Roman Wall admired the ancient buildings and visited the wonderful Cathedral promising ourselves we would return someday to spend more time there, there was so much to see.

The next day we set off for Llandudno and on one of those steepish hills Lucy played up again. George was tinkering about with the engine, without much success when a Limousine drew up and the driver came to offer assistance. He was an executive type with an obsession about old cars, so his wife told me, when I went over to apologise for delaying their journey.

"Don't worry," she said, "There's nothing he likes better than taking off his coat and getting his hands dirty. He is in his element now and I am sure he will get you going again, we had a model like that once and it was his pride and joy."

He certainly did the trick and we arrived safely in Llandudno. As you most probably know it's an attractive little town (not so little now) with the Great and

LUCY

Little Ormes dominating the landscape, and a long promenade where the seagulls swoop down to take bread from your fingers. The weather was good so we toured the area. We viewed the smallest house in Conway, watched the salmon leap at Betws-y-coed, had our photographs taken on the pier at Bangor, and marvelled at the Menai Bridge when we went to visit friends in Anglesey. Back in Llandudno, George announced he was going up the Great Orme.

"You can't come," he said, "I don't think Lucy could stand the strain."

"Thank you very much!" I retorted, secretly thankful that I was being spared this ordeal, but none the less anxiously awaiting their return.

"Took it like a bird," was his verdict. "She's a little marvel!"

I thought so too when she took us through the Bristol traffic. There we were, minute by comparison, among mountainous buses, and gigantic commercial vehicles and she didn't falter.

I remember thinking, 'if I ever get out of this alive I'll never venture in such traffic again.'

However, panic passes and she took us through various hazards after that.

Eventually there was little of the original Lucy left. Her wire wheels were replaced and she had two new doors fitted and a window that actually closed. The glass was missing from the original one, and when it snowed George had to put his arm through the aperture to serape the ice off the windscreen as the wiper lacked power.

When the Suez Crisis was over and driving tests recommenced, George took his in Lucy. Now my husband is six feet and the examiner was also a big chap so Lucy looked a little inadequate.

"Is this your car?" he asked in a surprised voice.

"Afraid I must plead guilty," admitted George, which made the great man smile. This all important test was taken in Cambridge no easy rendezvous, even in those days, so I waited anxiously for the result. When Lucy made her appearance again, George was looking very serious but seeing my disappointed expression began to smile.

"It's okay, we're in the clear," he said, apparently the examiner had told him:-

"I shall have to give you a pass Mr W. you can take those 'L' plates off now."

When no one was looking I gave Lucy a little pat, after all, that first time pass was partly due to her efforts she could so easily have ruined everything.

Then came a very sad day – we decided we should have to let Lucy go in favour of more modern transport. We found a Morris 8 in very nice condition to replace her and before he saw it the dealer agreed to take our old model in part exchange.

"Is this it?" he asked with a disparaging glance at Lucy, "Can't give you very much for that, but the battery might be useful!"

"You can't have that," said George, "It's on loan."

So, alas poor Lucy ended up in the compound to await the arrival of the scrap man and the end of her career. I don't mind admitting we felt like a couple of traitors and I shed more than a tear or two when we abandoned her to her fate.

The strange thing is that had we kept her, she would be quite a valuable asset today as you know vintage cars are at a premium.

*

The Tooth, the Whole Tooth and Nothing but the Tooth
By Pamela Joyce

I am very fortunate to still have my own teeth yet I have every sympathy for people who, through whatever reason, have to cohabit with the dreaded dentures.

We've all seen an assortment of folk struggling with these 'aliens' that rebel against the human race by refusing to stay up, stay in or stay clean. They are savage hunters who set out to trap every morsel of food, storing it securely under their plate.

Dentures never give up food without a fight! When dentures are first introduced to humans, both parties are reluctant to accept each other. However, the dentures do try to entertain their host's friends and family by making their male hosts do a pretty good impression of Dick Emery playing his vicar character, and their female hosts are excellent mimics of Janet Street-Porter. However, they soon tire of this and eventually most humans do graduate to become the master of the dentures. Our sympathies lie with those still studying.

Personally, not having had to cohabit with the beasts, I can only say that most of my experiences with them have been hilarious. I have found them to be very entertaining.

Dentures have been connected with my family for years. I recall my curiosity about the strange beings when I first saw them without my dad. They lurked in the bathroom, looking at me from the bottom of a glass. The fizzing, pinky water distorted their features making them appear bigger than they really were. Once, curiosity got the better of me, I poked and prodded them. Using my toothbrush I tried levering them out of the water for a closer look, but the little devils flicked off the end, right out of the glass and went splash into the toilet. Thankfully, I'd flushed, because I had to rescue them. They didn't tell tales on me to Dad – he never knew. They got their own back on me, because on occasions they'd twist and protrude hideously from his mouth. They'd make him screw up one eye, drop his shoulder and lope after me with his arm swinging and his back hunched. This 'monster' would chase me, my brother and often our friends around the house. Our terrified giggles and squeals would echo down the street. As I grew up, I recognised the impression to be the Hunchback of Notre Dame; it was good and effective at the time.

Those dentures eventually retired. The next set arrived, did the Dick Emery routine for a while and then appeared to settle. We were fooled. The previous lot must have left word about their escapade down the toilet. Unbeknown to us, this set was planning their escape. We took them on holiday to Germany. One morning Dad felt ill and while he was decorating the toilet bowl, they cunningly jumped out without him knowing, he flushed, and they were gone forever! I suspect they are now wallowing in German beer, writing a book called 'The Adventures of Dentures'!

After being raised with dentures, I suppose it was inevitable that I'd marry into another denture family. I have been lucky. Through the years, each generation has gone out of their way to entertain me. Many times I've laughed until the tears flowed. It's strange, because my husband who's been the host never seems to find their antics as amusing as I do. In fact, he tends to get annoyed first, but then he will gradually see the funny side and laugh with me.

My husband was approaching his twentieth birthday when we started courting and I was surprised that he already had a small family of dentures cohabiting with him. There were just two who lived in the front. I thought he was too young for dentures.

I discovered that he was about ten years old when he'd fallen over, badly chipping his front teeth, which eventually had to be taken out. I didn't pay much attention to these dentures throughout our courtship. They were a little small, but well behaved.

We married in 1971 and after spending a few months in an unsatisfactory flat, we had spells of living with both sets of parents, during which time our daughter Karen was born. At last the day arrived when we moved into our first real home together as a family. It was a two-bedroom bungalow. We were so excited. We moved in, dumping all the boxes into Karen's room. We sorted out the lounge and our bedroom, putting Karen's cot in with us for the first few nights, until we'd unpacked everything and put her own room straight. Karen went to bed and slept as if it had been a normal day.

It was late before Michael and I got ready for bed. Not wanting to put the bedroom light on for fear of waking Karen, we got undressed with only the light from the hallway. I got into bed and Michael went to switch off the hall light. The bedroom was plunged into pitch darkness. I heard him feeling his way back through the door when there was this big bang and an 'oofff', followed by a cursing groan. I immediately started to giggle. I couldn't see a thing, but I knew he'd stubbed his toe on the cot. His disembodied voice retorted with, "It's not bloody funny ..... I've lost my teeth!" With that, my desperate attempt to stifle my giggles gave way to smothering my laughter in the pillow. In the blackness, Michael was feeling carpet and bed for his departed dentures. He was not amused. I was getting hysterical. The more he hissed at me to stop laughing and be quiet, the worse I got. Finally, he decided he'd have to put the light on and take a chance on not waking Karen. Several seconds went by while he felt the walls before finding the switch. Both of us looked at the cot to see if our daughter would wake. Karen laid perfectly still, eyes wide open; she looked at us both then looked down onto her chest. There, grinning up at her, sat the dentures.

That finished me. I laughed helplessly, tears rolled and my sides ached. Michael, also laughing, popped the teeth back into his mouth, tucked Karen in, switched off the light and finally climbed into bed. The dentures had landed!

It must have been the bungalow that appealed to these two little dentures, because after that first night's escapade they seemed to pop out a lot. Michael claimed he'd outgrown them, but I think that once these little tinkers get a taste for adventure there's no stopping them.

THE TOOTH, THE WHOLE TOOTH AND NOTHING BUT THE TOOTH

It must have been a year later; Michael and I always took a hot drink and a biscuit to bed. This particular night, I put two Club biscuits on the bedside table and returned to the kitchen to finish making the Horlicks. Standing at the cooker, I could see Michael through the open door popped up in bed munching his biscuit. When he'd finished, knowing they were the last two biscuits we had, he'd started to tease me by threatening to eat mine. I had a running commentary as he slowly opened the wrapper and waved it in front of his open mouth. As I carried our drinks into the bedroom, he dived under the covers with my biscuit. I retorted jokingly by saying "Oh eat it ….. but I hope it breaks your teeth!" Giggling like a schoolboy, he'd been popping in and out of the bed covers, then there was a moment's calm. Michael emerged sheepishly from hiding, the two dentures in one hand and the plate in the other. They had managed to devour part of my biscuit, but the last laugh was all mine. Defeat of the dentures!

Michael's next set of dentures were a family of four, his mouth needing a few alterations to accommodate them. As they were much bigger that his first two, they mimicked Dick Emery for quite a while. In fact, they were rather a good comedy act, often larking about playing chase with Michael's gums, which never seemed to be able to catch them. Before long, they'd slip out to see what was happening in the outside world.

Those dentures saw the arrival of our son, Lee, and subsequently our move to a three-bedroom house. The dentures behaviour was still comical. They would entice Lee to put his chubby fingers into his dad's mouth. While he was making funny noise and expressions, attempting to entertain his baby son, the dentures would steal the show as Lee hooked them out!

Whether it was this tomfoolery that made their plate weak I don't know, but on several occasions it just cracked up. Michael was forever super-gluing them together and once or twice I'd rushed them through to the denture hospital for emergency repairs. Eventually, they gave up. The demise of the denture four!

Michael underwent more mouth alteration to accommodate his next set of dentures. We named these 'Full Top Set Dentures'. We went through the usual Dick Emery routine; poor Michael took some time to accept them. I think he still mourned the denture four's sense of humour, some of which must have rubbed off on him. One day he came in from work with no dentures. Sitting in the kitchen waiting for him was Sandy, an elderly friend of Michael's father, who wanted one of the budgies Michael had recently bred. I was preparing the evening meal. Stifling giggles, I questioned Michael as to the whereabouts of his dentures. Shrugging his shoulders, he explained that the window of his lorry was open, he'd sneezed suddenly and his teeth flew out the window. As he was on a motorway at the time, there was no hope of getting them. My stifled giggles exploded into laughter. Sandy sat there gaping at me in amazement and then declared he could see nothing funny. He said it was a terrible thing to have happened and dentures were expensive. Sandy's disgust at my reaction made me laugh even more helplessly; Michael also started chuckling. Sand just kept shaking his head in disbelief. I managed to control my laughter enough to explain my sick sense of humour. It wasn't the consequences that amused me, it was visualising what happened that sparked me off, along with the fact Michael looked and sounded funny without his dentures. Sandy, I'm sure, thought I was mad. They both went down to the aviary to sort out the budgies and I returned to preparing our meal.

They came back as dinner was served. Sandy was gathering his things to leave when Michael, seated at the table, put his hand in his pocket, withdrew his dentures and popped them into his mouth! He said, "Just joking!" I playfully swiped him with the tea towel. We both started laughing, but poor Sandy, amazed and disgusted, was now convinced we were both mad. Beware deranged dentures!

As the dentures aged, they did develop more of a sense of humour. One year, we had taken them to Cornwall on holiday. They had started to pop out a bit more, but Michael felt he could control them.

It was a glorious day on the beach. The surf was boisterous, it's waves lifting us up and carrying us giggling and squealing to shore. We stood waist deep in the water getting our breath back, away from where the waves crashed, their passing just lifting us off our feet. Michael had his back to the incoming tide. A big wave was building and heading inshore. I shouted "Look Out!" We all jumped, squealing as the wave hit us. Its passing left Michael grabbing frantically at the water as his dentures gradually swished side to side, as they sank gracefully to the bottom. The dentures only wanted to join in the fun, but with a near disastrous result; luckily, a moment's calm after the wave was just enough to snatch them from a watery grave. Just when you thought it was safe to go into the water – dentures!

Dentures never learn from their experiences with water. They have a 'devil-may-care' attitude when it comes to taking the plunge.

We were spending a week at Center Parcs, where the domed swimming pool complex is fantastic. Our favourite part is the outdoor rapids. This feature starts inside the dome, then moves outside down the fast, swirling rapids, until you end up back in the dome. Crossing over a final hump sees you submerged in the 'landing lagoon', where you surface and giggling, climb the steps to get out and go do it all again. It was great fun. We would race each other down. After about the third time, I was in front, gushing over the final hump I plunged into the lagoon. This wasn't a very large area, but the waist deep water was constantly turbulent with people splashing into it one after the other. On the side wall, a big grid let the water flow out causing a swirling current.

I surfaced to see Michael whoosh over the hump and disappear underwater. He spluttered to his feet, calling out to me with a look of sheer panic on his face. "My teeth ... I've lost my teeth!" I'm afraid, as usual, I saw the funny side and started laughing. Michael did not think it was funny at all. He thrashed about the small pool in his frantic search. Just as the water started to calm a little, another person hurtled into the pool. I was helping to look for the missing dentures, but hysteria was getting the better of me and frustration was getting the better of my poor husband. We floundered around for what seemed like ages; my sides ached with laughing. I'm sure Michael wanted to drown me!

THE TOOTH, THE WHOLE TOOTH AND NOTHING BUT THE TOOTH

At last, I felt the teeth on the bottom and held them down with my foot. I shouted that I'd got them. Michael came to me side, looked me in the face and with clenched gums said, "Don't move!" He disappeared under the water, his hands feeling down my leg to the foot that trapped his treasured dentures. He surfaced, popped them straight into his mouth and then saw the funny side. We clambered up the steps, both laughing.

These are just a few of the denture adventures I've been entertained with over the years.

Michael studied along time but he now has his 'Master of the Dentures'.

Nowadays, the dentures are much calmer and even tough I miss their zany antics; I have no urge to let any of them live in my mouth!

*

The Perfect Murder
By Phyllis Gall

To call the green expanse in front of William's garden a lawn would be to denigrate the work of art upon which he had worked for many hours. It was a poem in green velvet, a perfect greensward which, although not overly large, could grace any stately home. But the perfection of the grass was but a small part of William's life. The leylandi trees which bordered the garden were all clipped to a uniform height; the flowers were pruned and arranged to form regiments of carefully co-ordinated colour in equidistant straight rows. William was very proud that many people stopped to look at his garden. He pretended not to see them peeking over his perfectly clipped privet hedge. What he didn't know, however, was that although they admired the finished result, no-one wanted a garden like it, for it lacked warmth and spontaneity. It was a garden for looking at, not for walking in and enjoying; a showpiece with no personality.

This reflected William himself, for everything he owned, worked upon or gave his attention to had to look just right. He had bought the house for the symmetry of its façade, although the kitchen was old-fashioned and labour intensive; the bathroom was draughty and the lounge was stuffy in warm weather. But to William the appearance of the house more than made up for these minor irrelevancies, and to complete its perfection the curtains had to be arranged in order that an equal amount of material showed at each window. The result was a lifeless, two-dimensional image, but to William it was perfect.

He beamed with pride and rocked his fat little body backwards and forwards on podgy feet. His hands were thrust deep into his pockets, and the shiny seat of his trousers was pulled taut across his buttocks. The material around his not inconsiderable paunch was stretched to the limit.

William wasn't an easy man to live with as his anger was very quick to show itself. He didn't forgive slights or insults easily, whether real or imaginary, and the favourite butt of his temper was Beryl, his wife. He saw only his own point of view and could never imagine that another person's opinion was just as relevant. This was especially so with regard to Beryl.

She was the only thing which upset his perfect way of life. She had her uses he would be the first to admit, but he had never been able to train her to his ways. She obstinately refused to arrange things in the house to his satisfaction. The towels in the airing cupboard were an example: he constantly had to rearrange them to get all the corners in perfect alignment. He had instructed her tirelessly about how the cups should all hang the same way on the dresser, but she never seemed to understand and comply with his wishes.

With a sigh William realised that Beryl would never fit into his ways, and yet she had seemed such promising material when he married her: always neat and tidy in her dress, and appreciative of William's orderly ways. He had thought the matter over very carefully and decided that Beryl would have to go. Not that it had been an easy decision, after all, she was his wife, and he had vowed to stay with her 'for better or for worse'. But he had reached his limit, and reluctant as he was to admit it, with Beryl he had made a mistake, and in William's view all mistakes must be dealt with. The only problem was the method.

Not divorce, that was too long and too costly. He would probably have to sell the house to give Beryl a half share, and he was too old to start another lawn. No, there was only one way: Beryl would have to eliminated, and for William's peace of mind it would have to be the perfect murder.

For the next few days he mulled some ideas over in his mind. He thought of the pros and cons of various methods. He rejected shooting her as he had no gun and no idea of where to get one. It was too noisy, anyway. He could use one of his sharp garden knives to stab her; that would probably do the trick. But then he would have to get really close to her, and he didn't think he would have the nerve to carry it through. The same went for strangling and hitting with the proverbial blunt instrument and, after all, he wasn't a violent man.

He considered staging an accident, but this wasn't foolproof and it had to be done just right to look authentic. The only way left was poison, and for an instant William saw himself injecting a lethal dose of something into chocolates with a hypodermic syringe. But he had no syringe and Beryl was on a permanent diet. She didn't eat chocolate, although it made no difference, she was still plump.

The idea of poison seemed the best way and William was sure that if he thought about it long enough a suitable method would occur to him. The advantage of poison was that it wouldn't leave a lot of messy blood for him to clean up, which was very distasteful and quite unnecessary if the job was done correctly.

The idea for the perfect method came to him as he was reading the advertisements in the local evening paper, the corners of which were all perfectly aligned. Next week was their wedding anniversary; twenty five years of wedded mediocrity. He didn't usually acknowledge birthdays or anniversaries; he considered them a waste of time and effort, but he could say that twenty-five years was special and deserved to be celebrated in some way.

He would take her to the local restaurant he had been reading about, which boasted a romantic atmosphere, dim lights, soft music and tables for two. The perfect place for an anniversary tete-a-tete. In such a setting it should be very easy to slip a lethal tablet into her food or drink under the pretext of togetherness, although as togetherness had not been a feature of their marriage for some years he was somewhat out of practice in the art. He would blame the restaurant for negligence, threaten to sue and altogether act the part of the anguished husband. And, he pondered, if he did it towards the end of the evening he would probably get his meal for free as well.

Where, though, could he get a lethal tablet? That would have to be worked upon, but William was sure the answer to his problem would materialise in some way or another. Although he doubted whether there would be an advertisement in the paper for such a thing. He almost laughed at his own witty thoughts, until he saw

Beryl looking at him and quickly turned the laugh into a cough. After all, he could hardly tell her what he found so amusing.

The next morning he went into the garden for his daily inspection and noted that several leaves were dropping from the trees. He hated the untidiness of Autumn and didn't appreciate Nature's beautiful display of colour. He saw only the tiresome job of raking and burning dead leaves. It was also the sign of the end of Summer and time to do the job he had been anticipating for several months: clearing away the house-martin's nests. He had wanted to do it at the beginning of the season when the birds had first started building, but Beryl had been surprisingly adamant. She liked to see the birds swooping and diving around the house, and William had reluctantly agreed to leave them until autumn. Now, he told himself, autumn is here, her feathered friends have gone and those nests are coming down. Today. He had indulged her female whims for far too long. She had to be shown who was the boss.

Humming tunelessly he walked around to the back of the house on the concrete path which he, himself, had laid. It was a job he hadn't trusted anyone else to do to his standards, for he had wanted it completely smooth and even. The concrete had replaced a gravel pathway which frustrated his efforts to keep tidy. Much to his annoyance people such as the paper-boy, the postman and the council refuse collectors had pushed the stones out of place, especially onto his precious lawn. William would never concede, however, that in wet and icy weather the concrete was a hazard. To do so would be to admit error, and William could not concede to having made two mistakes.

He stood in the back yard looking up at the little muddy structures, which to him were eyesores, spoiling the symmetry of his wall. He didn't see a masterpiece of construction or marvel at the cleverness of the birds in getting all those small pieces of mud to stick together in such perfect formation.

Pretending not to see Beryl glaring at him, he fetched the ladder and made much ado of leaning it against the wall. He spent time getting it just right, all the time feeling her intense gaze through the kitchen window. The thought crossed his mind that Beryl didn't know she was next, after the birds. His Autumn clearing. He almost chuckled aloud at the thought.

He tried to whistle as he fetched the hammer from the shed in an effort to appear nonchalant, but whistling had never been his forte and it sounded like a discordant hissing from between his teeth. With the hammer he had brought a piece of plastic sheeting which he spread on the ground under the nests to catch the dirt. 'Must keep the place tidy,' he muttered.

There was a chill in the air and a faint, misty drizzle as William slowly and carefully climbed the ladder. He wondered if maybe he should wait until the weather was better, but no, he had decided to do it, and do it he would. It shouldn't take many minutes.

When William reached the eaves he was higher than he thought. Everything looked different from this perspective. It had all seemed so easy. Up the ladder, knock down the nests, down the ladder, clear away the mess. Simple. But standing on the ladder, which seemed to bow considerably under his weight, clinging with one hand whilst trying to knock away the nests was not so easy. Should he cling with his right hand and wield the hammer with his left, or hold on awkwardly with his left hand and swing the hammer with his right? Either way felt unnatural and dangerous.

He had demolished one nest, but as he had been unable to rest the ladder between the nests he had to lean a bit further to reach the other one. He contemplated getting down and moving the ladder, but decided not to do this. If he went down now he didn't think he would have the nerve to climb back up again, and the job would only be half done.

Hesitantly, an inch at a time, he leaned to his right the hammer extended. His heart lurched and he froze as he felt the bottom of the ladder slip. Instinctively, he dropped the hammer and grabbed the guttering with both hands as the ladder fell away from beneath him and crashed to the ground.

"Beryl! Beryl!" he shouted. "Come quick and help me." The edge of the metal guttering was cutting into his hands as he glanced down quickly to see if Beryl was coming to his aid. The ground looked so far away it frightened him even more. "Beryl," he shrieked, his voice almost falsetto, "Beryl, I can't hold on much longer. Help me." His arms felt as if they were being torn from their sockets but the fear of falling made him cling on desperately. All his confidence and aplomb had deserted him. He needed help. He needed Beryl. He saw her standing quite still looking up at him.

"Quickly," he urged, "put the ladder – Beryl, where are you going? Come back." She was walking away, back into the house. Why didn't she help? He listened intently as a noise came to him through the open bathroom window. It sounded like the vacuum cleaner, and Beryl singing at the top of her voice. He couldn't believe it. She never could sing. Surely she wasn't going to abandon him, to leave him here. After all he had done for her. Just wait till I get down from here, Madam, he thought, I'll show you who's boss.

He could see the bathroom window tantalisingly near. Maybe he could work his way along the guttering and reach it. The combination of the cold rain, which was falling steadily now, and the sharp metal meant he could no longer feel his fingers. He lifted one hand a fraction of an inch and a sharp pain shot through his shoulder causing him to wince. The movement put a strain on his other arm, which couldn't support his weight and with a scream of panic he fell to the ground – hard.

Beryl stopped singing and switched off the vacuum cleaner. She opened the back door and looked at the crumpled body of her husband lying on the ground. She knelt briefly by his body and looked at his open, vacant eyes and the trickle of blood from his ear which was gradually washed away by the rain. "Well done, William," she said, grimly, "you even managed to fall on your plastic sheet and not make a mess of the yard."

Smiling, she walked slowly indoors to telephone for the doctor.

*

Just A Thought
By Rita Carrol

I remember very well how it all came about. It was Midsummer's Eve, and unusually warm that year. The four of us were sitting in Jack's spacious garden, watching the sunset and drinking his home-brew. Jack was giving us his views on the EU but I was not listening, my thoughts lay heavily in another direction. Suddenly the deafening roar of a motorbike spluttering into life drowned Jack's words.

"That damned Dillon or whatever he calls himself," he shouted above the din. "I swear I'll swing for that little tyke!"

He jumped to his feet shouting obscenities and shaking his fist at the thick hawthorn hedge that separated us from the offending machine.

After a few more waves of his fist, Jack sat down again, red in the face and speechless, as much by anger as by the earth-shattering racket of the nearby motorbike.

Eventually, the unseen machine could be heard accelerating down the quiet village street, past the Post Office and off into the countryside.

"Coming up to Devil's Elbow," muttered Jack into his beer and then added vindictively, "with any luck he won't make it."

For a brief moment there was a change of pitch as the rider slowed to go into the bend. Surely he's going too fast, I thought to myself. The engine's roar, dulled by distance, faltered for a moment and then picked up again as Dillon safely negotiated the hairpin. The sound of his machine floated to us on the warm evening air, gradually growing fainter and fainter as it receded far into the distance.

The air seemed to quiver in the ensuing stillness and there was a heaviness about it that promised thunder. I realised that I had been holding my breath and let it out in a rush as I turned over in my mind the event I had just witnessed. I was surprised at Jack's reaction and the venom in his voice had unsettled me somewhat. It struck me, that despite knowing my companions ever since I came to the village a dozen years ago, I really did not know them very well at all. Take Jack, I thought to myself, retired businessman, but he had always been evasive about what particular line he was in.

The there was Eddie, an ex-policeman who must have been a fine figure of a man at one time, but who was now running to fat – and he was much too fond of his drink.

I looked across at the fourth member of our group, Phil, a Woody Allen look-alike and the only one of us who could not afford to take early retirement. He was also the only member our group who was still married.

It was Phil who broke the silence.

"Do you think it's possible to get at people, I mean do them harm, just by thinking bad things?" he asked suddenly.

We all looked at Phil with surprise as he stared back at us defiantly.

"Who's been getting at you?" asked Eddie.

Phil adjusted his spectacles and looked sheepish. He muttered something about double-glazing salesmen.

Jack leered at him and hiccupped, "I know just what you mean old son," he said confidingly. "Has that BMW dealer been sniffin' around your Brenda again?"

"No he has not!" retorted Phil, but we all knew he was lying. His software business had not been doing too well lately and the dreams of becoming a millionaire by selling it all to Microsoft had long since faded. Brenda had never forgiven him. Phil adjusted his spectacles once more and cleared his throat nervously.

"It's just that I saw a programme on TV about witchcraft – sticking pins in dolls and that sort of thing..."

"And we all know who you want to stick pins into!" Jack gave a knowing wink. Phil scowled back but said nothing.

"That reminds me of a book I once read," I said, trying to ease the tension. "About a woman who travelled in Tibet years ago, long before the back-packers came. Well, she met a wise old monk who taught her how to use the power of thought to make things happen."

"Like what" Jack sounded sceptical.

"He taught her how to make an imaginary person become real, just by using her powers of thought. She decided to test it out by imagining a fat little Tibetan monk. Eventually, after a lot of meditation and concentration, he actually appeared."

"Who did?" asked Jack.

"The fat little monk of course!"

"Did she know him before?"

"No!" I think I sounded exasperated. "That's the point! She conjured up a person who did not exist. She actually created him."

"Could other people see him?" Jack still looked dubious.

"Yes. Well I think so," I finished lamely.

"Load of cobblers!" snorted Eddie and took another swig of his beer.

"Well, I dunno about that," Jack said thoughtfully. "The mind's a funny thing Eddie, more things in heaven and earth and all that."

"I bet she was just having hallucinations," Eddie scoffed. "Or like a kid – making up pretend friends. Load of bullshit!"

"We could give it a try," Phil said thoughtfully.

"What? Dream up some fat monk? What the hell for?"

"Not a monk," Phil answered patiently. "It could be anybody. Perhaps some big bloke to put the wind up people like Dillon."

Eddie and Jack looked at each other and laughed.

"Yeah, why not?" Jack grinned.

"I don't think it's meant to be a group exercise," I said doubtfully.

"Who says?" Jack looked aggrieved. "Four 'eads are better than one ain't they?"

I was not so sure. I seemed to recall that the original exercise had called for a tremendous amount of concentration and sustained periods of meditation. I also suspected that it might have involved a diet and lifestyle far removed from Jack and Eddie's alcohol sodden habits.

"Tell you what," Jack said, laying his glass on the table and looking round at us, "let's 'ave a bit of method. First, we decided who we wants sortin' out and then we decide on the imaginary bloke."

It was the most ridiculous thing I had ever heard but Eddie and Phil nodded enthusiastically, like a couple of eager schoolboys.

"Top of the list goes Dillon," Jack said emphatically.

"Always seemed a nice enough lad to me," I said.

Jack gave me a contemptuous, pitying look.

"Trouble with you Geoff," he said, "is you're too soft. You ain't bin in the big 'ard world like me and Eddie. We know about young thugs like that Dillon, don't we Eddie?" Eddie grunted in the affirmative. "Whereas you, well, what would an 'asbeen accountant know about them sort?" He wiped his fat wet lips with the back of his hand and belched loudly.

I was trying to think of a suitable retort when Phil said quickly, "There's a few more could do with sorting out."

"Yeah, like that old cow from the Post Office," Eddie said bitterly.

This was one of Eddie's constant themes; he swore that harmless old Mrs Minkin regularly opened his private mail. I thought it most unlikely but Eddie would not have it otherwise.

"And that snotty Mitch who keeps the Four Kings!" Phil blurted out, his spectacles wobbling on his thin red nose.

"Dead right!" agreed Jack, "'e's well overdue." Mitch had been in their bad books ever since he threw them out of our local last New Year.

"What about you Geoff?" Phil asked me, "Who do you want sorting?"

I froze for a moment, trying to quell the unwanted memories that suddenly surged forward.

"Well, there are a few politicians I could name, and perhaps some white-van drivers," I answered lightly.

"Nah! Not them!" Jack snorted. "We all want them. No, you got to say somebody what we know."

I shook my head. "There's nobody that I can think of," I lied.

"How about that insurance salesman who's always 'anging around your Emma?" asked Jack.

"What about him?" I snapped.

"Knows when 'e's on to a good thing," smirked Jack and gave a knowing wink. For a moment I wanted to smash my fist into his fat, red face and it was only by an effort of will that I managed to control my temper.

"Emma's old enough to choose her own friends," I said rather primly, "and although I don't like him, Justin's always treated her very well."

"She's a nice kid," Phil said, "don't take any notice of Jack." He inspected the remains of his drink. "There must be somebody you'd want sorting out. I mean, what about that bloke that killed Maggie?"

He looked up and suddenly became aware of my stricken face. "Oh God Geoff, I'm so sorry!"

"Leave it out Phil!" chided Jack, "have a care. I swear your mouth will be the death of you!"

For the second time that night I felt a rising tide of emotion. I took a deep breath. "It's okay Jack. Phil meant no harm. He's right. If there's anyone in this world I'd like to see 'sorted', it's that drunken bastard that knocked down my wife!"

They all looked away, awkward and unable to cope with my attempt to conceal my obvious distress. Perhaps they were aware that it was the tenth anniversary of the hit-and-run accident that killed my Maggie.

"They never did find him did they Geoff?" Eddie asked gently. I looked across at him and saw that there was true compassion in those red-veined eyes.

"No, they never did," my voice was husky with emotion. "But I've tried to move on from that and I had little Emmie to think of as well."

"Your Maggie was a star," Jack said sadly. "Worth both my exes put together." He looked so pathetic, that for a moment I actually felt sorry for him. Then he regained his composure and stood up.

"'Ere, what say we top up our glasses and drink a toast to Maggie?"

And that's what we did, there in the gathering dusk of that warm summer evening. Somewhere nearby a bird began to sing, its sweet song penetrating the heavy evening air.

"Nightingale," Phil said softly.

"Magic," murmured Jack in appreciation and we all nodded.

From far away came the low rumble of distant thunder.

* * *

The next morning dawned bright and clear but I was in no mood to appreciate it. My head ached abominably and I felt completely wretched. Emma fixed me with an accusing eye.

"You've been drinking!" she said reproachfully. "What did you get up to last night? And what time did you get back? It must have been well after two."

I blinked at her for a few moments; I could recall very little of the previous evening after the thunder began.

"Honest Dad, it's about time you acted your age!"

"And I think it's time you went to work," was the best I could manage. She laughed, picked up her bag and left leaving me to nurse my hangover in peace.

A few days later I decided to seek Phil's advice over some software that I was interested in. He ran his business from a scruffy little office attached to his house and once we had finished, he invited me stay for coffee.

"Brenda's out," he explained unnecessarily; Brenda was always out.

As we sat in their cold, formal living room drinking coffee, I sensed that there was something bothering him, something other than his wife.

"Have you seen him?" he asked suddenly.

"Who? Jack? No, not since the other evening."

"No, not Jack!" he replied irritably, "Norman."

I looked at him blankly, "I don't know any Norman."

"Yes you do!" Phil became quite agitated. "You said we should call him Norman because it was so ordinary and we wanted an ordinary bloke so that he would fit in!"

He was string at me intently. "You don't remember do you?"

I shook my head.

"The other night over at Jack's, he explained. "It was your idea, thinking up some imaginary bloke who could go around avenging all the injustices. That's what you said!"

"I think it was Jack who said that."

"Doesn't matter," Phil said abruptly. "We all agreed to it. During the storm, remember? We all agreed what he should look like and everything."

I remembered nothing of this.

"Must have been a joke," I said. "Nobody took it seriously."

"You seemed to."

"Me? Surely not. Anyway, what of it?"

"I've seen him," Phil said simply. "I've seen Norman – and so has Jack."

"You can't have!" I protested. "He doesn't exist! Anyway, how do you know it was him?"

"Because Eddie drew a sketch of him. He's good at that sort of thing."

Phil reached into a draw and handed me a sheet of paper.

"Your copy," he said, "for reference."

It was a head and shoulders sketch of a man in his mid-thirties, clean-shaven, with shortish hair. It was an ordinary enough face, a complete stranger, yet, at the same time vaguely familiar.

"He took features from all of us," Phil explained. "Like one of those Identi-kit pictures."

Inspecting the drawing closely I could see my own eyes looking back at me. I could also identify features that looked similar to those of my three companions. In the corner of the picture, Eddie had drawn a curious motif consisting of four stars arranged in a diamond pattern.

"Tattoo," Phil said. "One on the back of each hand. Jack said the face was so ordinary we'd add a bit extra to identify him."

"Where did you and Jack see him?"

"Jack rang me last night and said he'd just seen this dead ringer for Norman hanging around the Kings." Phil explained. "I saw him this morning. I was standing outside the Post Office with Jack when this taxi went past and Jack said, 'That's Norman!' He was right, it *was* Norman."

I sighed. "You must be mistaken Phil. This man can't possibly exist. It just doesn't happen that way."

Phil shot to his feet. "I saw him Geoff!" he cried angrily. "I looked into his eyes and I knew it was *him*!"

He was mistaken of course – he had always been highly-strung and impressionable. As for Jack, I never believed half of what he said.

Later, in the sanity of my own living room, I took out the drawing and looked at it again. Norman the Avenger! The whole idea was absurd, how could Phil and Jack be so deluded? I filed Norman away in my desk and forgot about him.

* * *

Emma was home later than usual that evening and I was beginning to become worried. When I head her key turn in the lock I rushed to the front door, trying hard not to appear the over-protective parent. When I saw her face I knew that something was wrong.

"Hi Dad."

"Everything okay?" I tried to sound nonchalant.

"He's dumped me the bastard!"

"Emma!" I exclaimed, taken aback by her language as much as the news. Emma had always maintained a ladylike façade, at least in my presence.

"Sorry Dad," she smiled ruefully. I led her into the kitchen and over a cup of coffee she told me about Justin.

"I waited for him in the 'Kings' but he didn't show. He didn't have the guts to say anything to my face, just sent a text saying it was all off. Men!"

"Oh Emmie love, I'm so sorry."

She gave me a withering look. "No you're not!" she said crisply. "You never liked him Dad. Anyway, I think he was cooling off. We didn't have that much in common and everybody said he wasn't my type."

We sat for a few moments sipping coffee whilst I tried to think of something suitable to say. I was relieved to see that she was not particularly heartbroken.

"Dillon thinks I should go to Uni," she said unexpectedly. "I might still make it with a late application."

"Dillon?" I was bewildered. Had I missed something?

"He was in the Kings," she answered patiently. "He bought me a drink and was very kind. We talked about old times and had a good really good chat. He's actually very nice, much better than people make him out to be."

I recalled that Dillon and Emma used to go to school together.

"He said Mum was a brilliant lady," she said wistfully. "He remembers the day she died. It was his tenth birthday so it was a special day for him."

We sat together for a while, remembering and nursing our mutual sadness. Emma went to bed soon afterwards but I lingered for a while, my thoughts on Maggie and all that she had left behind.

* * *

The next morning the postman informed me that Mrs Minkin had been threatened by a stranger.

"Threatened?" I asked.

"Yeah. Some bloke came up to 'er just as she was closin' up last night. Told 'er to stick to 'er own job and not go interferin' with 'Er Majesty's Royal Mail – otherwise she'd get what for."

Alarm bells sounded in my head.

"Did she see who it was?" I was half afraid to ask.

"Nobody she knew. Just an ordinary bloke – but she did say as 'e 'ad tattoos on both 'ands."

The alarm bells in my head rang louder.

"Is she all right?"

"Oh yes, tough old bird that one. She 'ad no idea what this bloke was on about but she didn't 'alf give 'im a piece of 'er mind! I reckon it was 'im what came off worse!" He sighed and added dolefully as he departed, "we'll never 'ear the end of it now."

I found the postman's news disturbing in more ways than one. It occurred to me that if Eddie was the culprit Mrs Minkin would surely have said so, but Norman? No, that was impossible.

Later that day I met up with Jack, Phil and Eddie in the Four Kings. Jack was full of the news about Mrs Minkin.

"It's 'appening lads!" he chortled over his pint. "Our mate Norman is doing 'is stuff!"

"If you mean poor old Mrs Minkin," I said coldly "then forget it Jack, it's all a coincidence."

"Not so Geoffrey boy," He replied making me squirm with his unwanted familiarity. "It's not just Mrs M that's been sorted. There's Justin and now Mitch 'as gone missing!"

"What's happened to Mitch?" Phil queried, looking round the bar as if to find the answer to his question.

"Dunno!" Jack shook his head. "Nobody's seen 'im since last night." He leaned forward and lowered his voice. "Perhaps Norman's persuaded 'im to do a runner. I mean, I did see a bloke like Norman 'anging around 'ere last night."

"What about Justin then?"

Jack gave me a conspiratorial wink. "Mate of mine drinks in the same local as Justin," he explained. "Word is, Justin got done over by some bloke. Warned the little prick to stay clear of a certain young lady."

He smirked, enjoying telling the tale. "Total stranger it was, only distinguishing feature was tattoos on the back of 'is 'ands. Bet you anything you like they was diamond shaped!"

I shook my head. "All coincidence," I said.

Jack grinned and downed the last of his pint. "You wait and see," he answered. "Norman ain't finished yet!"

* * *

Mitch's body was found the next day, floating face down in a nearby pond. Eddie told me that the police were regarding the death as 'suspicious'. I studied Eddie closely; he looked terrible, the worst that I had ever seen him.

"What's wrong?" I asked. "Surely you don't think Norman..?

"Don't know what to think," he said miserably. "I know it's insane Geoff, but I've seen him. Norman I mean."

"Not you too Eddie! Where, when?"

He cleared his throat and began to recount the events in a formal manner, as if giving evidence. Old habits die hard I thought.

"It was about midnight last night and I was at Jack's place," he said. "it was getting dark so Jack went to draw the curtains. As he glanced out of the window, he caught sight of a man standing underneath the street lamp. He called me over to look. We could see the man's face clearly and we both agreed that it was Norman. Before we could do anything the man walked away and we lost sight of him."

I gave an involuntary glance out of my own front window.

"You were mistaken," I said. "It was dark and lamplight plays tricks. You know yourself how unreliable eye-witness are." I did not add that both witnesses in this case were almost certainly the worse for drink.

"I know what I saw," he said quietly.

He stayed for a while longer, but no matter how much I tried to persuade him otherwise, it was clear that Eddie was convinced that he had seen Norman. Once he had gone, I tried to think things over but my thoughts were cut short by a phone call from Phil. In a breathless rush he told me that the BMW dealer (Brenda's friend) had been roughed up by an unknown assailant.

"And I suppose he had diamond tattoos on each hand," I said wearily.

"I don't know," Phil admitted. "I'll have to ask Brenda."

"You got this from Brenda?" I asked incredulously.

"Oh, yes. She saw it all. The attacker just leaped out of the bushes and set on her, um, friend. I showed her the picture of Norman and she thinks it was him."

I said something about 'leading the witness' but Phil brushed it aside. We finally agreed to meet in the Four Kings later on.

When I entered the bar of the Four Kings that evening I was immediately struck by the subdued atmosphere. Mitch's death had struck hard I thought, but I soon learned that it was more than that.

"It's Dillon," Phil said sombrely. "Came off his bike this morning and was killed."

"Probably 'is own daft fault," Jack muttered. He seemed edgy and I could not decide whether he was glad or sorry about Dillon.

"At least that's one thing you can't pin on Norman," I said.

"I'm not so sure," Jack looked serious. "I mean, look what's been going on: Justin, Mrs M, Mr BMW, Mitch – and now Dillon. All the people on our little list! Makes you wonder."

"If Norman was any good," I said coldly, "the first person he'd get would be the bastard who killed my Maggie!"

Jack looked uncomfortable. "No-one knows who that is Geoff," he said quietly. "No witnesses, remember?"

"Perhaps. All the same, Dillon's death was an unfortunate accident, so it's all coincidence.."

"Dillon didn't have an accident!"

I looked up to see who had spoken and found that Eddie had joined us. He sat down, looking immensely weary. "I've been speaking to some of the lads investigating Dillon's death," he continued. "Looks like somebody set a trap for him. Stretched a length of rope across the road where he came off, just about chest height. The speed limit's sixty there, but most likely he was doling a ton. He wouldn't have stood a chance, poor sod."

"So it's murder!" Phil exclaimed looking pale.

"Looks like it," Eddie nodded gravely. "Mitch too."

"Do they think the deaths are connected?" I asked.

Eddie shrugged his big shoulders. "They're not saying."

"But who would want to kill Dillon?" I asked. "I know he could be a nuisance, but murder...."

"Norman of course!" Phil hissed trying to keep his voice down so that the rest of the bar would not hear. "He's doing what we wanted! He's gone through the people on the list!" He looked at me with wild eyes. "It's all your fault Geoff!"

"Don't be daft Phil!" I said. "Norman's not real, he's all in your head."

"Then 'e must be in mine as well," Jack said. "And Eddie's. We've seen 'im, remember."

We spent the remainder of that evening arguing over Norman. As the drink flowed, the talk became more animated. It was clear that I was the only one who thought that Norman was purely a figment of their imaginations. I pointed out how ridiculous and absurd the whole thing was, but the more I tried to be rational the more stubborn they became. I was becoming more and more exasperated with the three of them and the atmosphere was becoming strained.

Finally, I had had enough. "I'm going home," I announced as I rose to leave.

"Watch out for Norman," said Jack flippantly.

"No chance," I replied frostily. "Norman only appears to drunks and neurotics!"

Immediately I regretted what I had said. Jack laughed but Eddie and Phil looked shocked, I had obviously hurt them deeply. Embarrassed and ashamed at my cheap jibe, I muttered a hasty goodbye and left.

The village street was deserted as I hurried homewards. For some reason I found myself peering anxiously into shadows and jumping nervously at every dog bark and every rustle of the wind in the trees. It was just past the church that I realised that I was being followed. I froze for a moment then steeled myself to turn around.

"Phil!" I exclaimed as his figure emerged from the shadows. "Look, I'm sorry about what I said back there."

He shrugged. "Forget it. I've been called worse things. Anyway, I thought I'd walk back with you. To tell the truth, Jack's getting on my wick, he's so jumpy nowadays, real twitch."

We walked together chatting amiably until we reached my front gate. Phil hesitated for a moment as if about to speak.

"Something wrong?" I asked.

He looked at me thoughtfully then shook his head. "Nothing that can't wait until tomorrow," he said and continued on his way.

"Take care!" I called. He raised his hand in response as I watched his slight figure retreating towards his cold lonely house.

That was the last time I saw Phil. Next day I learned that Brenda had arrived home in the early hours to find her estranged husband murdered, his brains splattered all over their best living room carpet.

* * *

The next few days were almost as miserable as those following Maggie's death. I was the last person to see Phil alive – apart from the murderer – so I was of great interest to the police.

They were not convinced by my first statement and hauled me in twice more for questioning. They said I was not being completely honest. They were right of course – how could I tell them about Norman? Indeed, *should* I tell them about Norman? Would Jack and Eddie mention him? I tried to contact both of them, but without any luck.

The inner conflict between the urge to tell the truth, yet not appear a total idiot, began to wear me down, for the thing was, I was beginning to see Norman for myself. He began to haunt my dreams until I dreaded sleep and the prospect o his shadowy figure flitting through my dream world. On two occasions I thought I caught glimpses of him during the day, once getting off a bus and on another occasion going into the Post Office. Both times, when I looked again he had disappeared.

I was finally put out of my misery by a visit from Eddie, who, I noticed, appeared remarkably well.

"You look awful!" he said, coming straight to the point.

"And you look very well. What's your secret?"

"I stopped boozing," he said simply. "Your words the other night made me think."

I was about to apologize but he cut me short. "I came to tell you that Jack has been arrested for the murders of Dillon and Phil."

This was not what I had expected to hear.

"Jack had a secret," Eddie continued and then paused for a moment as if trying to find the right words. "It was Jack who knocked down Maggie all those years ago," he said gently.

I was so taken aback, that for a moment I was speechless. Then the questions began to flood in.

"But there were no witnesses so why kill Phil and Dillon?"

"Dillon saw something that day, something that could land Jack right in it. He was only a kid at the time and probably didn't realise what he'd seen. Perhaps it was the damage to the car, who knows. But Jack knew, and all these years he's been watching and waiting, always afraid that Dillon would put two and two together and make trouble."

"But after all this time," I said, "surely Dillon would have forgotten?"

Eddie nodded. "Yes, he probably had, but Jack hadn't and it's been eating away at him ever sine. Something like that can drive a man out of his mind."

I was still confused. "But how did he get away with it? The police had a nation wide hunt for that car."

Eddie sighed. "Jack always had a load of shady friends – the kind who would fix your motor up, no questions asked, then give you an invoice dated for whenever you liked."

He looked at me sadly. "Me and Jack go back a long way Geoff," he said quietly, "but I swear I never knew. He was a dodgy character, granted, but I never had him down as a killer."

"But why kill Phil?"

"Phil may have suspected something. At any rate, Jack was convinced he was a danger and got rid of him. They say the second murder is easier than the first."

"And Mitch?" I asked. "Did Jack kill him as well?"

Eddie shook his head. "He's not admitting to it. Anyway, Mitch had enemies of his own, so the case is still open."

As he got up to leave I suddenly thought of something.

"What about Norman? Did you say anything to the police?"

He grinned and shook his head. "No way!"

"Have you seen him again?"

"I never saw Norman at all," he said firmly. "What you said that night got me thinking. The only time Phil and I ever saw him was when Jack was with us. Jack can be very persuasive at times – and of course, I was always half cut, so I never knew what I saw. As for Phil, well, he didn't take much persuading."

"so you agree that Justin etcetera were all coincidences?"

Eddie shook his head, "No. I said I never saw *Norman*. What I saw was a bloke who *looked* like Norman. Probably one of Jack's dodgy mates. Remember, we only had my sketch to go on. Easiest thing in the world to bung a few quid to some look-alike and get him to do the dirty."

"And the tattoos?" I asked.

"Easy. Dab of ink – who would know the difference in all the excitement?"

"But why do all that?" I asked. "Why go to all that trouble?"

Eddie looked thoughtful. "It was Jack's way," he replied. "I reckon he likes to play games and manipulate people. It would suit him fine if we thought Norman was behind it all. Gave him a sense of power I suppose.

JUST A THOUGHT

After Eddie had gone I had a lot to think about, not least how to tell Emma. Then there was the prospect of Jack's hearing; Eddie had warned me that I might be called as witness.

As it turned out, Jack never did stand trial. He was found hanged in his police cell a few days after his arrest. At the inquest, the Coroner mentioned that Jack had not been considered a suicide risk and thus no blame should be apportioned to those on duty. However, it was noted that the deceased had been visited by his lawyer the previous evening and had seemed unusually subdued afterwards. The lawyer in question could not be traced and it was concluded that he was an impostor who had somehow managed to deceive the desk-sergeant with false documents. Eddie and I are sure that the bogus lawyer was one of Jack's accomplices reporting back to him.

After that, village life returned to normal. Brenda went to live with her BMW dealer and Mrs Minkin continues to tell the tale of her mystery assailant with relish. Justin was arrested for the manslaughter of Mitch – something that he vehemently denies, although there had been bad blood between them for a long time.

Emma obtained a place at university and is now reading for a degree in psychology. Indeed, it is for her interest that I am recording this account. I think she will find it of interest to see how easily people can be duped into seeing things that are not there, although I do not include myself in that category. She certainly seems to have settled well; she phoned last night to say that she had, at last, met the true love of her life.

"He's just an ordinary guy, not flash and shallow like Justin," she enthused. "He reminds me so much of you Dad, especially around the eyes. Weird isn't it? Oh, and his name, is Norman."

Emma is bringing Norman home to meet me next week. I look forward to seeing him of course but I must remember to take a good look at his hands.

*

A Real Bargain
By Ron Radford

Julie Mortlock hurried homeward from her job at the post office. She crossed the bridge, hurried up the lane and past the church. She was walking quickly, because she had felt a few spots of rain and the skies looked stormy.

Home was a pretty, red-brick cottage near Thetford, where Julie was born and had lived all her life.

Her parents had passed away some years ago and Julie had never quite got over her loss. Her father, James, had been a master builder, and had started building the cottage when her mother, Mary, and he had become engaged. It was finally finished in time for the wedding. Above the front door, partially obscured by the roses growing across the rustic porch, was a round, wooden plaque bearing the words *'Mary and James, 1943'*.

Every part of the dwelling held memories for Julie. The small bedroom that used to be the nursery was her favourite room. When she was a child, it used to serve as a doll's hospital, a general store, or an imaginary kitchen. In fact, anything she wanted it to be.

Julie now slept in her parents' bedroom. She remembered climbing into their bed when she was small and snuggling down in the warm, cosy space between them.

The whole building was still decorated in the style of the fifties. The scullery had an old cabinet with glass doors and a pull-out, enamel worktop. There was a walk-in pantry in the kitchen where years ago, Julie used to hide from her mother who always seemed to find her.

The lounge still contained the original furniture. There was a pendulum clock on the mantelpiece and antimacassars on the large, voluminous sofa and armchairs. In fact, the whole cottage was a friendly shrine to the memory of Julie's parents. She even kept their clothes in a large wooden chest in the bedroom.

* * *

Julie was addicted to car boot sales. She had staggered home with many a bargain. This particular day, she had spotted a leaden urn, decorated with four satyr masks round the side and coiled, serpent handles. She haggled with the scruffy old man who looked rather like one of the satyrs that decorated the urn. Finally, she managed to buy it for the modest sum of five pounds.

'It would look rather fetching in the front garden with some sort of plant in it.'

In order to carry the urn home, she had managed to get a taxi instead of her usual bus ride. The driver helped Julie into the garden with it and they dumped it in the middle of the path. She paid him and off he went.

She had spent longer at the sale than she had intended and soon busied herself with household chores and preparing a meal. When she eventually had time to relax it was getting dark. She stood at the door enjoying the cool breeze on her face. As it blew the branches of the trees in the garden, the moonlight shone through and flicked onto the urn.

Was her imagination playing tricks? The satyr faces were leering at her. Their eyes were alive and evil. The serpents glistened in the soft light and slithered upwards. She shuddered and slammed the door. This wasn't like her. What was wrong? She was trembling. Finally plucking up courage, she pulled aside the curtain and looked through the window at the urn. The shadows from the trees resembled dark figures dancing round it, half animal, half human. She bolted the doors and windows, went to bed and tried to sleep.

* * *

The next day, Julie washed, dressed and had her breakfast. She had to pass the urn on her way to work, so she sidled past it and tried not to look.

The morning went quickly. She hadn't told Miss Bentley at the post office about her purchase. Julie felt quite ashamed of her behaviour of the night before. On the way home she bought an ivy leaf geranium in full bloom. She stood back admiringly after planting it in the urn. It looked less sinister now. She moved it next to the porch, subconsciously placing it where it could not be seen from the window.

She settled down into her routine. She only worked mornings, so she had the rest of the day to herself. Once a week she hoed the flower beds. Although she was not much of a gardener, the garden looked very tidy.

After a busy afternoon, feeling quite exhausted she walked towards the front door. What was that on the urn? There, curled up and partially crushing the geranium, was a large black cat. It stared at her, daring her to move it. Julie threatened the cat with the hoe and for a time it stood its ground, arching its back and spitting. It looked so fierce and evil. Julie prodded it with the handle of the hoe and it leapt off. As it pushed away with its back legs, it toppled the urn onto the porch, snapping the main support. It was probably rotted through but the rambling rose prevented it from collapsing completely. The cat ran off and Julie propped up the porch with the urn, tying it with a length of rope round one of the handles. She squeezed through the space left and went into the kitchen.

Her comfortable home was gradually becoming disrupted. She filled the kettle, lit the gas and placed the kettle on the ring.

'*Was the urn unlucky? Everything was fine until I bought it.*'

She made the tea and stood thoughtfully at the sink. '*No, I'm being foolish.*'

After pouring the tea, she felt drowsy and carried it to bed. When she had almost reached the top stair the sight that greeted her caused her to stumble, drop the cup and twist her ankle.

'*That ghastly cat is asleep on my bed!*'

Julie limped quickly towards it. Sensing her rage the cat jumped through the window. She was past caring whether of not it had injured itself, and spent a restless couple of hours trying to get her ankle into a comfortable position.

Exhaustion soon overcame her and she slumped back onto the bed, drifting into a sleep of sorts, tormented by thoughts of the urn and the pain from her injured ankle.

She awoke some hours later to find the room in darkness. The sound of a storm raging outside had clearly been the cause of her being wakened so suddenly. As she listened, the noise outside grew gradually louder and louder, until there was a deafening clap of thunder overhead. By now, Julie's head was buried under the bedclothes. There was a brilliant flash that illuminated the room, followed by a crash and the sound of breaking glass.

Julie was too frightened to investigate and finally dozed off again into a fitful sleep when the storm passed over.

Next morning, she felt like a wet rag. Dragging herself to the kitchen she washed and dressed. As she limped to the lounge it seemed very dark. All she could see of the window was a mass of leaves and branches. The lightning must have struck one of the trees, which had fallen against the window. There was broken glass everywhere and branches were poking through into the lounge.

'That damned urn and its bad luck!'

Julie hobbled to the front door and squeezed through what was left of the porch. She was gradually becoming angrier by the second. The garden looked devastated. Shrubs and flowers were crushed and where the tree had hit the house, there was a large crack in the wall. She clenched her fists until the knuckles showed white. Then, on impulse, she limped to the shed, wheeled out her father's old wheelbarrow and trundled it to the porch. She cut the rope that was tied to the serpent handle of the urn and with great difficulty, managed to load it onto the wheelbarrow.

Her ankle forgotten, she wheeled the barrow down the path and through the gate. Then she headed down the lane towards the bridge that spanned the river near the post office. When she reached the river, she chose the deepest part and tipped the urn out of the barrow. She hadn't notice in her rage that she had stepped into a loop of the rope that was still tied to the urn. The bank had become muddy and slippery after the storm. The urn slithered and rolled down the bank, dragging Julie with it. She grabbed frantically at clumps of grass and bushes as the urn gathered speed, but to no avail. The urn hit the water with a great splash. Julie gave a piercing scream as the water closed over her head. There was a flurry of bubbles and then silence.

Back at the cottage, the black cat settled once again on the bed and gave a contented purr.

*

A Significant Tumble
By John Coyne

For once the forecast was correct. The day started off misty soon giving way to bright warm sunshine. Warm was an understatement, judging by the volume of sweat streaming down Jacob's face, as he performed the ill practiced manoeuvre of reversing car and caravan. Angela, his almost new wife; they had been married nearly two weeks, tried her best to assist, running to and fro shouting instructions. It soon became obvious her help was less than productive confusing 'left and right hand down' constantly.

"I think I can manage better on my own darling," Jacob remarked with well disguised frustration.

He jumped out of the car hoping to relieve the irritation of sticky clinging clothes. Walking slowly to the rear of the still attached caravan, he unbuttoned his sweat soaked shirt and removed it as though peeling off a parasite. It was mid June and certainly blazing. Normally he would be very pleased but not at present, finding concentration difficult, as he plucked his trousers from his inside leg. However, there was one piece of good news, the caravan practically lined up with their pitch.

He called to his wife, "We should be able to position it easier if I uncouple it and we both push it up to the electric hook up."

Angela appeared much less affected by the rapidly developing heat, her flimsy loose fitting dress showing no evidence of sweat marks.

She drew up close to Jacob, flinging her arms about his torso, recoiling rapidly at the touch of his cold clammy skin.

"Ugh! You feel horrible. Soon as we've got the 'van where we want it you must go over and get a shower."

It was fairly easy to push the 'van within reach of the designated hook up; the ground surprisingly level; the grass stunted mainly due to the closeness of the underlying chalk.

The pair unloaded their suitcases and placed them on the caravan bed. Jacob quickly connected the electric then sorted out a change of kit, stuffed it into a plastic bag and headed for the shower block, collecting his discarded shirt on the way.

"Don't be long will you darling," purred Angela framed in the doorway.

Jacob stopped. A cheeky grin spread across his face as he turned to face her.

"You won't have to wait long."

Angela was well acquainted with that look and tone.

She shouted after him, "You can get that idea right out of your head," and followed up with. "Make sure you have a really cold one."

Minutes later, he finished his shower, changed into his shorts and, reinvigorated, began the short walk back. Few of the pitches were occupied he noticed, except for two small groups of three or four, reminding him of covered wagons ready to repel red Indian attacks. Nearer to the site main building and toilet block, stood three expensive looking statics; all appeared unoccupied. May be Angie would like an ice cream he thought and diverted to the site shop. On second thoughts decided it could cramp his style and abandoned the idea, settling for four small bottles of chilled water obtained from the vending machine inside the entrance. Rejoining the path he felt quite pleased with the spot they'd chosen. Unless there was an influx of fresh caravaners they seemed quite isolated. Not only that, their 'van sat closest to the cliff edge and therefore the sea. Even so it was a good two hundred metres away.

When he got back, Angela had unpacked and hung most of their clothes in the small wardrobe. She had also brought in the cool box, erected the table, set two places and was in the process of dolling out sandwiches.

She heard his footfall. He closed the door.

"Keep the door open it's much too hot. Come and sit down and grab a sandwich," she ordered.

Disappointed, Jacob reluctantly obeyed, but first putting the water in the fridge. Sitting opposite his wife he gave her the hangdog look.

"I told you, you can cut that out," she said, hardly able to suppress a teasing laugh. "Be a good boy and you can have a bit."

Jacob's eyes twinkled, "Of Battenberg", she added.

About an hour later they both felt refreshed. Angela was on the move. She found her shoulder bag and opened the door.

"Where are you off to," queried Jacob.

"Thought I'd try and get down to the beach. There must be steps or a track some where near."

Jacob knew it was pointless trying to dissuade her.

"Ok, but be careful. Take this chilled water with you, the sun's very hot."

She took a couple of paces back into the caravan and accepted the sensible gift.

"By the way the water container needs filling and waste emptying. Perhaps you could do that whilst I'm out. If you've got enough energy, that is."

Jacob made a playful dash forward. She scampered out.

As she stood on the metal step the searing accumulated heat briefly penetrated the soles of her sandals. Gratefully she alighted on the spiky grass. Heat haze partially obscured sight of the sea; its rhythmic sound urging her forward. Several times she traversed the cliff top seeking a way down. On her third reccy she found a narrow gouged out gully just below the lip guarded by a dwarfish silver birch. She tugged two whippy branches aside exposing an almost non-existent track. It fell away sharply. Strewn with screed and larger boulders it looked dangerous and uninviting, causing a rethink of the whole idea of clambering to the beach. Grasping one branch tightly she ventured a stride down, then stood nervously for a minute or so surveying the rest of the track.

Further down it appeared less precipitous even levelling out before swinging left, with any further view obscured by clinging scrub. Angela felt compelled to follow it but, before moving off, looked down to the beach and out to the rolling sea. It was a difficult climb down to the small levelish platform, made more awkward by her totally unsuitable footwear. Most of the descent was accomplished on her bottom, creating a minor landslide as pebbles and larger stones cascaded to the beach, pursued closely by a dust cloud.

Here the cliff face was in shadow and pleasantly cool. She rested for a few minutes contemplating whether to go on or turn back. Seconds later the sky fell in as she lost consciousness, slumping forward and slithering lower still. Gradually, as her head cleared, senses kicked in. The first pain she became aware of was the dull nagging throb emanating from the base of her skull.

Vision returned patchily zooming in and out of focus as her brain sought to organise itself. Eventually the mists cleared and her view stabilised. Her restored sight revealed a restricted vista of leaves, plant roots and sandy shingle. She was lying on her side. Automatically she tried to stand up but a bout of swirling giddiness changed her mind.

Settling for sitting, Angela felt the nape of her neck. It was sticky, painful, and covered in blood. Gingerly she guided her hand over it and was unsurprised to feel a large pulsating lump rapidly forming at the base of her skull. She soon discovered touching was not recommended. A quarrelling flock of black headed gulls caused her to look up, immediately triggering more pain. Her whole body sweated profusely as she no longer remained in the shade; the sun, though lower, still felt pretty hot. She was near the bottom of the track. A welcome zephyr swirled soothingly round her body lifting her dress on its journey and wafting in the unmistakeable odour of the advancing sea.

In fact the breeze seemed a little too penetrative. To her horror her dress was in shreds, massive tears stretched to her waist exposing her knickers. That was one bit of good news, she still had them on.

Refreshed a little, she had another attempt at standing. Safely achieved, Angela took faltering steps to the beach. The sand radiated its stored heat and she searched anxiously for a cool spot. There, about a couple of hundred metres away on her left, a sizeable rock beckoned her. As it sat in close proximity to the lapping sea, she decided it must be cooler than her present position. Fortunately the beach was deserted so nobody could witness her knickers-flashing stumble to the rock.

The rock, worn smooth, was much bigger than first thought, but with a concentrated effort she managed to lever herself astride it. My! It was soothing and cool. The gentle coolness circulated through her battered limbs as she leant back on her hands, reminiscent of the Copenhagen mermaid.

She took a short respite and tried to recall events. That she had received a sickening blow to the back of her head was indisputable, the lump proved it. How it happened she could only speculate. She had seen no-one on the beach or track all afternoon. Apart from minor cuts and abrasions she was uninjured.

She took the opportunity to scan her surroundings. It was a very small cove. A line of semi-submerged rocks formed, pincer like to the left and right, greatly narrowing access to the beach. Thirst now became a problem though; she longed for the bottle of chilled water Jacob urged her to take. Anyway, where was the shoulder bag now? She deduced she must have dropped it somewhere on the narrow track leaving her with no option but to retrace her steps. As she straddled her unusual seat she was surprised how a lump of rock could feel so comfortable and swinging her legs over, slid off.

Unexpectedly it wasn't the feeling of noisy shingle that greeted her but swirling tepid water flowing round her calves. Unnoticed, the tide was coming in rapidly. This worried her. *I must leave the beach straight away and make for the high water mark*, she told herself. The loose shingle beach rose steeply and gave little purchase to her feet. With considerable difficulty she managed to scramble clear of the encroaching water and head for a line of jetsam some hundred metres away marking high water point. She scrambled towards this sanctuary and plonked herself down a few strides beyond and took another rest.

Cracked lips and a sore face reminded her she really needed that bottle of water. On reflection, she realised a number of other useful items were in the missing bag, Suntan lotion, spare caravan key, comb etc. above all, sunglasses.

Though most of the cliff was in shadow, her spot still had the sun, rendering it impossible to see the start of the trail. Shading her eyes she struck out in its general direction. A dozen steps on and she entered the shadow zone, permitting unhindered sight. She spotted the track and was about to hobble over to it when something, a sixth sense maybe, compelled her to look back to the sea. A lifeboat-sized craft headed to the point where she waded ashore.

A strong on-shore breeze had sprung up causing the boat to pitch and toss as it made for land fall. She noticed three figures, almost certainly men, expertly riding this marine rodeo. The powerful throb of its motor became the dominant noise, even drowning out the ubiquitous gulls. An inner voice kept nagging her. Hide! Hide!

She dropped down to a crouch, and, keeping as low as possible headed for a patch of scrub. Cover was at a premium. Clumps of coarse grass, sea holly and diminutive bushes were scattered unhelpfully over the area. Thankfully the patch of scrub did offer some hiding and Angela knelt carefully behind the leafiest bush to observe the trio's activities. The sun still dazzled so she was pretty sure they'd not seen her, though it would be stupid to stand up and risk dashing to the track. Her predominantly light coloured tattered dress would be difficult to miss. Attempting to darken it by smearing with sand, met with marginal success, as the constant needle like pricking of her unprotected fingers by dead, sea holly leaves, became unbearable.

Nervously she pushed the leafy twigs aside and watched the boat, now lurching much more vigorously, move ever closer. The beach still appeared deserted, which was strange on this hot day. Perhaps the dangerous and over grown descent had gone unnoticed; access by boat the preferred method, though even this was tricky. The sea breeze strengthened further and a choppy swell meant the three occupants were perpetually on the look out for the large rock that so conveniently provided Angela with a welcome seat. As they wrestled with the bucking craft Angela took the opportunity to seek a more protected position.

Half standing, half crawling, she made for a slightly denser group of vegetation, picking up a lump of wood on the way. Closer examination revealed it to be a broken paddle shaft. Any idea of retaining it as a weapon was quickly shelved. It would be a hindrance on the return ascent. Her new location provided all round screening, and in addition an excellently placed grassy hump afforded a ready made seat. With observation easier and safer, she confidently bent the obscuring branches clear, in time to see the boat crash noisily onto the shingle.

The motor was cut immediately. A frighteningly enormous bearded man leapt to the beach holding the mooring rope. Joined by a smaller man, wearing a light blue bobble hat, together they hauled the craft further up the beach. Both men then approached the near side of the boat and conversed with a third, who, standing at the tiller, appeared to be the leader. Allowing for the depth of the boat, he too was tall with distinctive close cropped ginger hair and wearing a black leather bomber jacket which had some sort of bird emblem, a hawk maybe, emblazoned on the back. Angela had become fascinated by these suspicious happenings, continuing to watching avidly. What were they up to?

Events unfolded in quick time. The smaller of the two men clambered back into the boat and with the help of the leader yanked a hitherto unseen person to their feet. The pair of them then roughly manhandled this fourth person out onto the beach. From its attire it was obviously a young woman. Expertly, the second man vaulted from the boat and joined the mini mountain.

Angela's blood froze as Blackbeard; she thought the name apt for the colossus, produced a large knife and approached the woman who was bound hand and foot. He brandished the weapon. His huge bulk hid his next move from Angela, who, when he stepped away half expected to see a crimson stain draining into the sand. She was relieved to see only the bonds had been severed round the young woman's feet. Run, run, for the love of Christ run! Angela almost shouted the words out loud. Standing drunkenly for a few seconds, the woman suddenly pitched forward into the sand. Dressed in a red top and beige skirt, she remained immobile. Leader gestured for Blackbeard to stand her up. He accomplished this by a sharp kick to the ribs and tugging on her long tousled hair. Once on her unshod feet she took a couple of paces then slumped into a motionless heap. The giant stood over her, then, in one swift move, hoisted her across his massive shoulders, like a slaughtered deer. Angela thought she must be dead, but breathed again when she noticed the captive kick out weakly. Not a sound came from the prisoner. She must be gagged surmised Angela, with duck tape no doubt.

Surprisingly, the three ruffians made a beeline for the base of the cliff, away from the track. Due to the contours of the cliff, Angela found it impossible to follow their movements and was about to step from cover to observe better, when the mobile hill and the leader changed direction and strode to the sea shore. Wading in up to his groin, the chest for normal people, Blackbeard turned to face inland. The leader promptly splashed water over the unfortunate woman. Satisfied she was still alive, they returned to their original tack. This time Angela remained hidden until persistent curiosity over came her and she decided to venture closer. She was in time to observe the smallest of the trio wander behind a large projecting column of rock and so out of sight. The poor woman needed help desperately. Against three tough thugs what could Angela hope to accomplish.

She deliberated for a few seconds wondering if she dare take a peek round the rock. No! She concluded. More sensible to climb back up the track as quick as possible and get help. If Jacob's mobile phone was working she could contact the police.

Stealthily she made her way to the foot of the cliff to begin her climb. Once there she tried to increase her pace but, a combination of dehydration and loose unforgiving terrain, cut progress to a snails pace. Dirty, puffing and blowing, she eventually arrived at the spot where she had been felled. Her shoulder bag lay partially hidden to one side. Hastily she grabbed it and finding the bottle of water took a long drink. Though it no longer felt chilled, it still refreshed.

About to move on, her gaze was distracted by a group of flying insects circling a small boulder. Curious, she hooked her bag over it and pulled it close to hand. The little swarm dispersed except for a couple who were stuck to a tacky substance. It was blood, her blood. Not only blood but a slither of flesh also. She felt nauseous. It must be a pretty big gash she'd received from this plummeting rock. Zipping up the bag she stood on the grass and not wishing to carry it, flung it towards the top of the cliff. Thankfully it stayed put somewhere. As she laboured higher the harrowing recent events flooded her brain. What had the young woman done, or perhaps not done, to warrant such cruelty. Her thoughts turned to Jacob; surely, by now he wondered where she'd got to. Maybe not! If he got the tele working and cricket was on, he'd be oblivious of time. It was then she heard a muffled bang echo around the bay.

Stunned, Angela instinctively knew a shot had been fired. Just a solitary one. Still, with a trussed up helpless female at your feet, one would be sufficient. Deeply saddened with the turn of events and trembling with fright she nearly released her grip on a tree root preventing her falling back.

At this point the track narrowed as it neared the cliff top and formed a gully. Wedging herself in, she scrutinized the beach below in time to see the three thugs strolling to their boat. All were laughing as Blackbeard thrust what appeared to be a gun into his belt. The woman was not with them. Fearing the worst Angela continued to watch them reach their boat. The giant began hauling the craft seawards but his way was barred quickly by the leader who produced a pair of binoculars from his jacket. At this range they appeared fairly small, '*small but expensive type*' she thought. He scanned the cliffs. Angela tried desperately to squeeze herself tighter in the gully. The scanning ceased as it centred on her position. She froze. No way could she be seen from down there, the gully was too steep and scrappy vegetation grew across it. Craning her neck and looking to the cliff top, the reason swung slowly above her. Her bag had landed on the bush that camouflaged the entrance to the track. Acting like a beacon, its red and white stripe stood stark against the sky.

Numbness was creeping into her legs and back. The man returned the binoculars to his pocket. Angela sighed with relief and shifted her position. Relief was short lived as the man exchanged the binoculars for a mobile phone, pointing out her location as he spoke. Clawing herself to the top, she snatched the troublesome bag off the bush, crawled on all fours for a few seconds, and then collapsed exhausted. Her raging brain permitted only the briefest of rests. Painfully she struggled to kneel and took one last sight of the distant sea. Did a light flash a couple of times on the horizon? She was unsure. Her top priority was to home in on their caravan and alert the authorities.

Painfully she arose and scrutinized the area. There it was, a little farther to her left than she thought, but definitely theirs, complete with Jacob talking to some woman dressed in the skimpiest of shorts. Talking to a woman! Was she hallucinating? He never talked to other women! He was too shy. Wasn't he? She waved frantically, trying to shout, voice, cracked and feeble due to her arid throat, produced little sound. Her energy ebbed away fast, exhausting totally a few strides further, as she slumped, slow motion to the grass.

She came round in the caravan with Jacob clucking anxiously over her. He dabbed her brow tenderly and, seeing her conscious, propped her up. Gratefully she took a long drink of the ice cold water. Alarm danced across her face as she attempted to relate the awful events. Still her voice box would not respond. Taking another drink she tried to communicate.

"Call police. Woman killed on beach." She managed to gasp the words till her vocal chords succumbed once more.

"Try and calm down darling. I know something nasty has happened. You look as though you've been in a fight. You're safe now."

Angela waved her arms frantically at him; desperately trying to make her husband understand she, and now they, was very much in danger.

Her brain reacted slowly to the noise. She motioned to Jacob to help her see out of the window. He quickly obliged. Angela saw a rapidly advancing dust devil close in on the site entrance. Digging her nails into Jacobs shoulder, she pulled him, protesting loudly, to the window and pointed to the commotion. She now realised what the sound meant. A powerful S.U.V. burst onto the site and stopped. Its engine bellowed like a Spanish bull ready to smash away the matador. Slowly the vehicle edged forward, as if seeking to flush out its prey. Shaking with fear, Angela drew back from the window.

"It's them. They're looking for me."

She choked on the words as she hid below window level.

"Who are?" asked Jacob, trying valiantly to mask the infectious fear.

The mystery female entered, beckoning to Angela to stay out of sight.

She obeyed and slid away to the floor. Bossy so and so thought Angela.

"What, in the name of sanity's going on?" Jacob's tone was hard and uncompromising.

"You'll be informed," replied the woman with equal harshness.

"Where are you from? MI bloody 5."

"Nearly."

"MI four and a bit?" Jibed Angela.

Her strength and mental clarity returned, she sat cross-legged on the floor. Her head throbbed still, but less severely. There was no doubt the presence of the other woman was acting as a catalyst in her recovery.

Edging forward on her bruised bottom, she tugged Jacob's shorts. He looked down and smiled.

"Who is she?" Angela mouthed words silently.

Even so Jacob knew it was not a friendly question.

Any reply was drowned out. The ominous low revving engine sounded much nearer. Jacob joined the stranger in the doorway. He could make out several passengers as the S.U.V. continued to sniff out its quarry, all the time probing deeper into the site. Carefully, Angela raised her head above the sill, hoping to observe the intruder leaving the area. It had stopped again and seemed uncertain the direction it should take. Their caravan being set apart from the two other groups, it swung towards them. This appeared to be a signal for action. A cacophony of sound rent the air, as trucks and vans erupted from the other two groups. At the same time a pair of large, un-noticed black vans blocked the site entrance. Disturbingly, the S.U.V. continued on its heading, picking up speed. The leggy woman shut the bottom section of the door. It was then Angela saw she carried a gun. She didn't know whether to feel reassured or not.

The throaty engine noise became deafening. Petrified, the newly weds clasped each other, whilst the gun toting woman remained, steely eyed, watching from the top section of door. Angela felt Jacob's strong reassuring arm about her waist as he guided her to the rear. They stared out of this window and the reason for a dramatic increase in the decibels was obvious. A second heavily armoured vehicle, similar to those used for riot control, had joined the fray and was headed on a collision course with the S.U.V.

Switching their view to the side, they were relieved to see the menacing vehicle veer away. The armoured car screeched to a halt, positioning itself close alongside them. Unfortunately, their view through the half stable type door was now completely obscured. The armoured car (later Jacob discovered it was a modified Landrover) had drawn up within two feet of the caravan, leaving barely sufficient room to exit. 'Skimpy shorts' was already out and talking to the driver.

In spite of its gloomy interior, the couple could pick out a number of figures. All appeared to be in uniform. After a short conversation the woman gave the cab a friendly pat and the vehicle moved off, not at rubber burning speed but still quite rapidly. Standing in the fully open door the young couple craned their necks to see where the Landrover was headed.

At this point Angela dug her husband in the ribs and repeated the earlier question. "Who **is** she?"

Her face had taken on an uncharacteristically hard appearance, eyebrows knitted firmly together, lips no longer full and inviting, nostrils flared to such and extent a small prominent previously unnoticed black nasal hair, bent under the gale blasting by it.

"Pamela," Jacob replied timidly.

The reply only increased Angela's anger. "How come it took you about three visits to mum and dad's before you knew our Jane's name? I've a feeling you discovered hers pretty quick."

Jacob sensibly stepped on to the grass. His wife quickly joined him and together they walked to where Pamela stood staring at the receding armoured car. Another, faster vehicle, clearly emblazoned 'Police' had joined the scene and gave chase to the bucking, swerving S.U.V. as it took avoiding action.

Suddenly, a noise not unlike a colony of bees searching to swarm, reached their ears; the unmistakeable sound of an Uzi machine gun. All three watchers noticed the muzzle poking from its rear window. Instantly the police car swung away and retreated at high speed. By now the armoured car had moved to intercept the miscreants. It stopped some distance away and two rapid shots rang out hitting a front and rear tyre of the escaping vehicle.

Moving on again, the armoured car closed swiftly on its target, which, because of the rapidly deflating tyres careered about madly. Blind panic took over as the passengers loosed off wild shots. Jacob and Pamela dropped to the ground but Angela took root. Seconds later she was yanked down by her husband as stray bullets struck the grass close by, raising spurts of white dust where as they smashed into the underlying chalk. A deadly game of cat and mouse ensued with the armoured car easily able to out-manoeuvre the stricken S.U.V. as it made one last bid for freedom. By some fluke it found increased grip and hared off along the cliff edge. The riot van stopped seeing a possible disaster in the making. Even in its semi-disabled state the criminals were able to coax a fair turn of speed from their machine.

Then, for some reason probably known only to the driver, he braked hard. Skidding completely out of control the vehicle slid towards the cliff. Two passengers jumped free and Jacob expected the cliff edge vegetation to arrest its progress. At the edge it did appear to stop. Unfortunately being a heavy vehicle, the chalk crumbled and it teetered drunkenly on the edge for a few seconds. The driver's door sprang open and the three onlookers watched in horror as the vehicle tipped uncontrollably forward and over the cliff before he could jump out. A pair of police cars hurtled up to the fortunate escapees who, familiar with routine dived face down placing their hands on heads. One of the black vans trundled over to the now hand cuffed criminals and unceremoniously bundled them in. The crew of the armoured car were all peering over the cliff at the point where the remaining villains had plunged headlong to the beach. Their group increased as the breathless caravan trio arrived.

They saw the S.U.V. had landed on its roof with the wheels continuing to spin ever more slowly as their momentum decreased.

"Looks as though the roll bar has prevented the roof being crushed," noted one of the coppers. "Perhaps the driver survived?"

A sudden whoosh caused everyone to retreat as the petrol tank exploded, showering burning fuel all over the beach and onto the sea.

"If he was in it, he's a crisp now," remarked another of the spectators callously.

"Sergeant Williams, why are these civilians here?"

The rasping voice of authority came from a very large stout man with bulging eyes standing behind the trio. He paced pompously to and from the cliff edge. Though it was late afternoon the sun still bathed the area and as all remnants of breeze had ceased, the heat became more oppressive causing the big man to sweat profusely.

"Well, move them from the area sergeant."

Angela realised this ill informed buffoon was addressing Pamela, who appeared distressed by its abruptness. For a time she felt sorry for the W.P.S. It soon passed.

"Mrs. Jenkins," she began causing Angela to spin round looking for another woman. She really must get used to her married name.

"Mrs. Jenkins can you and your husband please return to your caravan, Superintendent Rodgers will visit you and explain the situation." She fired off the last remark defiantly turning to her boss.

"We're not going anywhere until you tell me what's happened to the cruelly treated woman who was later shot", barked Angela, eyes flashing, hands planted firmly on hips.

Pamela was already on the move with a hand on Jacob's shoulder heading in the direction of their caravan.

The Super's loud threatening growl halted progress instantly.

"What the hell's this charming young lady talking about Williams."

He smiled at Angela, who, jolted by the about face, self-consciously, smiled back. It was then she realised all the officers were staring at her and smiling. Not the friendly 'Hello nice to meet you smile' but a lascivious sexual one. What she found particularly disturbing was the fact one female officer had an unmistakeable glint in her eye. In all the excitement she'd forgotten the state of her shredded dress. Thank God she'd not worn her thong.

Sergeant Williams regained some of her composure as she replied to her fuming boss.

"I'm not really sure sir. She was very greatly stressed and her speech garbled.

Angela hurled a fusillade of mental daggers at the police woman.

"I think we ought to hear it from the horse's mouth. Don't you?"

Correcting himself he said, "I mean young filly's mouth."

A signal from the police man brought over his chauffeured car.

"I'd like to change please before we move on," Angela said assertively.

Rodgers nodded in agreement, a hint of disappointment flickering over his face.

They all squeezed into the police car. And, after stopping at their caravan, where she re-emerged wearing jeans and top, they drove to a large rectangular mobile incident room.

Once inside, Angela related her experience, with her voice trembling emotionally as she described the events surrounding the unfortunate captive.

Superintendent Rodgers's mood blackened. He spoke to one of the officers manning the communications section.

"Get me inspector Steele on the radio. Now!"

He spun round and vented his spleen on Williams, "Next time Williams pay more attention."

Angela felt not the slightest pang of compassion for the sergeant; in fact the complete reverse. A wave of undisguised pleasure swept through her heart. Why she felt such hostility towards the police woman puzzled her.

"Got him sir," shouted the young communications officer, waving the mike at the super.

Superintendent Rodgers bustled across and grabbed the microphone.

"Where exactly are you Steele?" The super's voice sounded edgy.

"We've just finished checking out the site office sir. Found several interesting bits of contraband." Inspector Steele tried to conceal his excitement. This was the first big operation he'd participated in along side the legendary Rhino Rodgers.

"Forget about that for now. You know what you're looking for so concentrate solely on that goal." The big man took a paper handkerchief from a large box on the table and mopped his brow, then, placing the microphone next to it he was on the radio again.

"Still there Steele?" queried the super.

"Yes sir."

"Listen. We've reason to believe a young woman may have been executed. Shot in other words. So take extra care. What's your next move?"

The super wiped his face again and looked over to Angela and Jacob.

Both stood close together, fascinated by events.

Inspector Steele reported back. "There're only two more buildings to check out sir. Well they're more like sheds or shacks really."

Rodgers interrupted abruptly. "Skip the architectural lecture inspector, what's their functions can you tell?"

Feeling a little chastened Steele tried to put extra snap into his reply.

"One looks like a storage facility and the second almost certainly is a gas bottle compound. It's some distance from the other buildings though."

"How many men have you got?"

"Six, sir."

"Well split them in two and examine both at once."

"All ready done that sir." The rooky inspector hoped his initiative wouldn't go unnoticed.

Angela was showing signs of increasing frustration.

"Excuse me Mr Rodgers." Her tone betrayed the irritation. "The woman was landed on the beach then taken to some rocks at the foot of the cliff, and shot. Why are you messing about on top?"

Before he could answer a second radio officer waved urgently at the super.

"The coastguard have stopped a long boat size vessel and arrested the people on board. The tides on the turn do you want them to land some men and work from the beach?"

Frantic waving from Angela finally attracted the super's attention.

"Yes Mrs. Jenkins what is it now?"

"Ask them how many people they arrested."

Rodgers nodded to the radio officer to inquire.

For what seemed like an age the super chomped at the bit.

"Two, sir. They picked up two people." The officer beamed as he gave the info.

"There should be three," squealed Angela beginning to pace nervously around the control centre. "Tell them to describe the two under arrest."

Reluctantly, Rodgers again indicated to the officer to find out. As the answer to this last request would probably take sometime, the super reckoned it was time to check on progress with inspector Steele.

It was a jubilant inspector that reported. "We've found it sir, or more correctly we've found them, just as you surmised sir. What's your instructions sir?"

The big man smiled, *'so he was right after all'*.

"Stay where you are for the present. No heroics. Re-enforcements are on the way. You're getting four more men."

A message from the coastguard came in.

"S'cuse me sir," the radio officer interrupted hesitantly. "The coastguard's been on."

"Let's have it then man. Don't bluster."

"One's a dirty great big bastard with a beard; the other's a lot smaller, though still average height wearing a bobble hat.

Angela breathed heavily. "Look's as if the leader's got away then. Tell them we're missing another man, tall with a ginger haired crew cut."

Peeved through lack of involvement, Jacob went outside, soon to be joined by sergeant Williams.

Inside the mobile police H.Q. things were hotting up. Rhino Rodgers was having one of his happy/sullen moods. Happy, when he felt that within a few hours he expected to tell the commissioner all the gang were in custody. Sullen; because the commissioner contacted him too soon, before he could give the triumphant announcement.

With Rhino dishing out orders like verbal confetti, Angela decided to take a breather. Once outside she took a dawdle round the H.Q. and hearing voices close by, she recognised immediately; one was her husband's, the other rang a bell. Of course, it was that police woman, Pamela. Her heart began pounding and her head swam. She steadied herself against the caravan. Her first inclination was to spring out and confront them. Confront them, about what. She decided to bide her time and listen, that's if her heart didn't give her away, its thumping was so strong.

She heard Jacob say, "I thought you'd moved down to the smoke?"

"I did but the congestion and pollution's too much so I transferred back."

"Don't think you can take up where we left off. I'm very happily married and will become seriously vindictive if you harbour any remote thoughts of returning to our relationship." Jacob coughed as his throat dried up spitting out the invective.

"A bit presumptive aren't we?" Pamela replied, scornfully. "I've moved on way past you. Much bigger fish to fry."

"Just make sure you've not put a shark in the pan," sneered Jacob.

Angela felt more annoyed than upset. Granted she believed that there had been no serious romantic involvement before her and now it appeared there had. At least she could feel good about Jacob's vitriolic rebuff. Actually, thinking back, she could not honestly recall asking her husband about previous girl friends. She resolved to correct this omission. It was very difficult not to casually stroll round and accidentally meet the ex-lovers. After a little thought she decided to keep quiet and at some later date carefully steer the conversation around to old liaisons. Things had gone awfully quiet behind the caravan. She had sickening visions of the pair embracing feverishly. Unable to control her seething volcano of jealousy, she charged round the other side. Nobody there.

Her eyes scanned the surroundings finding it difficult to penetrate the lengthening shadows, whilst her mind raced through the distasteful possibilities of a continued liaison. Her preamble had now taken her back to the H.Q. and a shout from the steps reset her mind.

"The super's looking for you sergeant. Where've yer bin?" She was addressed by a second police woman who, by her unfriendly tone, probably empathised with Angela.

Deep down animosity to Pamela proved justified? The two female officers made burning eye contact before Pamela pushed past. Jacob held back, kicking idly at the short tufts of grass. He started to trundle away but was surprised by his wife's presence behind him.

Exhibiting masterful self control she said, "Got the same idea eh? Fresh air. Didn't see Sergeant Williams about did you, that dreadful superintendent's looking for her?"

"Yes I did. I've been talking to her."

Angela's heart sang with the sound of thousand violins. Jacob was going to put her in the picture.

"What about?"

She tried to stifle the excitement from her voice. Unfortunately events were on the boil in the mobile H.Q. and it was about to be moved.

Seeing this, Angela grabbed Jacob's arm and they boarded together. At first the second police woman barred their way saying, "I don't think you can come along I'm afraid."

"It's ok Baxter," boomed Rodgers. "Young Mrs. Jenkins could possibly help with identification."

The police woman helped them further in and smiling, whispered in Angela's ear, "He likes you."

Blushing slightly, she smiled back and stood to one side as inconspicuous as possible.

The mobile office gave a lurch and was on the move causing Angela to utter a cry of surprise. "Ah! Mrs Jenkins. Can I call you Angela? We're going over to link up with inspector Steele."

The journey to the second group of police was short and fairly bump free.

The H.Q. came to rest and everyone jumped out apart from the two communication officers. A beaming, very tall man, probably in his thirties strode purposefully towards them. Undoubtedly inspector Steele reckoned Angela. He went into a huddle with the Super for a few minutes.

The Superintendent stood on the H.Q. steps and addressed the group.

"Right, for safety's sake, Mr. and Mrs. Jenkins please return to the H.Q. with me, the rest of you follow the inspector."

Angela was far from pleased about this move but reluctantly obeyed.

"Superintendent Rodgers, there's an urgent message from the coastguard sir," shouted an officer waving a notepad.

"Let's have it then," growled Rodgers.

"The two suspects have been transferred to a frigate and questioned by the security forces. The mammoth sized bloke is singing like a canary and the big revelation is that there's a hell of a lot of fire power in that cliff."

"Damn! That changes things. I won't risk my officers until I know more about what they'd be up against," he bawled out loud.

The super sounded annoyed, his dreams of national fame were receding fast as other agencies became involved. Then, as if to compound the situation, a call from the chief constable resulted in a still more crestfallen superintendent. He addressed his team.

"There's a small contingent of S.B.S. on the frigate, which is holding station about a mile and a half outside the bay. The chief constable's been instructed that they must lead any seaward assault."

"Where does that leave us sir?" queried a clearly disappointed and frustrated inspector Steele.

"It leaves us inspector, with a task of our own to perform based on your information concerning the buildings you and your crew searched over there."

He stopped, wiped his face yet again, rolled up his immaculate shirt sleeves and pointed to the two shed like structures nearby.

"But before we proceed I want you, sergeant Williams, to run up to the lads in the armoured Landrover and get them here tout de suite. Oh and make sure they bring the ignition keys and their weapons. Don't want any embarrassments in front of the army do we?"

Happy to escape the super's gaze, the sergeant scampered away and soon had the armed officers striding purposefully towards the H.Q. Pleased with the response superintendent Rodgers stood imposingly in the door way, with his rolled up sleeves rapidly becoming unrolled. Clearing his throat he boomed out his orders.

"According to my information, both the sheds you can see about fifty metres away to the left, contain trapdoors leading to, as yet, numerous unchecked passageways riddling the cliffs. So here's the plan. At 19.15 hrs, armed units will split into two and enter the labyrinth. At the same time a unit of S.B.S soldiers will land on the beach and head into the tunnels. As we are the closest, all communications will be channelled through our H.Q. At least that's what the navy tell us."

He paused. Even his deep sonorous voice was beginning to show signs of wear.

A SIGNIFICANT TUMBLE

Inspector Steele took the opportunity to speak whilst his boss refreshed his vocal cords with swigs of water.

"Listen everyone, I've just been asked a very sensible question. Should you take extra lighting? The answer is no! From my cursory glance beneath one of the trap doors, the tunnels are lit up like the 'Underground'". He finished his address and showing signs of anxiety gratefully accepted a bottle of water, his hands shaking noticeably as he took it.

"You ok Steele," asked the super gruffly. "You look a bit white round the gills."

"Fine sir; just want to get on with it."

"Right! Three minutes to go. So the armed officers make your way to the shacks and enter when we flash our lights. Don't get carried away if there's any shooting. Leave it to the army unless it's unavoidable." Rodgers was beginning to enjoy himself again. He popped his head inside the H.Q.,

"Where's the chopper and reinforcements," he shouted to the officers manning the radio.

"I can hear it now sir and there are a couple of vans entering the site," one of the officers replied excitedly.

"Tell them to fan out on the cliff top and look for any possible breakouts. This scum could have numerous escape routes. It's like a rabbit warren."

A cry went up!

"We can see the boats sir. Four men in each, Christ they're really moving."

"Flash the lights," barked Rogers.

Through the open doors of the shacks, light flowed from the exposed trapdoors as officers streamed through them. For several long tense minutes nothing appeared to be happening. The S.B.S had landed and entered the hideout unopposed; the police met no opposition either. It was congratulations all round when the inspector emerged, dashed up to the superintendent and informed him the labyrinth was clear. A much more sombre message came from the army; a badly beaten young woman had been discovered in one of the galleries trussed up and barely alive. Forethought meant an ambulance was on hand, but, because moving her upwards to the cliff top was deemed more life threatening, evacuation to the frigate more sensible. An air of euphoria pervaded the police officers.

It was Rodgers as usual who choked off the self indulgence when he said, "Where's Williams. She's armed and should have stayed close by."

The assembled force all looked blankly at each other. She was missing.

"Forget that for now, she'll turn up with some excuse," he remarked calmly though he fulminated secretly. *Who the hell does she think she is disappearing at the critical time?* Turning to the inspector, he managed to modify his tone as he asked for verbal report.

"So what's in there, Steele?"

The inspector was slightly out of breath, being overwhelmed with excitement.

"A bloody supermarket, sir. A criminal bloody supermarket," he blurted out.

"Yes, yes, but what's there?" rasped his boss.

"Guns and guns, racks of 'em, plus thousands of rounds of ammo." He paused and inhaled deeply.

Rodgers sounded increasingly agitated as he fired off more questions.

"And, inspector, and. You said it was like supermarket. No supermarket I know only has two lines on sale. Did you come across the leader, ginger haired crew cut, as described by young Mrs Jenkins? In fact did you find anyone else there?"

I didn't go in very far. I thought you needed to know about the guns urgently," he replied, his voice betraying a sense of disappointment.

Detecting despondency, Rodgers thought he would pep up the inspector's ego a little.

"You and your team have performed very well, so I'd like you to take two more officers and spend the next twenty minutes searching as many galleries as you can. And make a note of what you find."

He was interrupted by a radio officer.

"The boat service lads have found a hidden dormitory. They think you ought to examine it."

"I'll say we did. Slight change of plan, Steele. Take your group to this new find and check it out. Be very careful make sure the army lads know who you are, I don't want a blood bath."

With a fresh objective, inspector Steele departed feeling much happier.

All this frenetic activity had bypassed Jacob and Angela who unanimously decided to return to their caravan. They left quietly and strolled casually back to it, enjoying the sun's last rays on their backs. As they approached their mobile abode, Jacob thought he noticed it rock momentarily. He grabbed his wife's arm preventing her moving any closer.

She looked at him inquiringly.

"I think somebody's inside," he whispered putting his fingers up to his lips as a gesture to keep quiet. Then he decided on a confrontational approach.

"Ok come on out, I know you're in there. There's a whole squadron of coppers just a shout away, so don't try anythin'".

A figure filled the doorway. A female figure; Sergeant Pamela Williams.

The sound and sight of this woman provoked instant uncontrollable reaction from Angela as she stormed into the caravan. Shocked, Williams backed hurriedly inside as a furious Jacob joined them. Pamela waved her cocked revolver ominously, indicating they should sit on one of the benches towards the front. The pair seethed with anger as they sat down. Jacob found his hatred immensely difficult to deal with, his strong fingers flexing and snapping continually.

Worse was to come. The galley occupied most of the rear area, but on the left was a door leading to a small wash room with shower. This door opened and their anger was replaced by terror when the missing ginger haired leader stepped nonchalantly out. He moved towards the couple, unfolding a handy sized table and placing it very close in front of them; the obvious intention being to prevent any sudden lunges. Angela was correct; he was pretty tall and dangerous. The butt of a pistol protruded from his pocket.

A SIGNIFICANT TUMBLE

Sliding over to the opposite seat he placed his gun bedside him. "Right my darling Pamela, where's my coffee?"

He spoke softly in an indeterminate accent, a mixture of Irish and South African.

"Now, my unlucky pawns, what shall we do with you?"

Jacob opened his mouth to answer but was sharply harangued by the usurper.

"It's a rhetorical question, stupid. My wife and I know exactly what we're going to do."

Don't make eye contact, don't make eye contact, Jacob kept telling himself, certain this man would be able to detect his simmering hatred and more importantly, his now lack of fear. He stared awkwardly at his feet; a wicked fleeting smile crossed his lips.

Married her eh! At least miss' poison ivy' seems to have met her match, he surmised.

"Our ticket out of here that's what you'll be. And if you're sensible and give no trouble you'll be unharmed. If you're really co-operative there will be a nice little bonus."

He unlocked a small suitcase. Picking up a tightly banded wad, he plonked it on the table.

"Anything happening over at the circus Pam?" he asked, referring disparagingly to police presence.

"No! All quiet. Probably having a conference or a tea break darlin'."

By using a term of endearment she secretly hoped to provoke jealousy in Jacob. She resented being dumped. With a smug look she placed a mug of steaming coffee before her husband.

Pamela's assessment of the lack of activity was completely wrong. The mobile H.Q. throbbed with expectancy. A whole host of information had been accumulated and passed between agencies. Inspector Steele had described the cache perfectly; a 'criminal supermarket'. Apart from the vast selection of guns, large quantities of plastic explosive and R.P.Gs, had been uncovered. As for the dormitory, that turned out to be a side line in prostitution, acting as a dispersal point. A hefty sum of cash, ready for laundering no doubt, was also discovered. The groups, both civilian and military, were in celebratory mood. Though, but for an officer desperate for a fag, they would have missed the subdued happenings at the other caravan. The young man clambered noisily into the H.Q. forgetting to extinguish his cigarette.

"Get that bloody fag out," bawled Rodgers.

"Sorry sir but the young couple seem to be getting ready to leave. Did you give the ok?"

"I sodding well didn't. Well spotted young man, but still put that fag out. Steele you've still got a gun, is that right?"

"Yes sir."

"Take two other armed officers and get into a car and be ready to intercept them if they move towards the exit."

Puzzled, he selected two men and jumped into a police car hidden from the view of the touring caravan.

The hostage takers were not exactly running smoothly along either. A couple of flaws had appeared in the getaway plan. Firstly, in order to prevent being seen, the caravan curtains had to remain more or less closed, thus making it practically impossible to see what was going on. The leader felt threats to Angela's life covered this one. Secondly, they hadn't bargained on Jacob's ingenuity. When instructed to hitch up the caravan, he'd apparently encountered a problem. No difficulty in reversing up to it, but, now with three unscheduled occupants its stability was all over the place which he soon discovered after raising the caravan's legs.

"I need some help. Angela darling can you come out and give me a hand," he shouted, loud enough he hoped to draw the attention of the coppers.

He walked to the caravan door and pulled it open. Poking his head inside he was greeted by the sight of a petrified Angela held down and a pistol pressed against her head.

"I suppose you think you're being clever," hissed the leader like an activated pressure relief valve.

"I can't move it about with three people in it," appealed Jacob.

"Pam," growled the unseen leader. "Change into some of her clothes and get out there and help."

"I'm taller than her," complained Williams.

"Well, find a dress and crouch down a bit. Don't forget your gun."

From the corner of his eye Jacob could see a number of officers leaning against the H.Q. and taking surreptitious glances in his direction. Next minute they were gone, but he was sure they had noticed him. Williams stood in the doorway clad in one of Angela's dresses. Though she was taller, she was a bit of a bean pole and where there should be bulges and curves, only flats. She jumped out onto the grass, positioning herself on the side away from possible onlookers. Jacob motioned to her to help steady the unwieldy mass.

"You treacherous bitch! You know you're dead don't you," he whistled through his teeth contemptuously.

Together they hitched up. One of Angela's sun hats suddenly floated onto the grass.

"Get it on," commanded ginger knob.

Pamela obeyed. With the wide brim pulled down, ostensibly to shade from the lowering sun, her face was shielded from prying eyes.

Deliberately playing for time, Jacob strolled to the driver's seat, at the last minute giving a hammy performance of tripping up and losing the keys.

"One more trick like that and I'll test fire my gun on your wife's knee cap."

Jacob knew by the cold venomous threat he dare not do any other than accept the situation. He thought to redeem himself.

"Is the bonus still on?"

"It's up to you and your missus. No more talk. Get in and drive steadily off the site."

The car's engine purred as he slipped it into gear and began to pull away. Slowly and sedately they rolled towards the exit. He took a glance at his passenger but the dipped brim effectively obscured her face. Lowering his gaze he noticed her knuckles showed white as she grasped the gun on her lap. She was frightened too.

His mind raced around examining escape possibilities. All were dismissed, meaning certain death to Angela. About fifty metres on a police car containing three officers drew along side. A very stern faced inspector Steele waved them to stop. Jacob felt he must obey. In a loud voice Steele said, "Sorry to delay you and your wife Mr Jenkins but did you realise your rear tyre is almost flat?"

The inspector casually stepped up to the driver's window and out of sight of the passenger, winked at Jacob.

Jacob replied with an almost imperceptible nod. "Are you sure," he said sounding concerned.

"Get out and see for yourself."

"Yes I will. Come to think of it the towing seemed a bit hard."

Keeping a wary eye on Pamela, he gradually eased out and made for the 'puncture'. The inspector followed him closely and at the back wheel they both knelt down as if to examine it.

"We've got about thirty seconds. Fill me in. Where's your wife?"

"Hostage."

"You've got to get the caravan door open on some pretext. Be very careful as you open it. I expect your wife will be standing there with a gun focussed on her. Signal to her to hit the deck when you do. Like this."

Steele held his hands out and lowered them. Before they moved off the inspector stuck a knife in a tyre.

"Don't want to give him a get-away car."

Fortunately Jacob had devised a plausible reason to get the door open.

He approached the caravan, his mouth ran dry and his throat closed up making swallowing difficult, so it was in a husky voice he said, "You in there, Ginger, don't panic I'm putting my key in the lock and need to open the door."

"What for?" snarled the hostage taker.

"My car's got a rear wheel puncture. We keep the spare wheel, brace and jack in there. It's happened before so we find it easier than taking every thing out the boot. Angela knows where they are. I'm opening the door now."

He turned the key but it failed to move.

"Take the dead lock off. If I mess about any longer the coppers will think something's wrong."

"Well, fumble a bit more whilst we put the things up to the door."

The sound of movement and items placed against the door were soon apparent.

"Ok it's open. No heroics."

Full of apprehension, Jacob pushed back the door. The spare stood propped against a cupboard just inside; the jack and brace next to it. He mounted the two steps and climbed in. Angela stood swaying, ashen faced, a short stride away, a gun pressed viciously in her ribs. He grasped the spare and rolled it outside, then made as if to move further inside. A thought kept nagging at him. *Ginger really can't see much so he's probably is unaware of two now hopefully positioned marksmen.*

Interpreting Jacob's move as hostile the gun man said through clenched teeth, "No further."

"I can't reach the tools," complained Jacob as he backed towards the open door.

"She'll push them closer," her captor growled.

Using her feet, Angela tentatively edged them nearer her husband.

"Bend down and use your hands," urged Jacob in a compelling whisper.

With her hands trembling like aspen leaves, she did his bidding. The next few milliseconds were a blur to Angela. Like a pumped up mongoose, Jacob struck, gripping his wife's arm, so tightly she yelped, and with a mighty heave, flung himself backwards, dragging his terrified spouse to the grass on top of him. Taken by surprise, the panicky gunman loosed off at the disappearing figure; two bullets smashing harmlessly into the floor. On the grass, the two targets rolled as one under the caravan. Furious, the gunman made a very rash move, jumping out and aiming at the cowering couple. A look of surprise lit up his face as the first bullet pulverised his elbow, immobilising his shooting arm. A second thumped into his back, spinning him completely round. He dropped face down, his shattered arm spurting blood as it lay at a crazy angle out in front of him. The falcon like emblem on his bomber jacket gradually turned crimson. Making a last desperate effort to stand, he failed to get past knee high, as a third bullet ploughed into his neck, his body succumbing to the fatal wound.

"He's dead," whooped inspector Steele and waved the rest of the group forward.

Jacob and Angela hugged each other as a patrol car drew up and Superintendent Rodgers told them to get in.

"Off you go constable, back to the H.Q. Take it steady." The super sounded in a jubilant mood and began to whistle.

"Where's that sergeant Williams?", enquired Angela, unable to cover the hatred in her voice.

"Gone. Should be enjoying a nice cell by now."

They stopped at the H.Q., Rodgers leading inside.

"In view of your tremendous efforts I thought it only fair you're put in the picture before the press mangle the facts. Oh and one last request. Take a look at this picture of the woman discovered in the labyrinth."

Angela scanned the photo for a few seconds.

"I can't be certain; I didn't see her that closely, but the clothes are definitely the same. Anyway I thought she'd been shot. I heard it."

"You heard a shot alright; a signal to the scum on the cliff top to come and collect her. But they couldn't, they'd already fled."

Jacob walked to the door and remarked, "I'd better stir my stumps and change that wheel before it's too dark."

"Already taken care of," warbled the super. "Oh! And charge us for a new one and any damage to your property. Must go and sort out the paper work."

Feeling warm and happy the pair stood holding hands and looking fondly into each other's eyes.

A young patrolman poked his head out of the window. "Do you want a lift back?

Together they replied, "No we'll walk thanks."

A SIGNIFICANT TUMBLE

Arms wrapped around their bodies they soon reached their caravan and were pleased to see that not only had the wheel been changed but the hook up restored.

As they entered Jacob whispered, "I definitely fancy some Battenberg to-night."

"Funny I feel a bit peckish as well," whispered Angela, with a twinkle in her eyes as she put the kettle on. "Can't beat an early night with hot chocolate and Battenberg," she remarked impishly.

She opened the fridge door to get the milk.

"The greedy sods they've used it all."

"That'd be Pamela she always liked plenty of......"

He tried desperately to suck the words out of the air, without success.

A withering look from his wife told him she'd heard.

Battenberg was OFF the menu.

*

Nowhere to Go
By Dianne Wilson

Lying upon a park bench, on newspapers for sheets,
A lonely old woman is trying to sleep,
Unaware of the action going on all around,
As people rush by with a deafening sound.

With no family or friends or home of her own,
She wanders the streets looking sad and alone,
Rummaging through rubbish in the hope to find food,
Devouring so ravenously a sandwich half chewed.

It must be good fortune because she has found,
Leftovers from a takeaway thrown on the ground,
She claims it with haste, like a hungry wild beast,
For this means survival and a veritable feast.

But now she must find shelter as it's pouring with rain,
Because she has arthritis which causes her great pain,
Her hands are badly twisted, her back and feet are too,
And being unable to hurry she quickly gets wet through.

At last she finds some shelter to help dry out her clothes,
Inside a warm shop doorway she crouches down to doze,
But soon she is confronted to be told she cannot stay,
So she slowly struggles to her feet and wearily walks away.

In Loving Memory
By Joan Barnett

Autumn met winter on that clear blue day

Our footsteps broke the ridges in the sand

Packed down and patterned by the rhythmic play

Of idle waves in swaying saraband.

The sea trailed lazy fingers through the shore,

And stole a watery kiss in slow advance;

Then ebbed a little, to return in evermore

Audacious mood, until the tidal dance

Forced our retreat. Our fingers inter-wound

Secure in love. The sapphire sky gave way

To silhouette against the roseate west

Skein after skein of migrant geese, all southward bound.

Now I'm alone. Sometimes when life seems grey

The memory of that day returns, and I am blest.

Hands
By Edna Stacey

It seems like only yesterday, but so far off in time
When you invited me to dance, your hand clasped tight to mine.

It seems like only yesterday, not fifty years ago
We walked together hand in hand and planned our future through.

It seems like only yesterday, we were no longer two
You placed a ring upon my hand and made a dream come true.

It seems like only yesterday, we held a newborn child
Then nurtured it and moulded it with hands so strong and kind.

It seems like only yesterday, you tended to the needs
Of all who were so helpless, your hands did all the deeds.

It seems like only yesterday, we sat down clasping hands
Just cried and hugged in disbelief, at cruel fateful words.

It seems like only yesterday, our hands then posed in prayer
To ask of Him a question, to help ease our despair.

It seems like only yesterday, I felt I couldn't live
Without those loving tender hands, always free to give.

It seems like only yesterday, for just one final time
The strength that faltered in your hands flowed gently into mine.

Reflections on a February Evening
By Joan Barnett

No life had shown in the garden that day,
Only reflections, super-imposed;
Transparent images, grey upon grey,
Mixed, like a negative double-exposed.
I saw the table, real in the room,
Set insubstantially on the grass floor.
My face was ghostly, afloat in the gloom;
In the dark shrubbery stood the white door.
Then, as I stared beyond the twin scene,
The bushes appeared in a gradual glow,
As sun pierced the mist to glitter on rain
Caught in the branches, and dropping below
On flowers emerging where bare ground had been.
Life was in the garden, I just had not seen.

Drought
By Elizabeth Canmelle

The drought is harsh.

Pollution rampant,

Species hover on loss;

But I have seen a holly blue,

A little piece of sky amidst the green.

I have seen a linnet sing

And heard a warbler trill:

The wild neglected garden end

Is graced with meadow brown and copper,

Tortoiseshell and white,

The white! So despised, common and pestiferous it was!

Now rare.

Therefore desired

To see float round the thistles.

Moths I see, a pretty green

And orange too, and scarlet underwing.

Where nature is left unmanaged,

Back they come, from the Lord knows where.

To hearten us again.

There is still hope in the world.

Autumn
By Anne Melville

The golden leaves of Autumn time
Fall with every fitful breeze,
That dances through the branches of
The patient, sleepy trees.

They fall and gather in the roads,
Carpeting the grassy rides;
Make beds for spiky hedgehogs brown
Whose bristles guard their sides.

They dance with little eddies slow
In the streamlet where they sail
Gaily, gold and brown and red,
Until their life's spark fails.

When We Were Young
By Helen Stevens

We did not have computer games like children have today,
But we had something better when we went out to play.
Imagination –
When we were young.

We had to mind our p's and q's;
There were so many don'ts and dos
That we obeyed –
When we were young.

Our clothes were often hand-me-downs
Yet we looked tidy, not like the clowns
You see today –
When we were young.

The days were long, the summers hot
And we played out, as like as not
All day –
When we were young.

At school we learned to write and read
And do our sums, and we paid heed
To Miss and Sir –
When we were young.

Like everything this did not last
Time changes all, but yet the past
Seems bright somehow –
Now we are old.

Heard in the Bar at the Agricultural Show
By Helen Stevens

"I suppose," he said, "You think she is special
But I'm afraid that I cannot agree.
I find that her face is rather quite strange,
And she looks like a nightmare to me."

"I'm sorry, but you are completely wrong,"
Said his friend as he sucked on his beer.
"She has actually been chosen as Best in the Show
And will reign for the forthcoming year."

"Best in the Show! Now that's a surprise!"
He replied as he finished his drink.
"As a Jersey Cow she looks really strange.
I don't care – it's just what I think!"

Beyond the Windowpane
By Jean Miller

I tiptoed to the window
pressed my face against the glass
and saw us in the drawing room
for it was Christmas.
Firelight flickered in the hearth,
apple logs trembled in the flames.
Against the dark mahogany
red candles glowed and, flushed
from cooking earlier in the day,
my mother sat quietly. She looked up
but didn't see my face against the glass,
My father busy pouring sherry, paused,
distracted and glanced towards the window.
Curled up on the settee my sister
was reading, lost to the world.
Suddenly I heard the iron gate
pushed open, childish voices
called to each other across
the grass. Who came carol singing
on Christmas Day?
Or was time up to some other trick?
I moved away, half hiding as
the lovely words rang out:
'Hark the herald angels sing
Glory to the new born King.'
The front door opened and the boys were
welcomed in.
Silently I left
and in my mind closed
the shutters on the past.

Tranquillity
By Louis Barrow

Now I dwell in spirit and am one with you, Luther, evermore to be at my side in my bosom.

'Smoke and flame grew rapidly, I was there upon my bed, I died in the blue mist. I passed over coolly into heaven.'

Now stars shine bright everywhere evermore; they spell peace and tranquillity for me.

My daughters; they lived upon earth, I left them sleeping; they come one with me in my soul of love. I am one with them, as one body.

I still sing sweet songs. I swim in the force of love, bathe with pleasure in the hot celestial sun, seeing pards.

I am soaked in kisses, I cherish you; come touch me laying and hold me. I am lucky to be in your company evermore. I see you trine.

I breathe in spirit of still peace.

I enclose my love, and wishes of my love, to be free evermore in the almighty One of heaven.

Change
By Mary Oldham

Carpet those woods, said the wind,
With flame coloured leaves,
And those lanes too,
Among their misty blue,
A glint and gleam of gold,
To give relief.

Strip all those trees, I think,
They are past their prime,
Yes, every bough –
They have no beauty now,
Then get the frost to come,
And silver them with rime.

Evening
By Mary Oldham

Woodlark of sea and sky,
Holding earth's tears,
Wind wandering softly by,
Hushing earth's fears.

White winged the ships go by,
Through opal seas,
Belted with orange, night
Steals through the trees.

The Loch Ness Monster
By Mary Wise

Now Monty the monster lived deep in Loch Ness,
He'd dwelt there for many a year,
And by devious means he had managed it seems
Of human affairs to steer clear.

Monty was old, just a million and one,
Without any ailment or shock,
He swam in the sea, sunbathed on the lea,
And sported sometimes in the Loch.

But there came a time when he wasn't content,
And didn't quite know what to do,
So he waddled along, as you do on the prom,
And nearly got caught for the zoo.

He hadn't gone far when he came to a road,
And he'd only been there a short space,
When a lady on wheels, seeing poor Monty, squealed,
(I don't think she quite liked his face.)

Monty didn't stay long, just put out his tongue,
And tucking his tail through one fin,
He hurried and scurried, looking frightfully worried,
('till back in the Loch he dived in.)

From that day the shore wasn't his any more,
For people from both far and near,
Came to tempt him with lines, and bait of all kinds,
Which filled our poor Monty with fear.

"Oh for the time before fame was mine,"
Cried Monty, and reached for his hat,
"A fellow's no peace, only noise without cease,
And I can very well do without that."

So now though they wait, from early to late,
All they see is a rotting tree stump,
They can all scan the view, until they are blue,
For Monty has taken the Hump!

I Think of You
By Phyllis Gall

When the house is hushed and quiet
I think of you.

I see your face, but only in my mind.
Your face comes to me through shadows of the past,
Young again, carefree and handsome,
When life was laughter, and the years were kind,
And you were always there.

In the bustle of the morning
I think of you.

I hear your voice, but only in my mind.
Words of tenderness and love,
As through our married life we wove
Our thoughts together, till we were as one,
And you were always there.

At the end of the day
I think of you.

I feel your touch, but only in my mind.
Arms that held me in a warm embrace;
The touch of your lips upon my face;
Hands that guided and kept me from harm,
And you were always there.

Now you are gone and I am alone,
I think of you.

I see you soar on a seagull's wing;
I hear your voice on the sigh of the wind;
Your touch is soft, as a wave on the sand;
Your face is warm as the colours of the land.

In the grey morning light
And the still of the night
I think of you.

That's Show Business
By Sandra Finney

I've got a little rabbit with a very nasty habit;
he sits in his hutch scratching his crutch,
no matter who is looking.
So I phoned the vet who made a bet
he could get him a nightclub booking.

Now the vet's got an itch that'll make *him* rich,
though I can't say where, I wouldn't dare,
it really would spoil the show.
The rabbit's whacked and the vet's been sacked
for wearing a little pink bow.

You may not think it healthy but it made me very wealthy,
so with the extra money I bought another bunny
but problems have begun.
The over-zealous vet became a trifle jealous
when the rabbit kissed a nun.

You might find it funny that I own a stripping bunny
but it wasn't simple to find a rabbit with a dimple,
so I advertised on the net.
Rabbits came flocking; one even wore a stocking
and one was dressed as a vet.

People travel into town, they come from miles around
to see my little rabbits with very dirty habits,
they really are quite jaunty.
But I'm in quite a fix, I've now got sixty six
auditioning for The Full Monty.

Summer's End
By Wyn Land

Although she wore her summer dress and sandals,

The September mist blurred the figures running for the bus.

What was it about this time of year

That made it so exciting?

Relief that long school holidays were over,

Meeting friends, starting on new coursework,

Clubs re-opening; the future appearing dazzlingly bright.

Breathing the crisp air, sensing the droplets upon her hair,

Knowing that noon would reveal the blue skies.

She was far too young

To associate summer's ending

With the onset of decay.

Time enough for realisation.

Don't suggest it, lest it mar her day.

When We Were Lovers
By Terry Schooling

There was a time when friendship became inadequate: a need for something more.
   A time when a simple touch of the hand became a lovers' secret, towering tor.
   The gentle kiss of goodbye between people fresh at ease each with the other
   And in its place the passion of longing and an indivisible oneness discovered.

   There was a time the privacy of separate worlds ceased to be important, instead
   The joy of each being in the company of the other shared moments ne'er were said.
   The laughter of joined pleasure of moments together were natural as breathing:
   The cliché of the quiet of a crowded room with two beings amongst the seething.

   There was a time the unseen passion spilled over to fierce consuming physical love.
   The thrust of female breast against willing male body: stirring attraction uncovered.
   The overpowering desire to consummate quiet tenderness with the wild communion
   Of something at once primeval: filled with animal lust and the need for nature's union.

   There was a time the physical passion so deeply felt and now the moment spent,
   Relaxed into the warmth of the shared embrace and the oneness closely felt.
   To be as one yet separate to savour anew the depth of the physical attraction.
   The wish to throw open the windows and declare the wonder of love's reaction.

   There was a time when the passion of the love became tainted by who-knows-what.
   A time when the company of companions became invasive; unwelcome; best forgot.
   When the presence of others seemed to corrode the love and dilute its very essence.
   When the passion of riotous physical love became tainted like whore's excrescence.

   There came a time when the love that was there became a duty: a lesser unholy thing.
   The purity of the pleasure of each other's being became secondary to trivial stings

Of the open wounds of criticism and hurtful words supplanting love with bitter taste,
Leaving lasting scars on the naked flesh of the love once nurtured like maiden chaste.

And then came the time of parting's balm to forestall the fatal wound that's signed.
The last goodbyes and slowly disentangled hands which still wished to stay entwined.
Better this than the alternative path of a love turned completely sour and bad
And thus remains a hidden part, which nobody sees, that remains forever sad

Flight
By Warren Scott-Morrow

In hummingbird stasis the VC10 maintained its fixed position over the vertical filament architectonic landscape.
    Parked on non-tactile atmosphere.
    No strings.
    No wheels.
    Slow motion reduced to zero point zero recurring.
    Billposter for impossibility.
    Advertisement for shattered reality.
    Still snapshot for aerial disaster epic ego budget film.
    Metal marriage with oxygen and nitrogen.
    Non-sentient troilism.
    Invisible hand of God playing joke on Heathrow?
    Hiccup in time and space?
    Inter-dimensional interference?
    Product of fantasy writer?
    Explanation is a theory with four sides. Each side is wrong.
    Two plus two equals zero.
    An answer? No answer.
    A phenomenon? Yes, phenomenon.
    Man's first bold moves into the air began with an aircraft leaving the ground, travelling through the air and returning to the ground.
    Progress to regress?
    The airliner has entered the air. It remains there.
    Stationary.
    Silent.
    Awaiting an event.
    Zeno said the arrow would never reach the target.
    Anglo-Bavarian Airlines must face the fact that the aircraft will not land.
    Two thousand feet above sea level and the terminal has been attained.
    Movement.
    Side door opens with heart valve precision.
    For the time light takes to travel from the sun nothing happens.
    Grey suited, bowler hatted, brief cased businessman appears in the door way, eyes superglue fixed to shimmer horizon.
    Apollo Eleven, one small step for man. One giant leap for mankind.
    Businessman in air board meeting.
    Gucci shoes on gossamer clouds.
    Plunge. Gone.
    Out of sight. Out of mind. Out of life.

With mocking bird repetition several dozen sartorially identical men make the drop.

Copycat sacrifices to the god of gravity.

VC10 cocks a snook to Isaac Newton.

Cockpit cock-a-hoop.

Gender switch.

Housewives, models, secretaries and stewardesses join the queue.

With vibration blur equanimity they too step into the void.

No screams. No anguished expressions. Only the sound of the wind as they plummet to meet terra firma.

Lemmings in high heels.

Pied Piper office blocks

Stygian ferry airliner.

Red spots speckle streets. Multifarious mockeries of fixed colour traffic lights.

Stop

* * *

Everywhere green.

Beautiful green.

Stinking green.

Living green.

Dying green.

Silent growing green.

Noisy moving green.

Green rich tapestry.

Life, gone. Aeons ago. Genetically 'remembered' by all twenty first century life forms.

Plant life rules the green. Animals are the juggernaut interlopers into the garden of Pre-Eden. Their time is yet to come. Conquerors in awhile.

For now they are content to crash through the tolerant undergrowth in search of nourishment, desire and violence.

In the waters they follow similar programmed routines.

And also in the air.

Screeching. Crying. Piercing. Grey leather wings flap. Assaulting the prehistoric gases.

Pterodactyl.

Rara avis.

Purring. Humming. Intermittent buzzing. Blue and white fibreglass wings juxtaposing with the natural sounds of the environment.

Cessna.

Rara avis.

The pterodactyl swerves from its flight path and circles the small plane.

Beady evil eyes focus on the prey. Curiosity, hate and hunger make a negative substitute in its tiny brain for faith, hope and charity.

Pterodactyl thrust.

Cessna parry.

Versatile puppet acrobats. Dancers on trembling airwaves. Duelling protagonists of a pseudo paradise. Sheer mountain manoeuvre trajectories. Constructive approach without destructive reproach.

Fusion checkmates fission.

Yin meets yang.

Two becomes one

Singular entity.

Mechanical and sentient union.

Hybrid.

* * *

Separation.

Gaps between each equal twenty five metres.

Enough width.

Too much space.

Outside lies nothing. Emptiness. Darkness. Silence. A true kingdom of the blind.

No stars. Not outer space. Not inner space. Waste of space.

Inside loves light. Full. Bright. Quiet. Land of the midnight sun or the light of love?

Keeping the light from the darkness stand the metal sentinels.

Six sides. Square box.

Cage.

Ersatz bird within. Bird in the light. Bird panics. Goes this way. Goes that.

Joystick jerk. Swerve alert.

Confusion.

Silence save for rotors and engine.

Pilot steers again towards a gap between bars. Enough room.

He does not get through. The helicopter heads directly at a bar and swings sharply away to avoid a collision.

Time passes. Attempts continue. He is a professional. Yet whenever he heads for a gap he is blocked.

Do the bars move to prevent his exit or is it some type of optical illusion or even a subconscious impulse to remain encaged?

Three explanations. One may be right. All three could be wrong. The man has no answer. The 'copter computer has insufficient data. His initial surprise at appearing in such unusual circumstances quickly fade as the urge to survive takes precedence.

Hover. Collect thoughts. Struggle for decision.

In his vision the bars move nearer to one another. Perspiration beads on brow. The bars close in aiming for anaconda hug.

Glove tight asphyxiation.

No motion of helicopter. Bars all around it almost touch rotor blades and tail.

Increased perspiration.

Accelerated heartbeat.

Nick of time reprieve.

Cage disconnects.

Bar spins away into limbo. Each takes a different route. Metal parody of Big Bang.

Aesthetic shrapnel.

Lungs inflate.

Hand wipes forehead.

Not finished yet.

Rotor blades separate and spiral into the beyond.

Tail rotor follows.

Wheels depart.

Outer panels peel off one by one and skip away into the darkness.

Computer detaches. Instrument panel follows. Controls and seats act in solidarity.

Everything bounces away in an avant garde choreography, the man remains. Frozen in nowhere.

A human island in a waterless sea.

He is alone.

* * *

You are alone.

Legs pound as pistons in sinking gunboat.

Lungs pump in fire fighter jet fury.

Heartbeat in Krakatoa reiteration.

You are lost.

You do not know what you are fleeing from or why. Neither do you know where you are heading to or what will happen if you get there.

With petrol bomb action adrenalin rushes to where it is required to give the necessary stamina.

Marathon runner you are not.

Every step is an effort.

Yet you cannot stop.

Subconscious compulsion maintains momentum.

Smile through sweat flood.

Grin and bear cage.

Venus carved image of her sculpted in your mind. You need her with you right now but she is not in your sphere of influence. You want her not as a sex plastic rose object but because you feel she can furnish the answers you seek.

Would it have consoled you to know that the answers are beyond the parameters of her knowledge?

With Grand Canyon bouncing echo ecstasy moans you hope your Adam inherited chest engine will not explode.

The real fact and file is not for you to understand.

A team of scientists, psychiatrists and philosophers would only respond with anti equation deceptions.

You run as if with a worth beyond all known verse.

You are alone.

Alone for all eternity.

Alone in flight.

*

Fallen Trees
By Mary Oldham

Yesterday they stood tall and fair,

Their branches stretched towards the sky,

Today they lie slain and fallen,

Their naked roots exposed to the air,

Why did God send such fury,

To ruin his wondrous handiwork?

Only He knows,

I cannot understand,

WHY?

The Old Apple Tree
By Mary Oldham

Tall and twisted, encrusted with lichen,
Widely spread roots clutching the earth
With the splayed feet of a giant
Its trunk knobbly with brown knotholes.
Its branches flung crazily skyward
It is always beautiful,
In April, bright green new leaves,
Sharp and delicate
Prickly painted with silver,
A mist of pale colour
Slowly studded with crimson
Points of fire then,
Suddenly submerged by a foam
Of pink blossom,
As petals pale drift away
In flakes of milky white,
The leaves reappear darker
Growing with exquisite spears
Of glossy green,
The apples come very early
So many of them
Round and small, deep red and shiny,
In winter, the snow lodges
In the tracery of the twigs
Making it seem weighted
With mid-winter blossom.

Ode to a Lover
By Yani Birt

My love, you are the world to me,
You're the shiniest bauble on my Christmas tree.

You're the ray of sun through my pouring rain,
The putty that holds in my windowpane.

You're the welcome glow that turns on the light,
You're the sweetest dream in my darkest night.

You're the written word on my empty page,
And the laughter lines that increase with age.

You're the teasing twang of an elastic band,
A flash of steel as you plough the land.

You're the rhythmic pattern of my conversation,
And the pioneer of my exploration.

You're the splatters of paint on my naked frame,
You're the one who comes when I call your name.

The Waterfall
By Mary Oldham

Holidaying in Bonnie Scotland,
We had to see the waterfall,
So five of our little band
Set sail in a fisherman's boat.

The beach was of shingle so white
And purling down the hillside,
The burn, tumbling through the sunlight
Twisting through heather and bracken

Glowing white at every turn,
Dancing In the gleaming sunlight,
Fringed with rushes moss and fern,
It was beyond all our dreams.

We swept passed a very high rock,
And the bay was revealed to us,
We gave a cheer to our Captain Jack
For bringing us such a wonder to see.

Reaching above the beach some twenty feet,
It leapt out over a granite ledge
Spurting down like a shining sheet
Into the silver pool below.

The Doorway
By Yani Birt

Everyday many people enter,
Some may leave.
For I am a celestial doorway;
A protector of the future and a keeper of the past,
I have witnessed births,
When joyous parents rush through me,
To tell the news to those they love.
I have stood in silent respect as tearful mourners
Follow the coffin through my comforting arms.
I am the doorway of mankind.
Man made or so they think.
It is I, who decides,
Whether they pass through into their own reality,
Or whether they enter another dimension,
Into a parallel world.
Those who displease me may vanish into an empty void.
But they do not know it is I,
The doorway,
That rids the present of an unpleasant existence,
They think it is just another casualty of their own,
Vengeful world.
So be warned,
Dare you enter the doorway?

Wildlife of the Roadside Verge
By Dianne Wilson

As you are travelling in your car along the busy road,
Have you ever thought about – no, not the Highway Code,
But of all the living wildlife that you miss as it emerges,
Throughout the grassy undergrowth of our roadside verges.

I see among the clover a spider's web so neatly spun,
And I hear the chirrup of grasshoppers basking in the sun,
Tightly curled up and fast asleep near to a narrow path,
A hedgehog finds some refuge amongst the tall, wild grass.

Carefully perched on top of a post I see a carrion crow,
Watching with its beady eyes as sparrows peck grit from the road,
So gracefully floating in the air a butterfly passes by,
So delicately painted with its four outstanding eyes.

Tiger striped caterpillars feed on some leaves,
Stripping them bare as they shuffle and weave,
Hind legs of bumble bees bulge like yellow pantaloons,
With large masses of pollen collected from blooms.

A piercing squeal is heard coming from a shrew,
As another invades his territory a vicious fight is due,
The hoverflies are undisturbed and do not show fear,
As they contentedly sip the nectar from the flowers so near.

Hastily scampering around the twisting paths and slopes,
A rabbit is disturbed by a questing stoat,
When he fails to catch the rabbit he takes little rests,
Then continues to search for birds' eggs in nests.

WILDLIFE OF THE ROADSIDE VERGE

As well as all wildlife there are many flowers too,
All clearly on display that make a splendid view,
So many pretty colours and so many different shapes,
Red poppies, white daisies, ragwort and rape.

Stinging nettles, dead nettles, dandelions and thistles,
Cowslips, buttercups and hogweed sprouting bristles,
Red pyramidal orchids, blue forget-me-nots and yarrow,
And the yellow treacle mustard stands so tall and narrow.

The rich colours blend together like a patchwork quilt,
No human hand can ever match what nature's freely built,
So remember, when you are driving please take extra care,
Watch out for all the animals and let their lives be spared.

Take Me Back
By Jean Miller

Take me back a while to where dwells
A countryman with undemanding ways
Among the lakes and moors and fells.
Let me see the larch send forth her tender shoots
And hear the curlew's haunting cry.
Just let me sit and think of days gone by.

Lead me to the garden of my dream
With childish voices calling to and fro,
To see if still there flows the darling stream
Which takes our sticks into a tunnelled gloom
And is the arbour still a place where children eat
Their sweets and laugh and squabble on a rustic seat?

I want to watch the swirling Derwent rise and fall
Where I can see the salmon leap in silvered arc.
I'll walk again with wild rose hedges and a dry stone wall
And forget the dykes and drains of this flat land.
Just let me touch a mountain with my hand.

Harmony
By Jean Miller

If I were blind and could not see
Would all the colours sing to me
In perfect harmony?
I'd hear the violin's gentle blue
Soar up and down to join the piano's
Infinite variety of green.
Deeper shades of purple would play
Upon the cello's mellow tone
And red and black would throb
On beating drum.
I would listen
Lost in melody and winging like
The lark high above earth's bounds,
And then I'd lay aside all cares and rest
A while, content.

Spider
By Sandra Finney

Like diamonds in a delicate net,
Dew fills the filigree formation.
Curious creatures will soon regret
Encroaching on spider's creation.

Till warm sunlight disperses dew
His artful web is benign.
Then lethal danger, hidden from view,
Displays no visible warning sign.

This finely woven intricate snare,
A seemingly flimsy frame,
Entraps all that dare to venture there;
Curious prey make easy game.

This deadly arachnid dictator
Waits with dogged determination,
A mute but lethal gladiator
Poised in ardent anticipation.

Engrossed in eager expectation,
The cunning arthropod starts to preen,
Awaits his victim's invasion.
Hunger gnaws, his appetite is keen.

Aberfan
By Terry Schooling

The irony of the assembly hymn was like a black satirical play.
The strains of "All things bright and beautiful" had barely died away.
Children suppressed excitement, the reasoning was clear.
School soon done, half-term holiday was very nearly here.

Classes filed to their rooms, chattering voices stilled.
By 09:15, lessons started, the need for quiet fulfilled.
Further up the hillside workers called their mates to run.
The mountainous tip began to slide, its parlous hold undone.

Some thought the noise was miners on the hillside tipping spoil.
Steadily and louder yet the noise began to boil.
Some said it was akin to jet engine's angry roar.
Quiet in the classes: outside the din began to soar.

Mr Williams looked at pupils filling rows sat to attention.
Glancing up in windows frame, he saw a boulder in suspension.
Spinning, bouncing, on it came, riding on the darkness.
Seconds seemed eternal: he sought sense within the madness.

He didn't move as liquid hell crashed against the glass.
Windows rent and frames gave way, nothing stemmed its pass.
Higher up the hillside, at early morning work and play.
A farmer's family, in their home, cruelly swept away.

Thrown against the classroom door, held fast by the stinking pile.
The teacher watched a little boy scramble over rubble, while
Classmates struggled all around, though none were overcome.
Kicked against the classroom door for fear he would succumb.

TERRY SCHOOLING

Children, workers, teachers all ran from the school in fear.
Others who were passing by, or close at hand, rushed near.
Each helped to rescue children, some of whom were neighbours' kin.
With bloodied hands against the chaos, they knew they had to win.

Miners from the Merthyr Vale' ran to the nightmare place.
Dirty faces, tired eyes, tears streaking many a hardened face.
They took over from parents, struggling amid the foul melee.
The young ones must be saved; everyone's unspoken plea.

By 11:00 o'clock that fateful day, all the living had been freed.
From that time on, to one week hence, despite heroic deed,
Only broken bodies now were brought out from the school.
One hundred and forty four lay silent in death's pool.

Half the Pantglas Junior' children died and were no more.
By the time all were taken out, their number near six score.
Tip Number Seven had wreaked its fury, its energy now spent.
Laid upon the shattered school where by fate t'was surely sent.

Nobody said 'I'm to blame', instead said, 'Nobody could know,'
'That underneath the coal mine's waste a spring maintained its flow.'
Undermining pit's black slag, on the land so quickly thrown.
In greed and in ignorance was the seed of destruction surely sown.

Committees sat and pondered how this tragedy came to pass.
Considering what and when and why and how this die was cast.
The reasons known and written down were clear for all to see.
For cruel death of innocents the coal mine owners held the key.

Aberfan is peaceful now: the scars are gone and in their place,
A low stone enclave stands instead of walls so long ago replaced.
Walls of the little school first sheltered, safe in the valley's arms.
But later sheltered, nay exposed, ahead of coal tip's latent harm.

ABERFAN

The tips are cleared and once again the sun shines on grassy hills.
Rows of tiny houses climb the hillside, as they did, and always will.
Merthyr Vale mine is no more, and in its place on valley's floor,
A landscaped open meadow covers pit's once gaping maw.

A salve for villages' grief and nation's conscience you may find,
But nothing can eradicate the image forever brought to mind:
Of stricken school and broken bodies on chapel's floor of stone.
Of weeping kinfolk standing by together; but suddenly alone.

Not so far away, lying peacefully in community's cemetery sun,
Two lines of stark white arches stand, their number eighty one.
Under every arch is named a child, most eight to ten years old.
Some carry a doubly poignant note: two infant's names they hold.

To stand before this peaceful place; vivid memories now shared,
Rends the heart and tears the soul, leaves emotion lying bared.
So many, many children left families bereft and lacking sleep.
So many mothers died soon after, no longer could they weep.

So many lessons here for all to take and consider them afresh:
The nature of the greed of man, he takes for nought the flesh
Of his fellow man, and the need to protect the poor and weak alike,
From man-made follies biding their appointed time to strike.

Close within all our hearts let the inner tears never be over,
But remember still a cold autumn day; the 16th of October.
When one hundred and sixteen children died in terror and in fear.
In the Valley of the Martyrs, is their smiling presence forever near.

Nostalgia
By Yani Birt

Faded photographs in a leather book,
Memories recalled with a single look,
Remembering places, when journeys took
You somewhere, some place, some time.

Forgotten letter at the back of a drawer,
What's this? I haven't seen that before.
Remembering a sweetheart you'll always adore,
As you read special words with affection.

I hear a song; it reminds me of you,
It makes me sad when the words are true,
Nostalgia sometimes makes me blue,
But what is life without memories?

A house is a place for things to go,
My home is a place for memories to grow,
So nurture life's plants and new seeds sew,
And water them well with nostalgia.

Saxophone Summer
By Yani Birt

Somewhere a saxophone plays,

Melodious sensuality on a soothing breeze,

Summertime seduction in a hammock made for one.

The sun smiles onto the sea,

Casting diamonds into the gentle ripples.

A sailing ship with iceberg sails,

Glides by on turquoise silk,

Accompanied by restful soul music.

Buckets and spades of my absent children,

Adorn the sun-bleached veranda,

Its timbers, the colour of yesterday's candy floss.

Eyes close, the time is mine alone.

Sweet summertime seduction in a sleep-filled moment,

As the saxophone plays on.

Awakening
By Jean Miller

Deep in the earth's core
hidden in primordial caverns
a pulse beats.
Faintly through layers of soil
a tiny utterance
stammers to the surface
stirring forgotten yearnings.
It is taken up in
tentative bird song,
in all the joyous cleaning of Spring
and the dust-dark turning out.
The murmurs grow
snowdrops pierce the winter earth,
crocuses splash colour on the soil
and daffodils trumpet forth
spun gold.
High in the sky
the first lark sings
and all the dark things
of our earth retreat.

The Hydra-headed Monster
By Jean Miller

Even the angels dancing

on needle tip feel sick.

Suddenly they stop

and form a glittering ring

around the earth.

Next the pale ghosts of Aberfan

rise up in mute defiance.

Yet still this hydra-headed

monster grows in our midst

taking a stranglehold on

decency.

Skylark Song
By Joan Barnett

Where East-Anglian waters run
By grassy banks, from far on high,
I heard a skylark hymn the sun
In a pale blue winter sky.
I felt that I as well could fly,
Singing to the new-born year,
But then a breeze began to sigh,
Bring Fenland transient fear.

And as the music soared and spun
Above my head, I wondered why
This out-of-season song was sung,
And followed with my earth-bound eye
The fragile soul that hovered nigh
To God, while angels paused to hear
The joyful sound. Did they pass by,
Bringing Fenland transient fear?

The air grew silent, fear had won;
Dark clouds rolled in to veil the sky.
The skylark's song that had begun
The day with praise to God on high
Was lost. I heard a mallard cry,
And saw how rushes lined the mere,
By north-east wind blown hard and dry,
Bringing Fenland transient fear.

Their heads were broken all awry;
I mourned the skylark, and could hear
And eerie, wind-sung lullaby,
Bringing Fenland transient fear.

Washday Blues
By Yani Birt

Oh washing on a washing line,
How your rainbow colours shine.
Baby bootees look divine,
Hanging in a pair.

Billowing sheets like a galleon's sail,
Trousers flap like a kite's long tail,
The postman gets tangled as he delivers the mail,
And I laugh from the kitchen window.

Sexy lingerie next to a holey vest.
Does your washing powder pass the test?
It leaves the blood stains but gets rid of the rest,
So no good for the perfect murder.

Blue sports kit hangs in a row.
My tights have tied themselves in a bow.
There is no telling where one sock will go,
When I fetch things in for ironing.

A dozen different shirts of every shade.
Some brand new, jewelled masquerade.
Others well worn and starting to fade.
Oh, no! The line has just broken.

Clothes are scattered all over the floor.
My new dress has got ripped on the old shed door.
I don't think I can take anymore.
And now it has started to rain.

I rush like a maniac, picking up clothes.
Now the doorbell rings; I don't suppose
It's the man of my dreams with a lovely red rose?
But no! It's the woman from Avon.

At last, the ironing's been done and the clothes put away.
Wash day blues over for today.
But the kids come home and they're covered in clay
Washday blues will be back with a vengeance.

Inheritance
By Marion Megit

"Come on! It's ready!"

The girl called impatiently as she scraped mashed potato from a saucepan in large dollops onto three plates.

"Come on!"

She called again as she turned from the table and slammed the empty pan down into the sink.

"Do you 'ear me?" her voice was shrill, "I've dished up, you lazy pair. I'll give it to the bloody chickens! See if I don't." She threatened.

"Stop your nagging gal."

A, middle aged man appeared in the doorway, a smouldering cigarette end dangling from the corner of his scabby mouth. The girl grimaced as he removed it and tossed it into the sink alongside the dirty pans.

"Where is he?" she said exasperated.

"How should I bloody know?" He sat down heavily and reached for the sauce bottle. "Said somethin' aboot goin' to Wisbech."

"That's good that is, no one tells me. I cooked for 'im."

He ignored her as he sat rubbing his chin and studying his plate suspiciously. Then pointing a fat finger at his plate, he growled, "What's this?"

"What's it look like?"

"A bloody road smash!"

He began shaking brown sauce liberally over the grey potato and greasy mince.

"Well if you don't like it, don't eat it. You wants steak you buy it."

He gave a resentful snort. "These tatters only fit for bloody pigs."

"Suit you then!"

His eyes narrowed menacingly and he raised a threatening hand. She stepped back quickly out of his reach and he saw the fear in her eyes, and he grinned with satisfaction as she took her seat dumbly opposite him.

"You'd better get down to Dobson's field, they've finished lifting there," he said.

"I'll goo later," she said sullenly.

"You see you do!"

He shovelled mince and potato into his mouth and immediately spat it out.

"I don't want more of this bloody muck," and he pushed his plate away.

"There aint nothing' else."

"Bloody pigs swill! Why can't we afford somethin' decent?"

"You knows why. You spends it on booze!"

He stood up, toppling his chair over. She cringed as if expecting to feel the back of his hand.

"I'm pissed off with the pair of yer," he snarled then staggered out of the room. A moment later she heard the television and knew he would be slumped in front of it drinking himself into a stupor. For a long moment she sat staring down at her plate, the untouched food rapidly congealing. Then as tears of resentment stung her eyes she began to clear away.

* * *

The sleek motor, like a TV advert, purred its way across the fens. Its driver, who was unaccustomed to the narrow roads that often ran alongside deep drains, was surprised by the flatness of the countryside, which even on this bright autumn day, looked desolate and did nothing to quell the feelings of doubt he was experiencing.

However, apprehensive as he was, he was greatly impressed by the sky. For here it was vast and all enveloping. The landscape became incidental as the great sky swallowed it up; and its hugeness filled him with a sense of exhilaration but it did not last for he soon began to wonder about the winter.

"What must it be like on a dull November day?" he muttered to himself. The thought of a grey flat sky covering a grey flat landscape fuelled his doubts even more.

To shake them off he reached for a cassette and slid it into the player and as the selection of foot tapping melodies started he began to whistle.

As he continued to follow the narrow road he was puzzled by the lack of activity. There seemed to be no-one working in the fields. The absence of people, to a town dweller like himself, only added to his misgivings.

It was then he noticed her. A slight figure, far out in the middle of a field, the black fen soil sharp against the blindingly bright sky. He slowed the car down to a crawl.

He stopped half on the verge and lowered the window down. He wanted to confirm he was on the right road and he was glad there was at last someone to talk to.

She was walking towards him. Her hair was long and blonde and tied back. On her arm swung a bright yellow plastic bucket and he was mildly amused to see she wore odd Wellingtons. A pullover several sizes too big contrasted with her skin-tight jeans, which showed off her well-rounded hips and he watched her admiringly. He turned the sound down on the cassette player. As she came within hailing distance he leant across the passenger seat and called to her.

"Excuse me!"

He waited for an answer but she failed to react.

"Excuse me," he called louder.

This time she responded by turning to face the car, one hand shading her eyes against the low sun.

"Could you direct me to *Goose Gander Farm?*"

She moved nearer and he waited until she stood a couple of feet away.

"This is Angle's Dyke Drove? I'm looking for Goose Gander Farm."

She put the bucket down slowly.

"Yeh, this is Angle's Drove, the farm's further up the road," and she pointed in the direction he had been driving. "There's no one there though!" she added and looking curious.

"Thanks very much," he smiled and added chattily, "Lovely day!"

"All right," she shrugged.

"You live around here?" His question was inane but he was in need of some conversation, no matter how trivial. She nodded and pointed in the direction he had come.

He glanced back, "It's a bit out of the way for me – no shops. Pub?"

"No! No nothin'," she said, "bugger all!"

He grinned. Looking at her he reckoned she was not much more than eighteen and he wasn't surprised she sounded dissatisfied.

"What do you do around here for entertainment?"

"Goo to Kings Lynn or Peterborough when I can."

"Many guys?"

"A foo."

He smiled, "I expect they queue up for you."

"Might do. Might not!" she said her eyes smiling back at him.

"Well if they don't they must be slow."

"On, why's that then? You so quick are yer?"

He laughed. "Well, lets say I appreciate a pretty girl when I see one."

She studied him, his brown eyes were twinkling and she liked the look of him. She picked up her bucket and with a flirtatious smile she said, "Well, you know where to look then."

Once more he laughed. "I think I'd better be going, it's been nice talking to you. Probably meet up again some time. Cheerio!"

He started up the car before she had time to say another word.

As he sped away he glimpsed her in the mirror. By now she was standing in the middle of the road her gaze following the car's progress.

* * *

When he found the house, it was almost obscured by wind-scorched shrubs and tangled briers. The wooden gate hung drunkenly from one hinge and the house looked neglected. He took the small bunch of keys from the brown envelope the solicitor had given him and found the one that fitted the front door. As he unlocked it the smell of damp hit him.

Slowly he moved along the narrow passage. On his right he saw through an open door a room crammed with old furniture. All was covered in dust and smelled of mould and he was sure he could smell mice.

At the end of the passage was the kitchen. With a look of disgust he gazed about. It would have to be gutted.

INHERITANCE

After seeing the ground floor he was in two minds about going up stairs but decided he might as well, now that he was here and they creaked alarmingly as he climbed them.

There were three bedrooms in all. In one was an old bedstead. He was shocked to see a chamber pot underneath and he bent down to take a closer look. A spider sat waiting at the bottom.

The stench of musty bedclothes, mildew and general dirt, filled his nostrils and clung to the back of his throat and he quickly returned downstairs.

There he flung open all the doors and windows, then pushed his way out into the overgrown garden. At the side he found an outside lavatory, hence the need for the chamber pot, he concluded. Thistles and nettles clambered outside and protruded inside. The whole place needed bulldozing, he thought angrily.

When he'd received the letter telling him of his inheritance, this was not what he'd expected.

Even if it had been half decent: what a God awful spot! Way out in the back of beyond. He looked at his watch. It would soon be dark and he had to find a place to stay. He locked up but could not think why he'd bothered. Then, he drove back along the way he came.

After about five miles he came to a signpost and it directed him to a village where he hoped to put up for the night in a hostelry.

In the *Crafty Fox*, after a substantial supper and a good stiff drink he tried to think of what to do with the old house. *Goose Gander Farm* had sounded so romantic.

The next morning he was up early and soon on his way back to London.

His friends and colleagues in the advertising firm he worked for were all eager to hear about his inheritance.

"How was it Ellis?"

Julian was the first to enquire. There was no point in his trying to evade their natural curiosity so, he gave them a graphic account, ending with, "And that's *Goose Gander, bloody, Farm!*"

Some laughed and treated it as a huge joke, one or two sympathized. Only Julian thought about it before passing an opinion.

"It may not be as bad as you think......."

Ellis gave a snort of derision.

"Listen to me," urged his friend, "You're fed up with the set up here. Aren't we all?" he added laconically. "You've been brooding over this novel of yours for what, a year now.....?"

"So, what's a run down old farm got to do with anything?" said Ellis impatiently.

"I think you should keep it, invite a few down to help with the cleaning up."

"Come off it! You haven't seen it. I'm not going back there, let alone ask anyone else to. Can you imagine Fiona? She'd.........." He was lost for words.

"Yes, I know all that. But if you do it up. Plant a few trees, that sort of thing," Julian said enthusiastically, "then you can use it as a kind of retreat. To write! Where no one - no one will disturb you. Am I right?"

Ellis stared at him. "You want your bloody head examined."

Julian shrugged then without another word passing between them, they began applying themselves to the problems they were paid to solve.

A week later, a convoy of vehicles followed like an invading army as Ellis, who had taken Julian's advice, blazed a trail along the fen roads.

When at last they reached the farm and the assortment of executive type cars had been parked along and around the property, there was a stunned silence.

Ellis slowly got out from his BMW and looked apprehensively around. He was sure, at any moment, the engines would start up and the half dozen or so cars would make a quick exit. Instead, very slowly, everyone began to emerge.

"Christ Almighty!" Declan was the first to speak.

"Look, I did warn you!" Ellis said apologetically. "Perhaps we should get the hell out of here right now."

"Don't be so defeatist," Julian grinned, "it's just a bit of a surprise that's all."

There were murmurs of, "yes," from the others and "not so bad, and needs a bit or work, but wouldn't take long."

Ellis looked around at his friends, "I'm really sorry!"

"Oh do stop apologizing," said Fiona. "I can see it now. Lots of trees and a pond! Didn't you say you found one? Well, we can make it bigger and.........the rooms, good bright colours, I think."

Ellis laughed with relief. Fiona dressed for the part too. She quickly changed into a trendy shell suit and covered her hair with a multi-coloured scarf and then plunged her well-manicured hands into marigold gloves.

Ellis was pleasantly surprised at just how much they tackled and by late afternoon there had been a great bonfire and already the house smelled less than before.

They finished the weekend off at the *Crafty Fox*. Their enthusiasm lasted for another couple of weeks, until one by one, his friends who had been so eager and enthusiastic to help, began to find they had urgent commitments and prior engagements.

Ellis well understood and did not blame them. In fact, he thought himself lucky they had stayed with it for as long as they had. Even Fiona had lasted much longer than he could ever have imagined, but the inevitable happened.

She broke the news over dinner.

"Darling, I'm going to France.....a catalogue!"

Fiona was a moderately successful model and very ambitious. This was an opportunity she could not turn down.

Ellis returned to Goose Gander Farm. He had not been there for over a month. It was winter and not only was it cold and wet but the land seemed empty and lonely. The sky now was overcast and a uniform grey. It hung low and gloomily over everything the horizon merging into its greyness so that it covered the land like a shroud. It was eerie too and the water in the deep drains was still and dark and he was depressed by it all.

Nevertheless, now that a start had been made on the house, he was determined to see it through to the end.

During the time he and his friends had spent there, they had seen little of the local inhabitants and he'd not set eyes on the girl he had first encountered, although he had looked out for her.

On his first night alone, Ellis found it difficult to get to sleep. He listened to his radio, hoping the companionable voices and music would help.

Just as he was beginning to doze, he was abruptly wakened by the sound of a vehicle being driven along the road, its engine being revved unnecessarily. He listened as it came to a screeching halt. He lay in the dark wondering. All sorts of imaginings were going through his mind and poachers were at the top of the list until he decided there was little, if anything in this district worth poaching. Then, he heard voices.

"Come on, don't be bloody daft."

"Bugger off Stevey!"

He was curious and wondered who could be having a row in the middle of a fen road in the early hours. He peered at his clock. It was 2.30am. As he listened, he soon realised that the less than dulcet tones of the young woman sounded like the girl he had spoken to all those weeks ago and he chuckled to himself when she told Stevey to piss off.

Eventually the disturbance ceased and he could only imagine the two had gone their separate ways. It was then he found himself wondering about her. He'd gathered she was not pleased with Stevey, that was abundantly clear but what was her name?

The next day he journeyed to the nearest town for some provisions. When he had finished his shopping, he went for a ploughman's. He sat by a window and absentmindedly gazed out at the crowds. It was market day and people were busy Christmas shopping. It was then he caught sight of her. She was with two other girls and they were laughing together. As he watched her she became lost in the crowds and he finished his lunch.

When he left the pub he made his way to the car park, he was about to unlock his car when he saw her again. This time she was standing at a bus stop. On impulse he hurried towards her.

"Hello, remember me?"

She looked him up and down then jerked her head in recognition.

"Can I offer you a lift?" he asked congenially.

"If yer like."

My car is over there." He began to walk away expecting her to follow. She stood for a moment hesitating then suddenly she hurried after him teetering on her high heels as she endeavoured to catch up.

As they drove out of town she said nothing and seemed ill at ease.

"Been Christmas shopping?" Ellis opened up.

"Can't afford nothin'."

"Oh, I see."

"I don't think you do."

He raised one eyebrow in surprise. "Of course I do. Things are expensive, everything seems to cost the earth."

"What would you know about that? By the looks of you, you got plenty."

He shook his head and laughed softly.

"I wish!" he said, "I have to work for my living. Bloody hard."

"Lucky bloody you. I don't 'ave that privilege."

She was obviously out of work and hard up, but that wasn't his fault. He thought her aggressive attitude uncalled for and felt offended, however, he did not want to deliberately start up an altercation between them and kept quiet.

She fumbled for her cigarettes.

"Got a light?" she demanded as she held one between her fingers and he saw the nicotine stains.

"There's a lighter," he pointed to the dashboard.

She lit up and drew long and hard before exhaling slowly and filling the front of the car with smoke. A moment later, she seemed to have second thoughts and stubbed it out.

"It's all right," Ellis attempted to reassure her, "I don't mind. I've given them up myself but if you want……."

"I don't want," she snapped.

"What the hell's the matter with you? If you don't like my company then you shouldn't have accepted a lift," he snapped back.

She gave him a sideways look. Then the corners of her mouth turned up into a slow smile. "Sorry! Thanks for the lift, that bus would've taken ages."

He relaxed. "Forget it. Let's start again shall we? I don't know your name."

"Diana Parker, but I'm no princess!" she giggled infectiously. "But I wouldn't mind 'er money."

"Money isn't everything," he said then wished he hadn't. It sounded so priggish.

He was expecting her to say he was a prat but she didn't; instead she said, "So, what's your name?"

"Ellis Brown."

"The ole man, who lived in that house you was asking about, was named Brown."

"Yes I know."

"What you doin' then, living in that ole place?"

He could tell by the way she asked she was dying to know.

"Believe it or not, Ernie Brown was my Great Uncle. I'd never met him, but as it turned out I'm his only relative and Goose Gander Farm is my inheritance."

He laughed at the thought and she joined in.

For the rest of the journey they talked almost non-stop and when at last he let her off, she had promised to pay him a visit.

* * *

Fiona had telephoned in the middle of the night.

"Darling did I wake you? I'm in the States. I've been offered a contract, some TV commercials. Isn't it wonderful? Miss you darling."

Ellis listened, muddle headed from sleep. He could only grunt in answer, but as he slowly came round, he began to ask, "How long? What about Christmas?"

Fiona had no idea how long. As for Christmas, it would be spent out there. She would naturally keep in touch but as she spoke, Ellis had the feeling she wouldn't.

When she had finally hung up, he lay in the darkness thinking about their relationship. He was surprised how little he felt about it. They seemed to have drifted effortlessly apart and it didn't hurt. He went back to sleep.

* * *

January brought with it a change of scene. Now the days were bright and frosty and once more the sky was the dominant feature.

On just such a day he'd risen early and made a start on the outside of the house.

"You're still busy then!"

He turned from the window frame he'd been engrossed in painting, to see Diana standing by the newly mended gate.

His look of surprise quickly changed to a warm smile, and as he descended the ladder he said, "Hallo, how long have you been standing there?"

"Not long. I've come to see what you've been up to."

"Sure come on in."

He looked pleased and readily replaced the lid on the paint can and ushered her inside.

She said nothing at first but merely looked about as if inspecting and comparing. He began to feel anxious, why did it matter what she thought? Yet somehow it did.

"Well, what do you think?"

They were standing in the kitchen, which had been repainted and fitted with up-to-date cupboards.

Her eyes went round the room, and they shone child-like as if she had been set down in a fairy grotto.

"It's bootiful!"

He was pleased she approved.

"Must 'ave set you back a lot! Bugger me!"

He grinned, "All thanks to Uncle Ernie. Come upstairs and see the rest."

He saw a glint of mischief in her eyes, "Oh yes and what's the rest?"

"Just the bathroom I've had fitted," he said innocently.

She followed him upstairs and Ellis opened the bathroom door. She stepped inside and gasped in admiration.

"A shower! Oh, I've always wanted one of them," she turned to him and with a look of glee she said, again almost child-like, "Can I try it?"

He was astonished to see she had already begun to take off the thick jumper she was wearing.

"Er....sure........be my guest......I'll get a fresh towel."

He sidled out and quickly went downstairs to fetch one.

He tried desperately to work out what she really wanted. Was she completely impulsive, like a child, or was she giving him the come on? He didn't want to misread the situation and therefore blunder and ruin the whole thing before it had even got started; so, he decided to play it cool and act the perfect gentleman. After all, if she did mean more, then there was plenty of time.

When she emerged from her leisurely shower, her blonde hair was a brassy colour and he saw the black roots.

As she looked up at him with her cornflower blue eyes, he tried to imagine the naturally dark hair framing her face.

"What you staring at?" she said tartly.

"You're a very touchy young woman. I was simply admiring your pretty looks that's all."

She studied him suspiciously for a moment then suddenly her face broke into a smile, "I've never been told I was pretty before."

"Haven't you? What about Steve?"

Her expression was one of surprise and her cheeks flushed.

"What you know about Steve?"

Her forehead creased as if perplexed at his knowing anything.

"I heard you having a bit of a tiff one night. It was you, wasn't it?"

"It might 'ave been. What's it to you anyway?"

"Nothing. I just wondered if he was the boyfriend."

"No. He ain't."

"Like that is it?" he said looking quizzically at her.

"Yeah! Like that, so don't make somethin' of it."

"You are a prickly customer," he shook his head. "I'm going to make a cuppa."

He turned and went into the kitchen.

"Care to join me in a cup of coffee?" he called.

"Okay."

He turned to see her standing in the doorway. He grinned.

"Well make yourself useful. Top shelf, left hand cupboard."

As they sat either side of the table sipping their coffee, he studied her more closely. He suspected that behind the brittle facade she was vulnerable.

He looked up at the kitchen clock. "I think it's about time I got a meal going. Care to stay and share with me? I'm not a bad cook."

She laughed a scornful laugh. "You cook!"

"You'd be surprised. I'm a man of many talents. Stay and you can judge for yourself."

She agreed and took delight in fetching and carrying for him. When the Italian dish was ready, she tentatively poked it with a fork before tasting it.

She looked up at him, "It's good! How did you learn to cook Italian?"

"I'm glad you approve madam," he gave an exaggerated bow. "I used to have an Italian girl friend; her father had a restaurant."

"Huh," she snorted, "I prefer Chinese meself."

"You perverse little cow."

She shrugged, in a couldn't-care-less manner but he noticed she ate every bit. As they washed up together, he began to question her.

"Found a job yet?"

She shook her head. "Got no qualifications. Used to play hooky all the time."

"How come?"

"Me mother, she was ill a lot, she died in Peterborough hospital, two years agoo. Cancer!"

"I'm sorry to hear that. Must have been tough for you and your dad?"

"O that ol' bugger. Me and 'im don't get on. He's nothin' but a bloody drunk."

He was startled by her outburst but said nothing as she continued, "So, now if I wants any work, I 'ave to take what's gooin'."

"What kind of work is there?"

"Veg. Packers! But they're hard to git into. Then there's fieldwork, strawberry pickin' and that, for the Gang Masters. But they treat you like bloody animals. See most of us are signing on the social, so it's unofficial like. We can't say too much, about there ain't being no facilities."

He looked at her enquiringly.

"Toilets! If we wants to goo, we have to squat in the field or in a ditch."

As he listened to her, he couldn't help wondering how she could be, if she was given the chance. She was equally as beautiful as Fiona with those huge blue eyes and that lovely complexion, not from a bottle either. It was shame. He liked her and wished he could do something for her. Then, suddenly it came to him.

"How would you like to work for me?"

She looked surprised. "What doin?"

"Well, I'm away a lot. I could do with someone to look after the place. Keep it clean, that sort of thing."

She looked doubtful. He could see she wasn't sure.

"How about £12 a week. How's that sound?"

"You're joking?" she said still not able to believe what he was proposing. "You want's me to be a well, kind of 'ousekeeper?"

He shrugged; "Well, yes, I suppose I am asking that."

She stared at him and he could see the incredulity in her expression. "What's the catch?"

"What do you mean? Why has there got to be a catch? If you help in the house I can spend more of my time writing. It was just a thought, that's all."

Her expression quickly changed. She was intrigued. "You a writer?"

His brown eyes twinkled with amusement, "Let's just say I try to be."

She was impressed. "Like Jeffrey Archer?"

He burst into laughter. "No not quite! I have had a few bits published but as for a blockbuster. No! But who knows my novel might well be," he said teasingly seeing how she was viewing him in a new light.

"All right, I'll do it. Be glad to," she said in a rush.

* * *

Their arrangement was working out well and he had been getting on with his writing without too many distractions. However, he'd hit a period where he was finding it difficult. On this particular night it was gone midnight before he finally went to bed and quickly fell into a deep sleep.

He was awakened by the sound of movement downstairs. He got up and crept onto the landing and listened. He could hear voices: the front door was open.

"Leave me alone Stevey, I told you, it's finished."

"I told you gal if I catch you with that smarmy bloke, I'd break your fuckin' neck."

"You shut your mouth Stevey, he's not like that. Not like you, you bastard."

There was the sound of scuffling and then he heard a quiet cry. He was spurred into action and thundered down the stairs.

"What's going on? He shouted, "You all right Diana?"

"Yes. Yes. I'm fine. I'm sorry I woke you up." There was surprise in her voice, as if she were not expecting him to be there.

"It seems a good thing you did. Where is he?"

She had shut the door and was standing with her back to it.

"It's all right, he's gone now. He was just being a bit awk'ard. It was the drink talking."

As she spoke, her voice sounded different.

"What's the matter?" He couldn't see her well enough in the light from the landing above and he reached out for the light switch but she stopped him.

"I'm fine. I only come here 'cause you said I could stay here, I'll goo now. I didn't know you'd come up today. I never saw the car! I'll see you in the mornin'."

"Don't worry. I managed to get away sooner than I thought," he said then hesitated before asking, "Who was it? Not that Steve guy?"

She did not reply and he put out his hand and could feel her trembling.

"Look it's very late. You can't walk along the road on your own at this time. If you don't mind you can sleep here."

"No it's all right. It's only a short walk. I'll be all right."

For a long moment they stood silent until he reached out to her and his fingers clasped her hand.

"Come on," he whispered and submissively she allowed him to lead her up the stairs.

The next morning he awoke early and went downstairs where he made coffee and took some up to her. He found her fast asleep, curled in herself, like a pink shrimp. He put the mug down then gently shook her by the shoulder.

She started then realising where she was, sat up, still full of sleep.

It was then he saw. "What in God's name has happened to your face?" He could not disguise the shock he felt.

Quickly she put her hand to her right cheek. It was badly bruised and swollen.

"Nothin', I just fell, that's all."

"Oh yes, and how did you fall?"

"I was on me bike and I fell off."

"How?"

"I just fell off, no partic'lar way, how does anyone fall?"

"When did this happen? I didn't know you had a bike."

"Bloody hell! What's this, twenty questions?"

"Was it just that? Because..........if it was that Stevey guy?"

"Oh yeah, and what would you do about it, if it was?" She spoke mockingly.

"I'd go after him."

"And what good would that do. Just get yourself bloody beaten up. You ain't no match for 'im nor 'is mates. So mind your own business."

"All right!" he said, his anger rising. "If that's the way you want it. Get on with it."

He turned from her and stomped downstairs, but by the time she came down he had calmed himself and was preparing breakfast. He watched as she slurped the porridge he had made and could see every mouthful was painful. But he said nothing more.

The rest of the day he locked himself away and wrote. It was about 2pm when he heard a soft knocking on the door. She had prepared a tray for him.

He looked up at her and smiled. "Is that the time? That looks lovely, thanks, I could do with it."

She sat down and watched him eat. She looked apprehensive and nervously twiddled her fingers.

"What's wrong? You look worried. How's your face? It still looks swollen."

"Oh, it's okay. It don't hurt," she said dismissing his concern then, she said hesitantly, "I was wondering. If you don't mind, if I could stay here for a while."

"Sure! You can stay here for as long as you like. Permanently, if you've a mind to. But what about your father? Will he mind?"

She looked surprised, as if to consider what her father might think, didn't even enter her head.

"Huh, he wouldn't care. Wouldn't notice if I was gone or not."

"Well, that's settled then. Move in whenever you like."

The next day she trundled an old shopping trolley along the road; its bulging bag in danger of splitting. On top was balanced a ghetto blaster at the same time she managed to carry a small holdall, which was also packed to bursting.

When he saw her he was surprised and asked why she hadn't asked him to give her a lift in the car. In answer she merely shrugged and began unpacking the bag and then took everything upstairs to the back bedroom and finished off by pinning a poster of her favourite group on the wall.

* * *

Neither of them could have guessed what would happen. They certainly hadn't planned it. She had been sleeping at the house for two nights when she woke up in the early hours on the third night and went to his room.

It was as if she needed comforting. She climbed into his bed and lay still beside him. Waiting.

His fingers reached out in the dark and touched her, exploring slowly and gently. He did not rush her. He waited for her response. He covered her body with tender kisses while she sighed and uttered small cries of pleasure.

She tasted sweet. As he took her she arched her slender body wrapping her young arms around his waist and pulling him down on her and he felt her tremble beneath him. It was slow and lasting and when they were fully satisfied they were wonderfully tired. From that night, they shared his bed.

One evening when they were sitting idly together, he asked her what she had been doing with the yellow bucket all that time ago, when he'd first set eyes on her.

At first she looked puzzled, and then she remembered and grinned mischievously.

"I was shacking over a tatter field."

"What?"

"I was picking up the ones 'ad been missed."

"I didn't know you could still do it, glean I mean."

"Why not? Never been told can't!"

He looked at her, her bronze face like a ripened peach. Now she had let it grow out, her soft brown hair reminded him of a polished chestnut and he steeped himself in her wonderful blue eyes. He felt lucky to have her.

She was starting to take an interest in other music other than the top ten and he had carefully introduced her to some reading. At first she had grumbled, because he chose not to have a television, but now she was content to sit by him engrossed in a book.

But what she enjoyed most were their trips to Cambridge and Peterborough but when she had wanted to visit London he had put her off.

Then one night after they had made love and were falling into a comfortable sleep, they were jolted wide-awake by the sounds of vehicles speeding noisily along the road. One slammed on the brakes right outside and there were sounds of doors being slammed and raucous voices whooping and calling. A radio blared, adding to the cacophony. The culmination of this was the loud banging on the front door.

"What the hell's going on?" Ellis exclaimed in a hoarse whisper.

"Come out here Diana. Come out or I'll come and get yer."

Ellis recognised the rasping voice of Steve.

Diana quickly jumped out of bed and began to dress hurriedly. Ellis sat up and stared at her shadowy figure silhouetted against the window by the bright moonlight outside.

"What are you doing? He hissed, "you're not going down there to that prat."

"I must, or there'll be real trouble."

"What trouble? I'll ring for the police." He reached out for the phone but she put her hand on his urgently.

"No Ellis! Please! It's all right. He just wants to see me that's all. I'll be all right, I promise. He's just a bit pissed. Don't ring the police, I don't want them poking around here. It's my business, if I choose to goo, I'll goo."

He could hardly believe what she was saying. He threw back the bedcovers and began to pull on his trousers.

"I'm telling you, you are not going down there. Not until I know what that madman wants."

She did not answer but ran downstairs with him following. She opened the front door and a hand shot out and grabbed her.

"Let her go you bastard!" Ellis shouted and tried to pull her back. It was then he felt the blow. A fist hit him full in the face, his head jerked backwards and he staggered, as the door was slammed shut, leaving him dazed and bleeding in the dark.

He felt humiliated; she was right, he was no match for the brute and his mate. His humiliation quickly turned to anger. Why, he thought, why had she gone and so quickly? What kind of hold had that toe rag got over her? Why did she run the moment he commanded? Again he thought about the police, but he knew it would probably take them ages to get there. He had no idea where they had gone. He couldn't describe the cars or the occupants and to top it all she had gone with them willingly. There was nothing he could do.

* * *

She had been gone for two days. He decided to go and look for her. He got into the car and drove the couple of miles along the drain until he came to the rough track that she had told him led to the cottage she shared with her father.

When he reached the badly leaning slate roofed house with its two high steps leading to the front door, he stood staring at it. It seemed deserted. He went up to the door and knocked. There was no answer so he walked round to the back of the house, he tapped on the back door and it swung open. He leaned inside and called.

"Anyone in?"

"Who the 'ell is that?"

He stepped inside: he was in a kitchen. There were two saucepans on a small electric stove with something simmering in them.

"Hallo!"

"In 'ere."

The occupant's guttural voice came from the next room. Ellis walked into the sitting room. Sprawled on a settee, he found a man, who he judged to be in his fifties. He looked unwashed and there was several days, growth on his face.

Ellis stood staring down at him.

"Well, who are yoo?"

The man stared back at Ellis through slitty eyes, his crumpled features bloated and purple.

"I'm looking for Diana."

"Are yer now?"

The man, whom Ellis took to be Diana's father, lifted his bulk and sat up. His beer belly quivered through his grey string vest.

Ellis watched as he reached out for one of the cans of beer standing on top of a small table in front of him. Ellis waited, as he took one and guzzled down a great mouthful, then wiped the dribbles from his whiskered chin with the back of his grimy hand.

"What makes you think she's fuckin' 'ere anyway? Can you see 'er?" He waved a fat arm in the air.

Ellis could feel his anger rising. "I take it you're her father?"

"That's right! Not that it's any bloody business of yours." And he rolled over onto his side the effort turning his face puce. "Ain't she shacked up with you now? You that bloke down the road, ain't yer?"

"If you mean is she staying at my house, the answer is no. Not at the moment. I haven't seen her for two days. Do you know where she is?"

"I don't know or care where she is. Probably with Stevey." He grinned a yellow grin and winked suggestively.

"I take it you don't mind her being with him," said Ellis.

The man began to laugh, a drunken cackling laugh, spitting and dribbling beery saliva down his chin and onto his already heavily stained vest. "Why should I?" He finally spluttered.

Ellis looked down at him with disgust.

The man's expression suddenly changed from one of humour to one of contempt. "You ain't sharp, you ain't. I told yer I don't buggering care where she is. So clear off."

Ellis started to say something, but then decided it wasn't worth the bother to argue with the obscene figure lying in front of him. Instead he turned away and went outside. He stood by his car for a few moments wondering where he could go. He had no idea where to look. In the end he gave up and returned to Goose Gander Farm.

He had to wait for another day before she returned. She gave no explanation and looked defiant and unrepentant.

"I've been worried sick about you," he remonstrated, "Doesn't that mean anything to you?"

"I told you I can look after meself. I don't need anyone to *worry* over me," she sounded adamant.

"I went looking for you!" he said.

"What d'you mean?"

"I went to see your father. I asked him if he knew where you were?"

A look of horror crossed her face, "You got no right gooin' there. You ain't got no 'old over me. I come and goo as I please. You shouldn't have gone there, Ellis. I can look after meself. I told you."

He was unable to contain his anger any longer.

"Well, that's fine by me. But don't expect me to let you stay here. You can go."

She looked shocked. She had returned expecting to take up where they had left off but he was not prepared to.

"All right!" she said petulantly. "I'll get my things," and she ran to the stairs but he stopped her.

"God Diana! Have you no idea what you put me through? I didn't know what had happened to you."

She looked contrite. "I'm sorry."

"Your dad said you were with Steve. Is that right?"

She did not answer but cast her eyes downwards.

"Why? Why? Just give me one good reason. What can he mean to you for pities sake?"

He held her tightly by the arms and she pulled away from him.

"You don't understand. I 'ad to goo with 'im. He don't mean nothin' to me. Honest! It's just I've known 'im all my life. But I left 'im for you. That must tell you something. How I feel."

This time he could see tears forming in her beautiful eyes and he relented. He was just thankful to have her back.

"Yes, I know," he paused, "but you can't simply go off like that; without a word. If it's really over between you and him then it's over."

He took her in his arms and held her. He could not bear to be without her.

"I won't share you with anyone Diana," he whispered.

That night they made love and she made up for all the hurt and confusion she had caused him and for the next few days, things were peaceful between them.

* * *

He had been working, cooped up in the house, all day and felt in need of some air. He was about to go outside when he heard the familiar sound of a pick-up. He looked out of the window and saw it was parked across the road close to the drain. He guessed at once who it was.

He hurried outside to where already there were young trees planted in groups and beginning to change the look of the place.

It was then he saw them, Diana and a thick set man, whom he guessed to be the infamous Steve. They were standing together in animated conversation and didn't see him.

He stood behind a shed to observe them. He was angry but wasn't sure what he was going to do about it.

As he watched them, the man Steve attempted to put his hands on her breasts. Diana pulled away, and Ellis heard her say, "Stop it Steve." Steve's response was to give a cackling laugh that reminded Ellis of Diana's drunken father.

They began to walk towards the road and Ellis was able to hear some of their conversation.

"You comin' tonight then?"

"No I ain't. So stop goin' on about it."

"Listen gal, you're expected. It'll be good! Plenty of E."

"I don't care. I'm not interested."

"Why not? You used to be bloody keen enough before you met up with that poncey bloke." He looked about him, "Where is 'e anyway?"

Diana looked nervously round, "He's inside working. So shut up and goo."

Once more Steve gave an ugly laugh.

"Why's that then? Frightened what he might do to me if he catches me 'ere?"

As he spoke he played with the chain that hung from his leather jacket and Ellis could see the studs, in his ears and nose, quite clearly.

Diana hung her head and did not speak.

Steve hooked his arm around her neck and pulled her towards him.

"Come on! You know you'll like it. You're coming right?"

Diana started struggling to free herself. At this point Ellis moved impulsively into view.

"Let her go!"

Steve looked surprised at first but then as he released Diana he began to smirk at Ellis, daring him to make the first move.

"What are you doing here? Get off my property right now."

"Oooo," Steve threw his head back and roared with laughter.

"What's this bloke then, Di, what's he reckon he's goin' to do then eh?"

She looked angry and afraid at the same time.

"Ellis he's just goin', so don't start anything," she said anxiously.

"No don't start what you can't finish boy," Steve raised a tattooed fist and moved aggressively towards Ellis. Diana stepped quickly in front of Steve and pulled his hand down.

"Please Steve! Don't! I'll see you later. Now goo."

Steve glared at her for an agonising moment.

"Yeah, he ain't worth the fuckin' bother," his lips twisted into a smirk, "don't forget what I said Di. I'm expecting you."

"Just goo," and she pushed him away from her.

When he had gone, Diana turned her fury onto Ellis.

"What were you doing standing behind the barn spying on me?"

"I wasn't spying," he said, his face flushing with anger and embarrassment. "I heard the pick-up. If he keeps coming here I'm calling the police. I won't have him near you."

"What did I tell you," she screamed at him. "I don't want no soddin' police. It's got nothing to do with them. You're just being bloody stupid. I've known Stevey all my life, I told you. He just wants me to goo to a Rave. That's all."

This time it was he who could hardly contain himself. His anger contorted his face as he yelled back at her. "Then go to your blasted Rave. Go on; go with the rest of the brain dead."

Before she could reply he turned on his heels and stormed back into the house. She heard the door slam shut, as she stood alone and forlorn with tears of anger and regret stinging her eyes.

* * *

He had motored to London and as he drove, he pondered on selling up and moving back there. He told himself he'd get rid of *Goose Gander Farm* and her, all at the same time. He was mad putting up with her ways.

He was glad he hadn't put his old flat up for sale, at least he had somewhere to stay and he could easily put Goose Gander farm in the hands of an estate agent from there.

When he arrived at the flat it was cold and looked much smaller than he remembered.

The next morning he decided to call on his old friend Julian. He arrived about three in the afternoon and it was Beth Julian's wife who opened the door.

The harassed look she had been wearing quickly faded to one of pleasant surprise.

"Ellis!"

In the kitchen it was warm and smelled of baking. Beth had obviously been busy.

"He's out stocking up on booze," she smiled "don't mind if we stay in here?"

He perched on a high stool, "Of course not. It's lovely to see you Beth, how are the kids?"

She rolled her eyes and laughed softly, "Tom's at university, and Wendy is taking her exams and hoping to follow him and at the moment it's chaotic."

"Have I come at a wrong time?"

She shook her head. "No, of course not, just that I've got some people coming to dinner, well not exactly me that is,....." She sighed.

"Oh, I see. Who are they overseas? After a contract is he?"

She nodded. "What else. He needs it too Ellis." He detected an anxious tone.

"Well, can I help? I'm not bad at peeling spuds or whatever…"

She laughed. "Yes, I remember… its all right, most of the hard work's been done," then she glanced nervously at the kitchen clock. "Goodness knows where he's got to."

As she said the words the bell rang. "Oh he's forgot his blasted keys again I bet they're on the bedside table." She began to hurry to answer, but Ellis stopped her. "I'll let him in."

As he opened the door an equally harassed looking Julian stood on the doorstep holding a cardboard box loaded with bottles. When he saw it was Ellis he nearly dropped it in astonishment.

"Bloody Hell! Where did you come from?"

Ellis grinned. "Nice to see you too."

Inside the kitchen Beth gave her orders and Julian did everything he was instructed to do.

Ellis looked on smiling to himself. Julian would be lost without the support of such a lovely woman like Beth. Yet at the same time he detected a tension between them. Julian who had always been so relaxed seemed to be edgy.

Later when Julian had taken Ellis into the small junk room he called his study and they sat together over a drink Ellis began to question his friend.

"I hear you've got company to night."

"Yeah, did Beth tell you? Germans. We stand to get a good contract if all goes well. By the way has she asked you to stay?"

"What to dinner. No of course not, you don't want me hanging around, not when its business mate."

Julian suddenly looked very serious and said "As a matter of fact I'd like you to Ellis. If I don't get this bloody contract tied up...... I really need it Ellis. Things haven't been going too good lately and I need to come up with a real special deal otherwise old man Bond is going to start looking around for a replacement."

"I don't know Julian. I've been out of it all for over a year now."

"Come off it, Ellis you were the tops, you know you were and still are as far as I'm concerned." He paused, then got up and went to the cluttered desk in the corner, "Here take a look!" He handed over a folder and poured Ellis another drink.

Ellis reluctantly opened the file and began to look over the detailed report and plans for the advertising campaign that Julian had produced.

After an hour he closed the file and looked at Julian.

"It should knock them dead. It's bloody good. I'd buy it any day."

"Come on, give it to me straight. I've seen that look."

Ellis grinned. "Okay but honestly, it's just a matter of it being a bit rough round the edges so to speak, look this is what I mean."

They immediately fell into a huddle and another hour had gone by when Beth knocked on the door and called to Julian to start getting ready.

The dinner party was a great success and the German guests went away satisfied and very impressed and a contract would definitely be signed.

Beth looked tired and said she was going to bed and said Julian was to lock up.

The two friends sat in the drawing room and shared a nightcap.

"Thanks for your support Ellis my old mate!" Julian saluted Ellis who grinned back at him.

"Any way what are you doing up here? I thought you were gone for good hidden away in the flatlands writing your best seller."

Ellis did not reply.

Julian studied him for a moment or two. "Look as though it hasn't been all you thought it would be. You're not thinking of coming back are you?"

Ellis laughed. "No. Don't worry. I have no intentions of coming back to the rat race. However, you're right it isn't quite working out as I first thought. I've got a publisher and so far that side of it is going smoothly."

Here he paused.

"Well, what is it?" Suddenly Julian grinned. "Not got some local gal pregnant."

"No not exactly. But there is, or was a girl. She's quite a bit younger than me, and well at first it was going well. But now its time to move on."

Julian studied his friend again.

"In what way. Move on."

"I'm thinking of selling the place up. Moving back to town."

"Why should a girl make you do that; unless she means more than you're letting on? Or has she dumped you?"

Ellis looked at Julian then sighed and got up and poured out another drink for them both. When he sat down he found he needed to talk it over with someone so it might as well be Julian.

When he had finished Julian thought for a while.

"Well as I see it. You've got it bad. And what you've told me about her she seems worth it. Get this other prat out of her life; marry her Ellis it's about time you settled. You've had your fill of the Fiona's of this world."

Ellis grinned, by this time they were both somewhat inebriated and Ellis leant forward and said earnestly looking into Julian's bleary eyes, "If only I had someone like your Beth."

"Well you haven't 'cos I have her," Julian hiccupped.

"You won't for much longer if you two don't get yourselves to bed."

They looked up at an angry Beth.

"You can sleep in Tom's room." She instructed Ellis who dutifully and without another word obediently ascended the stairs Julian staggered behind followed by and being pushed, by a long-suffering Beth.

* * *

He spent a week in London but the whole time couldn't stop thinking about her and wondering. Finally, taking Julian's advice, he swallowed his pride and went back.

He found her in the house; she had kept it clean and full of fresh flowers. He was ashamed and full of remorse.

When she saw him she could not disguise her relief and happiness at his return. She ran to him and flung her arms about him and kissed him with a passion that sent his blood running.

That night they were hungry for each other. Ellis needed to claim her. His passion was so great he was unable to hide his jealousy of Steve who without doubt had treated her badly. And yet she had left Ellis to go with him. His jealousy caused him to push her down onto the bed almost savagely.

"Is this what you want? How you prefer it?"

His words stung her as his mouth found her breasts and his hands thrust roughly between her legs. She cried out, but he took no notice until he suddenly realised that she was quietly weeping. He stopped abruptly and pulled away.

"Oh God!" he moaned and rolled to one side, "What's happening? That bastard! I'm not like him! In not like that!" His voice cracked and his words came chokingly.

She put an arm around his neck and stroked his hair.

"I know," she whispered. "I know my love. It's all right."

She kissed him, her tongue finding its way into his mouth. This time he responded with tenderness, his hands exploring her until she lifted her legs and wound them around his buttocks.

"Love me Ellis," she whispered pulling him down on her.

Tears stung his eyes as he thrust harder and deeper feeling her tight around him his quickening movement enticing her to respond in harmony. She arched her back pushing upwards until at last they reached an eruption of intense pleasure. When their appetite for one another had been satisfied they, curled exhausted, in each other's arms and slept.

They lay sleeping, for about an hour. Ellis was still asleep when she slipped out of bed and went to the bathroom. When she returned he was sitting up and waiting for her.

"Again?" he said greedily.

But she sat on the edge of the bed, silent.

"Come on, what's wrong?" He pulled back the bedclothes and she slid in beside him; his hands went to her breasts.

It was then she told him. She whispered in his ear.

"You sure?"

"Yes. Of course I'm sure," she said and snuggled against him.

"What are you going to do about it?"

There was a long pause before she sat up and with her back to him she said,

"What do you want me to do Ellis?"

"Surely that's for you to decide. I mean, are you sure, who's........"

"Say what you really mean Ellis," she said and turned to look at him. "You want to know if it's yours."

"No. I didn't mean that," he protested but that was exactly what he meant.

She held him in a steady gaze. "Who else's could it be?"

He didn't answer. His thoughts were racing. He wasn't prepared. He didn't want the responsibility. It would interfere with his writing. Why couldn't it be as it was, simple, uncomplicated? Besides she couldn't blame him for wondering.

His silence told her everything. She could guess what he was thinking and inwardly she was crying out: the hurt and rejection stabbing at her heart. She thought he'd be pleased. She wanted him to take her in his arms and kiss her and laugh and be glad for them both. But he was like all the rest: Steve the Gang Master and her brute of a father.

Without another word she got out of bed.

"Don't get up!" he said peevishly.

Suddenly there was the sound of vehicles being driven at high speed. Someone was making wild whoops and cries.

"Oh! Don't say it's those morons again," he cursed. He was desperately trying to think and all he could hear were the mad noises outside.

"Di-an-a, coo-ee. Come on gal. You're wanted." Steve called mockingly.

She began to dress.

"What are you doing? You're not going out there to him! I won't let you."

"Why not? You don't want me!" She answered tearfully.

"Of course I want you. It's been a bit of a surprise that's all. What did you expect me to say? I thought you were on the pill. I didn't expect this. I need time to think it over." His voice was hoarse and urgent.

"What's there to think about Ellis?"

"Where are you going in the middle of the night? Don't be so silly. We can talk about it. Come back to bed."

All the time there were the shouts and laughter in the background distracting them. Diana pulled on her coat and ran out of the room.

She stood outside in the moonlight as several cars raced up and down. Steve was driving one of them and as he saw her in the headlights he leant out of the window and began cat-calling.

"Come on gal. You're wanted."

"Clear off Steve and let me alone," she called back. Then she hurried along the road in the direction of the home she hated. She had no choice.

The motors suddenly stopped and the drivers switched off the headlights. There was an eerie silence; the moon hid behind a cloud and the darkness took over.

When Diana left him Ellis was mortified. He was ashamed. He quickly jumped out of bed muttering: "Stupid sod! Of course it's mine. Why did I let her go out there, to that bastard?"

As he castigated himself he pulled on his trousers and threw on a thick jumper. He hopped about as he pushed his feet into his shoes and then ran downstairs and outside to look for her. He told himself that she couldn't have gone far. He would bring her back. He loved her.

He started up the car and drove slowly along the narrow road, his headlights on high beam as he looked for her.

Suddenly, the glare of lights from another vehicle was reflected in the rear view mirror and he could see it was approaching fast.

What was happening? Who ever it was must be able to see him? He cursed, as he lowered the window and could hear, above the noise of revving engines, maniacal jeering.

He cursed again: it was that madman Steve and his lunatic friends.

The back of his car took the ram with a thundering crunch. He put his foot on the accelerator and sped forward. The lights in the mirror dazzled him as they took up the chase. Then he saw two sets of headlights side by side appear out of the darkness and coming towards him at frightening speed. It was as if they had been lying in wait.

"They must be mad!" he cried out and then he saw her, she was standing on the grass verge; for a split second he took his eyes off the road. That was all it took. He was conscious of hearing her scream as he tried desperately to take avoiding action but he had no option but to swerve and as the wheels went into a skid he realised too late he was heading for the drain.

* * *

As the vehicles came to a screeching halt their occupants jeered and chanted. In their drunken state they fiendishly took pleasure in seeing the car skid helplessly into the deep water.

Then they became aware that Diana was screaming. Her tortured cries seemed to bring them back to reality as they realised what had happened.

But it was too late to do anything. Diana stood by the roadside crying hysterically, "You've killed him. You bastards! You've murdered him."

Steve got out of the pick-up and hurried to her. He took her by the shoulders and shook her violently. Her head jerked back with a jolt silencing her into quiet sobs.

"It were a fuckin' accident you stupid cow." He looked at the others who had gathered round, "every one knows that."

His companions were looking stunned and one was being violently sick.

"Better telephone for help," another said lamely.

Steve nodded, then took hold of Diana, "Come on Sis. It probably wasn't his anyway."

Drained of all emotion she dumbly surrendered. He helped her into the pick-up and drove her back to the only home she knew.

*

Shall I Be Mother?
By Sandra Finney

I try to focus on something, anything that will take my mind away from the inquisitive mumblings and fumblings. The clock ticks loudly.

"Just let your knees flop outwards," he snaps.

I raise my head and look down. My knees are drawn tightly together whilst my outspread feet, hanging at a ridiculous 120 degree angle, are cradled in a pair of rough canvas slings. Stirrups he called them. Can't imagine why, I can't remember ever riding Eric in this position. I snigger at the thought.

"Do try to relax, dear," moans the balding stranger as his head emerges from between my thighs.

The only bald head I wish to see emerge from my thighs is a ba----

Shall I be mother? Yearning gnaws at my empty womb.

Depriving me of any remaining vestige of dignity, rubber-clad fingers prod at my secret places, probing my very soul—fingers—sponge fingers, chocolate fingers with tea. I snigger again.

Shall I be mother?

Tick-tock, tick-tock. I fear my biological clock has ticked its last. The clock on the treatment room wall sounds louder than ever. The red second hand jerks impartially on.

A gentle hand squeezes my shoulder. "Shall I be mother, dear? I've made some tea. You must have gone sound off. I hope you didn't mind me letting myself in, but I was worried when you didn't answer the door. I've put your pension in your purse, dear. Shall I be mother?"

*

The Ten Minute Job
By Phyllis Gall

For the first eighteen years of my life I lived in the small village of Christchurch, situated in the heart of the Cambridgeshire Fens. They were very happy, untroubled years and many memories stand out in my mind. Memories of harvesting, but not with the giant combines of today: those were the days of the binder, and the threshing tackle, when stooking was done by hand, and no burning stubble polluted the air.

As children, my brother and two sisters and I played in grassy lanes and green fields, by hedgerows filled with wild flowers – buttercups, cowslips, violets and bluebells, which we picked and carried home in hot little fists to be put into water-filled jam jars on the kitchen mantelpiece.

One particular incident I recall happened in the late 1940's when self sufficiency was a necessity and not just an idea for a television programme.

Most of the families in the village kept some kind of domestic farm animal to supplement their income. In our case, besides the flock of Rhode Island Red chickens which supplied us with all the eggs we needed and plenty left over to sell, we also raised pigs. Two piglets were bought from the local farmer, reared, fattened and sold at the livestock auction at the nearby market town of March, or sold direct to a local butcher. Two more piglets were bought and so the cycle went on.

Our pair of porkers were kept in what would now seem luxury conditions for doomed animals. There was a large shed, deeply lined with straw in which they slept, with a fenced in yard where they had plenty of room to run about.

On of the jobs involved in back-yard pig rearing was to put a ring through the pig's nose, whilst it is young, to prevent it rootling in the ground, or under the fence and escaping its fate. The ringing is a comparatively simple job requiring two people: one to hold the pig and the other to insert the ring into the pig's snout using a specially designed pair of pincers.

Just a ten minute job. No trouble. But first catch your pig!

This lot usually fell to my grandfather, who was not inexperienced in these matters. He was quite a character: a small man, with bandy legs and a lugubrious face which was as wrinkled and brown as a walnut. He wore a flat cap, corduroy trousers, a collar-less shirt and a neckerchief tied under his chin in a complicated series of knots.

When it came to pig-ringing Grandfather had a well-used routine which, up to now, had never been known to fail. On this occasion, Grandfather opened the gate to the pig yard and went inside quietly and cautiously. He approached one of the pigs and stood facing it, his flat cap held in his outstretched hand. He intended to catch the pig's snout in his cap, thus enabling him to grab the ears and hold its head steady, ready for the pincers.

'Here, pig, pig,' cooed Grandfather, softly. 'Come on, old pig.'

THE TEN MINUTE JOB

This particular pig, however, had a very suspicious nature and did not altogether trust what he was seeing. With a grunt and a snort it charged straight at Grandfather and ran between his legs. Grandfather was not quick enough to take evasive action and, with a look of pained surprise, sat with a thump on the animal's back facing the tail.

The pig took great exception to this very unusual burden and began rushing around the yard, squealing loudly, trying to unseat its unwelcome rider. In and out of the shed it ran with Grandfather bumping his head on the low doorway each time they jogged through.

The other pig, alarmed at such unexpected activity, began running around in circles hampering Grandfather's porcine steed. For a while complete pandemonium broke loose with both pigs squealing, Grandfather shouting for someone to 'Stop the bugger!' and the family looking on, doubled up with laughter, enjoying the unorthodox rodeo. Afterwards no-one would admit to shouting out 'Ride him, Cowboy!' although we all had our suspicions as to who was the culprit.

Eventually the pig deposited Grandfather in the least salubrious corner of the yard and ran into the shed, grunting indignantly. Fortunately the only thing hurt was Grandfather's pride, although I do believe he had to buy a new cap, and it was generally agreed to leave the pig-ringing until another day.

*

Say It With Flowers
By Sandra Finney

Something was seriously amiss in the judging tent. Piercing screams smothered the affable chatter of the visitors to Little Houghton's flower show. Merriment evaporated abruptly in the heat of the hot June afternoon and silence hung like a fog.

Inside the tent the ashen-faced parish councillor, Mrs Mountford, was kneeling beside the body of a young woman whose neck was tightly bound with green garden twine. The bloated face was a mottled greyish-blue and her hands clutched a posy of African violets.

"Oh, dear God, no!" Reverend Speedwell was the first to speak, "Lord have mercy upon her soul." Crossing himself he moved swiftly over to where the body lay. "I'm afraid you can do nothing for the poor soul. It's a matter for the police now, dear lady." He offered an outstretched arm to the distraught Mrs Mountford, "Come along, my dear." He helped her to her feet and onto a nearby chair. She was no lightweight and the slightly built vicar grunted from the exertion. His kindness was the key to the floodgates. Mrs Mountford let out an eerie wail and her matronly figure quivered with violent sobs.

"Oh, Vicar, what on Earth is happening to our village?" She snuffled into a white lacy handkerchief, "Poor Daphne Burke last week and now poor Erica; so young too. My husband would turn in his grave."

The annual flower show had been set up in memory of the late Edgar G Mountford, the founder of the Gardening Club. It was the pride and joy of what was known locally as the four Houghtons. Great, Little, Upper and Lower Houghton each took their turn to host the event and the prestigious Mountford Memorial Trophy was a much coveted award.

"I agree wholeheartedly, dear lady, I can't make sense of it at all," the vicar rummaged about in the pocket of his threadbare tweed jacket. He withdrew a large antiquated mobile telephone and punched in 999. "The police I'm afraid, dear," he spoke quietly into the mouthpiece. "Yes, hello, this is Reverend Speedwell, Little Houghton. I'm afraid it looks like another murder, Sergeant." He explained the details and returned his phone to the fluffy recesses of his pocket. He turned to the crowd, now a cauldron of restless speculation and buzzing chatter. After clearing his throat he elevated his voice by several decibels.

"I'm afraid there's been a dreadful accident," he spoke loudly but as diplomatically as he could, "the emergency services are on their way. Please clear the entrance to the field but I must ask you all to remain here until the police arrive."

The chatter subsided slightly and a man's voice called, "What's wrong, Vicar?" The question came from the churchwarden, Peter Critchley. Relieved to see a familiar face, the vicar beckoned him to come forward, "Ah, Peter, perhaps you could get a couple of chaps to help you organise everyone." Dropping his voice, he murmured, "We have another murder on our hands but just tell them someone's fallen or something."

Standing head and shoulders above the vicar, the burly ex-sergeant major puffed out his chest. "You leave it to me, Vicar." His white moustache bristled, "I'll sort 'em for you." Turning on his heel with military precision he bellowed, "Right, you 'orrible, nosy little gits, we need to get an ambulance through here shortly. Now there's nothing to see, so can you all face the other way and proceed in an orderly fashion towards the refreshment marquee. You can either do it now or let the coppers sort you out."

Groans of dissent rumbled through the crowd.

"Well, what's it to be?"

Grumbling, they turned and shuffled towards the marquee. The wail of a siren cut through the noise and a police car screeched into the field parting the crowd in a manner that Reverend Speedwell could only compare to the parting of the Red Sea by Moses.

* * *

Pouring herself a very large sherry, Mrs Mountford crossed the room to the bureau by the window. Placing the glass on the desk, she sat in the swivel chair and gazed out of the window. Something was gnawing at her insides and it wasn't the pills the doctor had given her. They'd gone into the aspidistra pot when he wasn't looking. She chewed at her bottom lip. There was something she couldn't quite put her finger on.

Meanwhile, at the vicarage in Great Houghton, the vicar and Peter Critchley remedied their shock with a bottle of ten-year old Highland malt.

"The police said they'll need statements from everyone in the village, that'll take a time." The vicar's sharp features creased into a frown, "Who could do such a vile thing, Peter?"

"I can't make head nor tail of it all, Vicar. You must wonder what you've come to with only taking over the parish last year." Critchley swirled the whisky round his glass, gazing thoughtfully at it, "The village has never known anything like it. Then out of the blue, two murders in less than a week. First poor old Daphne, then Erica. The killer must have some sort of conscience though don't you think? Leaving posies in their hands?"

"You knew them both quite well didn't you, Peter?" the vicar asked, "must be harder on you than you let on."

"No, not really, Vicar. It was a shock right enough but they were more friends of the wife than mine." Critchley took a long drink from his glass.

The vicar jumped to his feet, "How heartless of me keeping you here. She must feel dreadful. Shouldn't you go home?"

"She'll be all right, Vicar, she don't confide in me no more." He drained his glass and heaved his strapping form from the armchair. "Another one for the road, Vicar?"

The vicar cleared his throat. "I'd feel much better if you went home to your poor wife, Peter. Under normal circumstances she may well be independent but she's just had two of her friends murdered. She must feel pretty vulnerable."

Critchley glowered at him, "You don't know her like I do," he growled, "still, I suppose you're right, I'd best get home. By the way," he smirked, "it's a good job they never got round to judging; my blooms would have well beaten yours this year, I reckon, Vicar."

The following Sunday, after conducting Communion at his own village church in Great Houghton, Reverend Speedwell held a memorial service for the two murdered women at St. Paul's in Little Houghton. A shortage of ordained clergy meant that he had to rotate church services between the four Houghtons. He worked it so that he attended Great and Little Houghton one week and Upper and Lower Houghton the following week. Apart from a few regular stalwarts, Sunday morning congregations were usually sparse but this week St Paul's was packed to capacity. What a pity it was, the vicar thought, that it took two murders to goad his flock into church.

The interior of the church was a mass of flowers donated and arranged by the Mothers' Union. They encircled the huge stone pillars, the pulpit was festooned and the altar could barely be seen through the extravagant displays at the entrance to the chancel. The organist played the gently haunting 'Nimrod' as the church filled.

"Morning, Mrs Mountford," Peter smiled, handing her a hymnbook.

"Good morning, Mr Critchley," she acknowledged, "by the way, I thought you handled the crowd extremely well last Saturday."

"Well, I wasn't a sergeant-major for nothing— but thank you."

After genuflecting in the aisle she shuffled along the second row of pews and sat beside Violet Critchley. "Good morning, my dear," she whispered. For some inexplicable reason she always felt sorry for the woman. Looking older than her fifty-nine years she invariably appeared to be carrying the troubles of the world and this morning she looked as fretful as ever. Mrs Critchley's smile manifested itself as a grimace. The older woman dismissed it as a reflection of the sombre occasion.

* * *

Later that evening Mrs Mountford had cause to remember Mrs Critchley's odd demeanour.

Just before ten o' clock the front doorbell shattered her tranquil Sunday evening. Tutting, she put her book on the coffee table and struggled up reluctantly from the sofa. As she struggled to push her swollen ankles into her slippers the doorbell shrilled again and this time the caller kept the button depressed. "All right," she shouted crossly, "I'm coming as quickly as I can." As it was almost dark outside she peeped through the spy-hole before opening the door to an extremely distressed and dishevelled churchwarden. "Mr Critchley," she gasped, "Come in, man, you look dreadful."

"I thought she was with you, I thought she was---"

She grasped his wrist and pulled his huge frame gently towards the sofa, "Sit down and gather yourself, I'll pour you a brandy, you look as though you need it."

"Whatever's wrong?" she inquired when the brandy had restored some colour to his cheeks, "You said you thought *she* was with me; whom precisely?"

"Violet—you sat with her in church this morning— when she didn't come home I assumed you'd invited her to lunch." He shook his balding head as though trying to clear it. "I should have gone looking for her sooner, I'll never forgive myself."

She recharged his glass.

"We've not been getting on lately so I thought she was just making a point, stupid sod I am."

"You're not making sense," Mrs Mountford was puzzled.

He glared wildly at her. "She's dead! My Violet's dead, murdered---and in the churchyard too----I don't---" his voice trailed off in a stifled sob.

"Surely not," she said inanely, unable to take it all in. "When? What did the police say?"

He clutched the top of his head with trembling hands, "They don't know yet, I've only just found her."

"For God's sake, man! Are you sure she's dead? Come on," she urged. "Now!" she shouted urgently, "Take me to her, she may need an ambulance."

Grabbing his hand roughly this time, she dragged him through to the hall where she shrugged her bulk into a capacious overcoat. Removing her mobile telephone and a torch from the drawer in the hall table she rammed them into her coat pocket and virtually pushed the dazed churchwarden out into the balmy June night. Cursing herself for not keeping the car and learning to drive after Edgar's death, she stumbled along through the village dragging the reluctant Critchley behind her.

Violet Critchley was laid out beneath a crumbling angel on the mouldy tomb of some long dead soul.

"Good God, Critchley, this is ghastly, you poor man."

Even before she shone the torch on her face it was plainly obvious that the woman was dead. Bulging eyes glared sightlessly from a bloated face, purple with blood that had suffused into the tissues when the belt around her neck had throttled the life from her. Lifeless hands clutched a clump of *hedera helix*. Plenty of that in the churchyard, Mrs Mountford thought, but it was too precisely arranged to have been clawed at by a woman in the throes of death.

* * *

Some hours later, with the body removed, police statements taken and Peter Critchley safely sedated at home, a shaken Mrs Mountford gratefully accepted the vicar's offer of a lift home. It was just as well that the police had contacted him.

Although it was two-thirty a.m. and she was shattered, sleep evaded her, even after a relaxing warm bath and a large brandy. She still couldn't shake off the gnawing sensation in the pit of her stomach. What was it? As she agonised over the tragic events of the past few weeks, she knew she was missing something— but what?

The police collected more statements, fingerprints and DNA samples from everyone in the village but made little progress in tracking down the murderer.

June rolled into July and after the funerals of the three women village life settled back into its usual prosaic pace. Although Little Houghton would never be *quite* the same again, the village became a rural idyll once more— outwardly at least. Suspicion turned neighbours against each other. Nothing was put into words but there was a palpable undercurrent of mistrust. Only the men dared to venture out alone at night.

The congregations in Reverend Speedwell's churches dwindled back to the usual few. After the overflowing collection plates at the funerals and memorial services, the meagre Sunday offerings took some getting used to again.

* * *

At the Parish Council meeting in July the chairman announced that the four Houghtons had been selected for a royal visit.

Mrs Mountford could barely contain her excitement. "I met her Majesty once," she bragged, "I invited her to tea if ever she was in the vicinity." She peered over her gold-rimmed half-moon spectacles, "Mind you, it was few years ago now, I doubt if she'd remember."

Contrary to expectations the sovereign had agreed to open the new village hall at Little Houghton on the twenty fifth of August. The vicar was ecstatic and persuaded the Mothers' Union to *'lay on a spread fit for a queen, so to speak'*. The children of the Sunday school and the local primary school, coached by the

vicar, perfected a choral rendition of the National Anthem in its entirety. The inhabitants of each village joined forces to tidy the verges and give all the fences a lick of paint. Little Houghton hadn't been so busy since entering the 'best kept village' competition two years previously. Every house was spruced up, dustbins were removed from view and gardens became a sea of colour. Having been nominated to cast a critical eye over the preparations Mrs Mountford was overjoyed with the results of everyone's labours. "This is just what the village needs after all that dreadful business in June," she told the vicar.

"How right you are, dear lady."

* * *

It was a schoolboy who discovered Ivy Jackson's body behind the new village hall on August the tenth after sneaking behind the building for a smoke. The boy had gone screaming to Peter Critchley's house as it was next to the hall. By the time the police arrived it was difficult to tell who was more distressed, the boy or Critchley.

"The poor man's in a terrible state, Mrs Mountford, and understandably," the vicar informed her when he called to break the news, "yet after the initial shock, the boy was more concerned that his father should discover he'd been smoking." He seated himself on the luxurious Chesterfield sofa stretching his legs out in front of him.

"Ah, the resilience of youth," she sighed wistfully. She handed him a large glass of sherry and settled herself in the armchair.

"Quite so, my dear, those were the days, eh?" He sipped delicately at his sherry.

"I never did thank you for running me home after that awful business with Violet. It was a good job the police informed you."

"They didn't."

"Then how did you know?"

"I was still in church after evensong and heard the rumpus."

"Just as well you did," she said earnestly. "I understand poor Ivy was found with a posy too?" she fished.

"Yes, some clematis or other."

"You don't know which one, by any chance?" she pressed.

"No idea, dear lady, but I managed to acquire a couple of pieces when the police weren't looking," he withdrew an envelope from his inside pocket.

"Vicar, you're a marvel," she beamed. "Now, I don't want you to feel I'm rushing you off, but I need to consult my gardening book. It's my oracle on all matters horticultural; a bit like the Bible is to you I suppose."

He smiled as he reluctantly left the recesses of the Chesterfield, "I must admit, my sermons would be a bit grim without it."

After closing the front door behind him, she walked briskly into the study and emptied the contents of the envelope onto the desk. It was clematis all right but two different varieties. She thumbed excitedly through the index in the gardening book and turned to the section on clematis.

In a flash she knew what had been troubling her these past weeks. She felt giddy as it all slotted into place. "Of course, why didn't I see it before? You stupid woman," she chided herself.

Each victim had been given a plant representing the name of the next victim.

First there was Daphne's murder and she had a posy of heather, otherwise known as Erica. Erica had a posy of violets then poor Violet Critchley was murdered.

Her insides went cold. Violet had a clump of ivy and Ivy Jackson had just been murdered. Something still niggled at her about Daphne Burke. Daphne was the name of a plant too. She was the first victim but surely the murderer would have been unable to resist giving some sort of clue as to his intentions.

Of course— that Sunday in May. That pretty pink shrub in a pot by the pulpit, how could she forget? She'd thought it so pretty that she'd rushed home and looked it up----*Daphne burkwoodii*. What on earth was wrong with her memory lately?

If the murderer didn't reside in Little Houghton he would have escaped DNA testing. That would explain why he had not yet been apprehended.

The vicar didn't live in Little Houghton.

And, being an expert gardener, why would he pretend he had no idea of the name of the clematis? Skimming down the page she soon identified both clematis; the small pink one was *Clematis Montana Elizabeth*. The pretty double white one was the *Duchess of Edinburgh*. She dropped heavily into her chair. "No, it can't be, he wouldn't dare," she said aloud.

Then another realisation jumped into her head. Speedwell was the common name for *Veronica*--- from which the anagram 'one vicar' could be derived.

Veronica Mountford's doorbell was ringing ....

*

Time Wins
By Warren Scott-Morrow

"I still maintain that time travel is an impossibility, no matter what you say."

"It all depends on your approach, Adam. The conventional idea of sending a solid object through the time barrier has been proved to be mere idealistic claptrap. Wells' time machine was no more than unenlightened fantasy. I have studied this subject from every conceivable angle."

"And you believe you can send me into a future zone?"

"Absolutely, though not your body. After all, you were selected out of all the potential candidates because of your own rare gift."

"Astral projection."

"Exactly. So few individuals have the ability to use mental power to cause their spirit to leave their body."

"True, but there are limits. Over the years I've caused my ectoplasmic form to travel all over the world but not even spirits can travel into the past or future."

"Just because it hasn't been done doesn't mean it can't be. I'm convinced that my machine can actually send your ethereal form into a pre-determined future for a limited duration."

"But why astral projection? Can't it send a man's spirit ..."

"No. Your mind has to be the agent to remove the spirit. The machine cannot actually extract the soul from a person."

"Well, I'm prepared to give it a try. It's worth the risk element. When I succeed it'll be the greatest moment in world history. It will even shadow the invention of the wheel, the moon landing or the American-Russian peace treaty. The name Adam Pope will go down in history."

"Indeed it will. We can learn so much from the future. I'd rather use this method than sending a solid body anyway."

"Why?"

"If a man could go in physical form he would not only be detected but could tamper with the destiny of humanity."

"I'd never be so foolhardy, Doctor Garvey."

"Perhaps not intentionally. Yet you might be inadvertently set off for some sort of disaster. Alternatively, you might be apprehended, which would lead to awkward circumstances."

"But this way I'll be like the invisible man."

"Yes, if you want to use another Wells analogy. Yet you will be more than just invisible. You will be tangible. You will be able to study without fear of interruptions or complications."

"So all you want me to do is observe."

"In a way, but more specific. The subject that you will be investigating will be yourself."

"What?" gasped Adam, who had been relaxing in an easy chair. Jumping up, he stormed across the room and stared down at the little bespectacled scientist who sat calmly with his chin resting on his folded hands.

"I don't know whether I much like the idea of that. With all the places I could go and all the people I could see there doesn't seem any point …"

"It will be far easier and more rewarding for your soul to seek out its own self. It will do so by instinct."

Without moving, the scientist glanced up at his test subject, who was pacing the room deep in thought. Pausing for a reaction, which did not come, he continued, "You will be able to discover something of the circumstances of your future self's life and read the mind for information on the state of the world. You will also register the emotions of your future self at the point of your arrival."

"But won't the future me realize?"

"No. Although you will be aware of your other self's thoughts you won't be detected by him."

"That doesn't make sense."

"Oh, it does. On previous occasions when you have projected you have observed people and events, but has anyone ever noticed you?"

"No, but this is different. As it will be a version of me, surely …"

"No, no, no. It will be the same as if you are studying someone else. The only advantage is that you will be able to read your own future mind. Although, of course, no one else's."

Adam hesitated and sitting down again, frowned in silent concentration for a few moments before speaking again.

"It all sounds fine so far, but one thing is still troubling me. As I've no idea of my lifespan, what happens if I appear in a time after my death?"

"I had already considered that. I can determine the exact amount of time I send you. Initially, you will only go a year forward. Due to your youth and good health it is statistically improbable that you will die within that period, though it's not too late to opt out."

"I wouldn't dream of it. I've taken risks with less excitement or potential gain that this."

"Splendid. Now let's get to my lab."

* * *

Going out of the friendly, relaxing living room and into the stark, chilling atmosphere of the laboratory, Adam felt an involuntary shudder. Ignoring the feeling he laid down on the hard couch, where he allowed the scientist to fit a cold, metal frame to his head. Plastic leads led to a large, steel cabinet with a colourful array of switches, buttons and dials on the front.

"I won't bother you with the technicalities of the process. It would be beyond your comprehension."

"Fair enough. Science never was my strong point. Well, I'm ready. How long will I be there?"

"A few minutes. Until we are certain that everything will be fine. It's best not to overdo your trip. When the panel lights up I want you to relax and send your astral form into the machine. Oh, and good luck."

Pressing a button, Garvey watched the pulsing activity on the instrument panel and listened to the steady, low tone commence.

Moments later, Adam experienced the familiar sensation as he rose from his body and entered the machine. Before he could contemplate the strangeness affecting him, he was whirling in a vortex.

Without even a moment to panic the spinning had ceased and he felt himself standing in a road in the centre of London. Traffic passed around and through him. Everything seemed just how he had always known it. Yet was it? He began to notice changes. The fashions were unlike any previously known to him. A row of shops had been replaced by an office block. There were several new models of cars.

A roaring sound caused him to look up. A squadron of jets raced across the sky. They were of an unrecognisable type. The world had progressed greatly for a mere twelve months. Before he could speculate further he sensed a strong presence nearby. He was in contact with his own mind. The feeling was from straight ahead. Although he knew that he was facing his other self he could see nothing. Yet he could sense the emotion.

Fear. Dominating and gripping fear.

As he attempted to ascertain the cause he began to regret his trip. Could it be that he had been detected and diagnosed for what he was? The desire to get away tugged at him, but he could do nothing until recalled.

Tense seconds weighed him down until he felt the machine drawing him home where he hasted into his prone body.

After a few moments of stunned thoughts he rose slowly to his feet.

"How are you feeling?" enquired a worried looking Garvey.

Shakily he poured out the details to his listener.

"I can explain the part concerning the fashions, buildings, cars and planes. Due to a slight malfunction your spirit was sent ten years into the future."

"I thought you had everything under control", snapped the time traveller, more in fright than anger.

"You are forgetting that we are still at an experimental stage."

"What about the fact that I couldn't see my future self?" asked Adam, somewhat calmer. "And what about the fear that I clearly picked up?"

"Regarding your first question, I don't know. As for the fear, I believe some outside influence was responsible. If you had been spotted the reaction would more likely have been surprise and curiosity."

"So, what happens next?"

"That rather depends on you. The fact that you went nine years too far disturbs me. I'd rather not send you again until further tests have been made."

"But if I did travel ten years it doesn't mean the machine is at fault. Maybe I was guided there."

"Hmm. Maybe. Perhaps there was a threat to your future self and your spirit can be of some help."

"Well, then, what are we waiting for?"

"I don't know." Doctor Garvey paused briefly. "If you're prepared to risk it again we'll do it. This time I'll set the dial for ten years."

"Give me longer this time. At least now I have some idea of what I'm going into."

"Very well. You can have fifteen minutes. Now, if you're ready, please lie down and we'll repeat the process."

Flashing. Humming. Spinning.

The same road in London. Yet was he on a road? As he looked down he saw smooth, glowing metal. In alarm he spun round. There were buildings, but composed of the same glowing metal as the road. They were without doors or windows. Making his way down the road he could see no end to the identical structures. There were no signs of inhabitants.

His attention was attracted to a light in the far distance. In a moment it had flashed past, shining like a miniature sun. Its speed was incredible. Other frightening thoughts crawled into his mind. Was he still on Earth? Glancing upwards he was relieved to see the sun, blue sky and the familiar clouds of home.

Then he began to sense that someone was close by. Perhaps watching from one of the strange buildings. Instinctively, he began to make his way towards the person.

Stopping in an empty square, he realized that it was immediately in front of him, although invisible. It struck him that he was again in contact with his future self. The fear was there but still no reason. All he could see were the buildings and they looked innocuous enough. What struck him as strange was that his future self was stationary.

Determined to find out if there was anything in the buildings to cause consternation, the time traveller drifted through them one by one. He found them to contain highly advanced technology, which fascinated him without appearing threatening. A he started to return to his future self he felt a sudden spinning and was back in the laboratory.

The scientist dashed over in alarm. "Are you alright?" he asked in a rising tone. "Tell me what happened."

Quickly, Adam related the story. Garvey listened before interrupting with a gasp of disbelief.

"That's impossible. You must have been mistaken. You can't have encountered your other self."

"But I did. It wasn't imagination. The feelings were as before. Anyway, why do you think I couldn't?"

"Because I set the controls for ten years but you were transported a hundred years. If your other self had been alive in that time he would have been a hundred and twenty eight."

Adam blanched at the news. "But that's absurd", he burst out, "the time dial on your machine has to be wrong."

"I doubt it, especially when considering your description of the world then. Do you seriously think that it could have only been ten years ahead?"

"I suppose not", he answered with a worried frown, "yet how could my future self still be alive?"

"Maybe it was some kind of medical breakthrough to prolong the human exis …"

"No. I can't accept that. My other self was the only person there and scared to death of goodness knows what."

"Look, perhaps it's time to call it a day. We're getting way out of our depth!"

"No chance! I'm determined to get to the bottom of this mystery. I'm sure you're equally anxious for results."

"So you actually want me to send you back again!"

"Too damned right! This time, send me one hundred years and we'll see what the outcome is. And keep me there for an hour. Hopefully I'll learn something relevant."

"Very well. It's your decision. I can't doubt your courage, but I must warn you that it may lead to as yet unexpected circumstances."

"Don't lecture me. I'm game for whatever may happen. Surely you don't think I could go through the rest of my life with this on my mind? Don't you understand? I've got to solve the matter once and for all."

The scientist nodded in resignation as he turned to the machine to set it up for the next trip, while the time traveller took his place on the couch.

* * *

This time, his arrival shook him far more than on the previous occasions. As he looked around in horror he could hardly believe what he saw. In every direction was total desolation. He was on a bleak and rocky landscape pock-marked with craters. It was hardly recognisable as the Earth. Wondering if he was still on his home world he gazed up into the black sky to see a full moon. A study of the stars showed him that they, too, seemed to be in the right positions.

Yet what had happened to the world? What tragedy had turned it into a dead planet? Was it a natural or man-made disaster? How far was he into the future?

It was patently clear that the trip was a waste of time. There could be no possibility of encountering his future self. Even if the theory of his prolonged lifespan had been correct he could never have survived such a holocaust. No living creature could.

The next moment a strange manifestation began to make itself known to him. He was not alone.

Intolerable. It could not be real.

Yet he had to face the facts. He had to believe the evidence of his senses, otherwise he must be insane and that was one idea he could not accept.

Consequently, it was not something conjured up by his imagination. It was all so incredibly real.

In a world where the human race was extinct his future self was still living. Alive and terribly scared. The fear that he had detected on previous trips was much greater. So unexpected was the encounter that he began to feel terror welling up inside himself. He turned and fled. Losing all track of time and distance he raced away across the burned out terrain. He seemed to have been fleeing for an eternity when, with relief, he felt the spinning sensation grip his ectoplasmic form and whip him away.

For a while he lay in a state of shock oblivious to everything around him. Garvey realized Adam was in a desperate condition and injected a tranquilizer into his arm.

Several hours later the amorphous mists began to dissipate and Adam Hope returned from his enforced slumber feeling much better. Slowly, as if reliving the experiences, he related the events of his nightmare trip. Garvey was more shaken by Adam's experiences from the future. Adam was to learn that he had travelled forward a thousand years.

For a long time the two of them discussed all the mysteries since the commencement of the tests. Adam began to wonder if something had happened, or was to happen, to make him immortal. Immortal in the spiritual rather than physical sense, like some ghost forever chained to the Earth. If the human race was extinct a thousand years hence and no other spirits had been detected, then presumably they had gone on to heaven or hell. If that was the case then why had he been left behind?

There were so many questions, yet no answers were forthcoming. Only the theories remained to taunt them both.

As the last trip had been so negative Adam was resolved to make no more until Garvey had given the machine a thorough overhaul. On that point they were in agreement.

ONE YEAR LATER

Adam Hope was once more lying on the couch. The fear of his last trip had worn off with the passage of time and with his faith in Garvey's abilities. The controls were set for exactly nine years into the future to give Adam a second chance to find a clue to the enigma. His astral self made its familiar journey through the machine.

Arriving at the London street from his first time trip he soon sensed that he was being observed by someone who was showing a strong interest in him. Yet how could anyone be aware of him? At first he was unnerved and then he became afraid as he could find no logical answer. Shortly, his observer vanished, which made him relax and feel safe again. Then he was whisked back to his own time.

Not wishing to discuss the matter yet, he asked permission to be sent ninety nine years. The scientist was too pleased that his machine was no longer playing up to pursue any line of interrogation at the moment.

Back to the scene of the strange buildings went the intrepid Adam. 'At least there is no one here to watch me.'

Once again the feeling was with him and once again he was afraid. Still there was no sign of the other party. After a while his unseen watcher moved away in the direction of the buildings. Had he come from one of them? No, they were uninhabited. His previous visit had proved that.

His previous visit!

A thought began to evolve as a possibility occurred. He laughed to himself.

Back in his time zone he explained all.

"So", Garvey smiled in satisfaction, "the watcher who had frightened you was your own spiritual self from the initial time trips. The reason that you could not observe your future self a year ago was that you were not studying your real future self by your astral form from these two recent visits."

"Obvious when you know, isn't it? That's why I still seemed to be living in a hundred years and a thousand years. And as there were only two of me, it is clear that I won't visit those particular time zones again. Yet I'll have to go back nine hundred and ninety nine years and be afraid or I'll be causing a paradox."

"How can you be afraid if we've already found the answer?"

"I don't know. I'm sure there's a perfectly simple explanation, but you've got to admit that I have to go back to that final zone."

"Yes, it's obvious that you do, so you must, but don't worry about a thing. I'll bring you back in a few minutes."

"Fine! Let's get it over with."

* * *

And so the trip was made. All progressed smoothly and Adam was back in the dead world.

The next moment a searing flash ripped painfully through him and he knew what had happened. Something had gone wrong with the time machine. His physical body in the laboratory had died. His spirit began to fade. He was more afraid than he had ever been. He did not want to die. He was too young.

With his last remaining thought he sensed his self from the previous time trip starting to materialise. Frantically, he attempted to send out a warning to his other self. It was no good.

However the laws of time worked they would not allow him to change his destiny.

A year in the past he had thought he was immortal. A thousand years in the future the human race was no more but his astral self was still alive and in two separate entities.

In the present he was dead.

*

My Chosen Path
By Wyn Land

Having had the advantage of knowing the names, some verbal anecdotes and the approximate locations of my eight great grandparents, gave me plenty of scope when I started to delve into my family background. I had no particular priority, expecting little more than basic records of birth, marriage and death of my humble, impecunious relations. I obtained a number of essential certificates, running up quite a bill, knowing that I must assure myself that I was following the correct trail before I launched into researching parish records.

At the time, journeys to London, heaving large heavy ledgers of
Indexes at St. Catharine's House and train journeys to Record Offices, followed by stays at B&Bs were necessary. These visits had to be undertaken on holiday dates as I was working full time. The limited time available heightened my resolve and interest; how I enjoyed all those hours of consulting books, culminating in finding, or hoping that I had found the right ancestor, before I ordered a certificate. Much time at Record Offices was spent in copying information from original registers in pencil. That evening was spent having fun sitting up in bed sorting the various names and discovering which family was mine, then drawing the appropriate trees. Ancestors originated from a number of villages in Gloucestershire, Dorset, Somerset, Devon, Wiltshire, Oxfordshire and Ireland to date. It was in the nineteenth century that work brought the various branches to Bristol where I was born.

Knowing that my husband was always interested in places and travelling, was a help, we camped at different sites near villages which I wished to explore, or close to Record Offices. Whereas I would keep my eyes glued to parish registers and scribble happily all day hardly stopping for lunch and refreshments, my "other half " soon learned to sneak off for a coffee. I must admit that he was much better than I was at deciphering old writing, reading wills and managing fiche and film technology. I used to set him a particular task whereas I consulted all kinds of indexes and books, looking up more and more surnames as I discovered the maiden names of brides every time I found a marriage. Peter took interest upon finding historical references in the registers. He was intrigued to find mention of a cook to Napoleon on St. Helena during a search at Trowbridge, the Wiltshire Record Office.

Snatching coffee in rooms set aside for this purpose often brought us into contact with other researchers and we enjoyed exchanging experiences. One does meet the occasional bore who insists on relating details of his famous or affluent forbears, however most people are very pleasant and sometimes suggestions of new avenues to find missing relatives were exchanged. At Gloucester, we found a nearby café that sold a variety of quickly prepared snacks. It was called "Fat Mamas", we thought this was hilarious and on subsequent visits made a point of visiting it.

So much research turns out to be frustrating because of missing registers destroyed by damp or mice years ago, and wills destroyed in the second world war bombings. Many births and christenings were not recorded; some couples did not in fact marry and if a common name is sought it is possible to buy a number of wrong certificates. On the positive side many family history societies have indexed a number of parish and census records. General Registrar records can now be accessed on-line thus future research should not be so arduous. Family History societies provide magazines and lists of members' interests, which can often be a great help. During the course of seeking ancestors one inevitably comes across remote cousins, sometimes one finds second or third cousins of whose existence one was unaware. Usually we meet up – in one case an Australian third cousin looked us up when she and her husband were in the UK. Such meetings give great pleasure, sometimes we learn of all kinds of scandal and folklore and of course sad events. One needs to be cautious that information received in this way is checked and that one is not taken advantage of by a few researchers who want to receive the results of someone's hours of work without reciprocating at all. At one point, arriving at a marriage of a John Smith filled me with despair. Which of four possibilities was mine? I left it for several years! Then I tried again – still no evidence, but I contacted another researcher. After three months I put it out of my mind, then I received a lovely letter from a remote cousin who had been very busy. Through his information I was able to ascertain the correct line and was led back on several other lines. The moral is, "do not despair," even with common names.

It is surprising sometimes to find that families who appear very poor might have descended from skilled forebears who wrote wills. These are most helpful, especially in the case of relatives without children who often named other relatives giving married names and specific relationships. Early wills appear very quaint to contemporary readers. They invariably start bequeathing the writer's soul to God and stating in which churchyard their body was to be buried, often giving money to the church for the benefit of the poor. The terms of the will follow which usually shows the occupation of the deceased, as animals, scythes, bushels of wheat or looms make clear. Clothes were shared between beneficiaries, particularly if a woman was bequeathed an item of clothing such as a best petticoat, a second best petticoat and various kerchiefs. Beds and flock mattresses were mentioned in a similar way. A "potte" was a three feet metal cooking pot which could stand over a fire. "my chamber whooleye" probably meant that Maurice Sparke who wrote a will in 1551 was bequeathing his room to his wife. I keep checking to see if names mentioned might prove or disprove that Maurice is my ancestor. He was obviously a yeoman, or maybe I have descended from one of the other Sparks men, copies of whose wills I have, one of which was a weaver. Hope springs eternal that another early will might refer to a married daughter, which could be the link I seek to give proof. Another approach might bring results if I traced who inherited a particular plot of land or left a record of selling it to another resident. If I could fill the gap in my records of the continuity of this family for the next hundred and fifty years or so, it would lead directly to my maternal grandfather James Samuel Sparks. Apparently, on one occasion, as part of the mounted police escort to a royal visit to Bristol, a lady, who considered him to be handsome, pointed him out. My grandmother, who happened to be standing in the crowd, turned around and proudly announced that he was her husband. James was far from pleased with Emma some time later when he learned that she had been out with the suffragettes! Early nineteenth century wills are still deferential to the church, but make conditions for a wife who must not be co-habiting with another man if she is to receive an inheritance. How life has changed in the following two centuries in so many ways. Witnesses can be used to show that a person was alive at a specific date or alternatively may be able to distinguish between two people with identical names. Early burial registers do not give ages; there is not always sufficient evidence to be sure if the entry refers to an adult, child or infant.

Information about how to explore one's roots is widely available in books, libraries and on-line. A warning about proof needed to prevent incorrect lines is vital. Spellings vary over time of both names and places they are easily corrupted, or wrongly deciphered. Son-in-law could mean stepson, godson possibly might mean grandson. Sometimes a brick wall really is a brick wall. Often it is possible to circumvent the problem by coming from another direction. It is always a challenge, but the detective work involved makes this hobby exciting. It can be left and picked up again at any time; we cannot hurt past generations or alter the course of their lives. A visit to Kew to consult the National Archives needs careful planning if full use is to be made of documents, which have to be ordered. Some army records are on film or fiche the amount of information gleaned varies considerably, it could be a lot or very little. Furthermore some records were destroyed in the war. Early records require dates or regiments in order to locate them. If lucky, physical attributes, medical details and places of service can be quite revealing.

Often because of the temptation to explore as far back as possible, more recent history is ignored. In order to preserve as much as possible, a niece helped me pool our old photographs and we now have a number of named transparencies from which copies can be made for interested parties. At the time, this niece was living in Bristol, and I was able to stay with her and her husband. On one such occasion a cousin of mine, hearing that I was around, invited me to her daughter's wedding, the reception being held at home in the garden, I knew they had little money, both bride and groom having just completed their university courses. It was a lovely simple wedding, made all the more enjoyable as I met four cousins, several of their children, and an uncle and was able to catch up on family news. I treasure this memory; it was made all the more poignant as this lovely girl developed Hodgkin's disease not many years later and sadly died. I can remember her happy smiling face very clearly, but know that the immediate family must have had to see her slowly decline. It seems to make no sense that someone with so much to live for is snatched away at such a young age.

I made another visit, staying with my niece when I planned to visit my sole remaining aunt who was living in a village not far from Torquay; I left my grip in a left luggage compartment at Bristol Temple Meads and continued on my journey to Devon by train, then by bus. I had not seen Aunt Ethel for a long time, I wondered if I'd recognize her. She was quite short and slim, but as soon as she spoke, she sounded just like my other aunts, her sisters whom I had had more contact with as they had remained in Bristol. I think it should be described as a family voice! She offered me a glass of sherry. I smiled, recognizing that offering sherry reminded me of that branch of the family who did just that each Christmas. Ethel was my father's youngest sister, she always remembered his birthday and sent him a card; I knew this pleased him as he always wrote her a letter in reply. We began to talk about the family; she chuckled telling me how my father who had worked on the railway, often on night shifts once put the tin kettle on to make a cup of tea, fell asleep so burnt a hole in it! She was eleven years younger than he was, when he brought my mother home one evening, she was obviously in the way so he gave her 6d. to make herself scarce. Looking at one of the shelves in a china cabinet I recognized two cups and saucers with a red and gold band that exactly matched two we had had at home. "Oh yes," she commented, "they came from my grandfather's house, as we shared the set between us all." I still wonder if the date of 1823 has significance that has eluded me. Our conversation turned to living family members and not wishing to appear too obvious I stored the details and wrote notes on the return train journey. Showing her a photograph, I was pleased when she said, " I think that is my grandfather." Just what I wanted to hear; the time spent together had been full of interest. Aunt Ethel would not hear of my taking the bus to the station, she arranged for a neighbour to take us there, "I shall pay him", she assured me - actually I was more concerned about the poor chap's emphysema, his breathing was very laboured, but we arrived in good time to catch the last train to Bristol and say our goodbyes.

Arriving at Bristol, I had a mad dash to recover my grip before finding the appropriate platform for the London train. I had told my son that I hoped to be home late that night, but not to worry as if I missed the last train I'd find somewhere to stay and return in the morning. Arriving at Paddington, I realized the pointlessness of catching a tube to King's Cross in time to take the train home, I must find somewhere to stay. A huge brightly lit sign advertised a local hotel, goodness that would be expensive I decided, knowing that I'd already spent a lot on train fares. I started walking outside the station, believing that the bright light I could see in the distance was a small hotel; I crossed the road, thinking that if I could stay there it would be good to get off the streets at that time of night. The light was still some way off when I became aware of a small establishment in the open doorway of which a man was standing. I asked if he had a room and paid the £12. he asked for it, after enquiring if it was just for one. His next remark I thought very odd. "I'll give you the family room, it wouldn't be fair to ask you to go upstairs." Having asked what time I'd like breakfast, he showed me the toilet, gave me the room key and said goodnight. There was a large double bed, a couple of singles and a washbasin, I noticed that the towel had an iron mould stain and looked none too clean. Suddenly there was a very loud mechanical noise; some sort of vehicle I presumed. I discovered in the morning it was the train using the post office line to the main post office sorting office at Mount Pleasance. No one could possibly sleep as it made a thunderous noise at fairly frequent intervals but it did stop in the small hours, giving some respite. Then I heard a couple of men's foreign voices nearby and felt uncomfortable, I was lying fully clothed on the bed, thinking "at least I'm off the street", more loud roaring of the train. A little later, an Asian voice could be heard saying "hullo" several times, he repeated this knocking at a door, was it mine or next door? I froze, there was only one thing to do, keep perfectly still and hope he'd go away, which after another attempt he did. I made sure that my grip was fully packed, eyed the window, and assured myself that no escape would be possible. About half an hour later, a lot of girlish laughter could be heard, footsteps running upstairs. If anything happened to me, none of the family would have a clue where I was. My husband was in Europe on a Mountain Leadership course, one of the girls was on holiday in Europe, the other working away, and no doubt I'd survive until the morning when I could make a quick get away. For breakfast I was offered tea and toast, another middle- aged German lady, was also eating. I suppose this episode could be explained as "an experience". Should I ever again need accommodation in similar circumstances, I'd plump for the expensive hotel. On the next occasion I took off on my family search, Peter's parting shot was "and don't get yourself in a brothel".

I became expert at making the best use of opportunities. After child minding in London, I stayed an extra night in order to spend a day at the Genealogists. Sometimes I was able to add to my information; always I had a fascinating time browsing all kinds of books not otherwise readily available. I was not pleased on one such day when there was a security alarm concerning the I.R.A. but the society provided us with a free coffee at a café a few streets away providing us with an unintended opportunity to talk to other members. Findings were invariably of infant and children's burials, accidents to breadwinners causing wives to apply to the parish for relief and the need to take in washing or lodgers. Very many remarriages were made most likely out of necessity, in order to look after children. It is a bonus if an accident was reported in a local newspaper. My paternal gt. gt. grandfather's case illustrates this perfectly. George Needs was badly injured when his pea jacket was caught in machinery that he was using on board a tugboat docked at the Mardyke on the River Avon in Bristol. He died the next day at the Infirmary; records held about the hospital admission showed the extent of his injuries. Several family members have felt as shocked as I was and we needed a little while to grieve, he was our direct ancestor, it seemed sad that we had known nothing about it, but it must have been much more terrible for his family. He was forty and was described as a mariner on boats travelling between his home city and Waterford in Ireland. Often coroners' reports have been lost so the only hope of finding out the full facts is from a newspaper. Many details are distressing, families losing many infants, children, or young adults. One single mother mentioned in a bastardy case was very, very, young. I can only guess at the circumstances, which resulted in this event, believing that she was probably working away from home. Her son's father was named, but my attempts to trace him have been unsuccessful. My Mitchell line includes a wife-selling incident. A Simon Stone Mitchell sold his wife, Sarah to a man called Larcombe; she bore him a number of children. When he could no longer support her because of his age and health, Sarah applied to the parish for help. Simon stated, that none of the children were his although they all bore the name Mitchell, as she was legally still his wife. My connection to this story occurs as my 3x gt. grandfather, a lath maker was his uncle. It is no wonder that I am careful if researchers on this line at this time make contact, they may be unaware of the circumstances, so far none have.

Sometimes I only have a name in my records. It gives me pleasure to know that Hugh & Alice Watts at Sydling St. Nicholas in Dorset, and Thomas & Susan Stinchcombe, living at Tortworth in Gloucestershire were ancestors of the fourteenth generation and William & Joanne Battman at Bitton were also direct ancestors of the thirteenth Generation. It so happens that this latter couple are also ancestors of W. G. Grace, the cricketer. Being a doctor and a surgeon, it is also of interest to find that he signed the death certificate of a relative on another line. It is indeed a small world, one can never be too sure of what we might find, both good and bad, our forbears were just like us, human with strengths and weaknesses. There has always been a lot of upward and downward social mobility in Great Britain, unfortunately, records of the most humble are usually only found in settlement, removal, criminal or transportation documents, other than basic christening, marriage or burial records. Every discovery might bring a surprise, or shed light on a character.

Although I retain a wealth of knowledge about family matters, I am selective about information I write about or pass on. It is particularly important to consider the feelings of those living relatives about not only themselves but their memories of those close to them who have died. A few confidences I would never reveal, most make interesting or comical snippets; one or two I have passed on verbally, to be recorded by trusted family members when the older relatives are no longer around. It would be so nice to be able to harness the energy of younger relatives who have computer skills, unfortunately, they are all busy studying, earning a living, or are involved in the general whirlwind of life. I have my uses as a consultant when the national curriculum specifies that an assignment about the Second World War requires the verbal input of someone who lived through it. All I ask is that my files are not disposed of, they may be shared between the various branches, as modern life separates us from our roots and technology, with compact discs and digital cameras items can easily be replicated. I am hopeful that someone will be able to help me consolidate my findings. I have various stories and interesting facts, each in its own transparency, and quite a collection of copies of wills, The family trees are safely stored on CD's and I have a programme with the facility of adding photographs to each individual. Perhaps one or two of my relations will meet up one day in order to complete the family saga if I cannot.

It is obvious that to write a good family history one needs to be focused, keep to one main family surname and define a time scale. I concede that I have done none of these things, although I have tried to be rigorous in factual detail, some will find my approach very fuzzy, for which I make no apology. It has been my choice to indulge myself on an enjoyable journey, being answerable to no one. Had I been a millionaire, genealogists could have been employed, conclusions would have arisen sooner and more facts might now be available, but what fun would have been missed. This type of research has to be of the stop-go variety that fits in with family responsibilities, work and other interests. It can be left and picked up at any time, and puzzling over the next move helps washing up and ironing to be less of a chore.

Every town or village has a point of interest or someone famous connected to it. Bristol will always be associated with Isambard Kingdom Brunel, he designed the famous Clifton Suspension Bridge, which spans the river Avon, and the S.S. Great Britain, which was brought back from the Falklands in 1970 and is a great tourist attraction. The Theatre Royal is the oldest one in Britain still in use. All my family and friends worked in firms, which are well known, such as Frys, Wills, or B.A.C. It is to be hoped that even those who profess no interest in their roots might find something to interest them in the growth of industry in the city. Often a place has been important at a particular time in history, it is when one embarks on an ancestral hunt that these facts emerge. Maybe the fact that my ancestors walked past the Tortworth chestnut tree when they walked towards the church might provide some with a feeling of awe because it is now at least 1,000 years old. So much more remains to be discovered, did the Paul family originate from Europe and were once named Paulet? Maybe my Irish Protestant family members came from Scotland or emigrated from England. I have learnt an awful lot from my individualistic approach, from which it must be obvious that I am as enthusiastic as ever about researching my family, I can thoroughly recommend it.

*

Once We Were Famous
By Edna Stacey

Sometimes a small part of history becomes so intriguing that one is compelled to seek an answer. Such is the question I felt over a local landmark - The Stone Cross. I have looked at early town history and tried to piece together plausible evidence. What I found was a large, disseminated jigsaw puzzle, which when put together does make sense. Here are the results of my findings and the suggestion that March was once a very important place.

In the Middle Ages it was almost unknown for anyone to take a holiday as we know it today, but the origin of the word 'holiday' comes from the many 'holy days', which were observed all those years ago by the church. Occasionally, in time of great disasters such as flood and plague, those that felt the need, travelled to far off places to seek spiritual advancement by getting as close to the roots of their beliefs as possible. As people were converted to Christianity and learned about Jesus of Nazareth and Mary his mother, they wanted to feel part of that revelation. Those who could not travel to the Holy Land travelled within their own country to visit the many shrines, which were either buildings that contained the relics of those who had done much good within their community or had been built on the site of a religious experience. These travellers were called pilgrims. Pilgrimages were not grim occasions even though the journey had its hardships. There was a holiday atmosphere with singers and pipers in attendance. There would be nobles and their retinues and poorer folk on foot. Travel would be slow with frequent stops at churches, inns and religious houses on route. Soon the church began to insist some sort of approval for the journey from the bishop. This meant that intending pilgrims would gather at a designated church for a blessing, wearing the pilgrim garb of a long smock with hood, a staff, and a large hat. Pilgrims were called palmers after earlier pilgrims who had returned from the Holy Land with palms or leaves and sometimes a palmer would undertake a pilgrimage on behalf of someone else. Each shrine had its own symbol, which would be worn with pride. A cockleshell depicted a completed pilgrimage to Compastella.

The Pilgrim's badge found at Doddington in 1976.

Walsingham seemed to favour badges depicting the Annunciation, while others issued leather flasks to hold water from holy wells and sacred springs.

Such a well existed at Exning near Newmarket called St. Wendred's Well. King Anna lived near there. In 1976 a pilgrim's badge, authenticated by the British Museum, was found a Doddington. This suggests that pilgrims did pass through the area on their way to Walsingham and maybe Doddington was one of those special churches where the pilgrims met for their blessing.

On the eastern side of England the main sites were Lindisfarne, Walsingham and Canterbury. Walsingham shrine was founded in 1061at the time of a great religious upheaval in the Holy Land and was a copy of the house at Nazareth; during the reign of Edward I it became known as 'England's Nazareth'. By the end of the 15th century it was the most important and popular pilgrimage site in England. Pilgrims travelling to this place would plan their routes to coincide with places that could offer them sustenance and a bed for sleep. Such journeys could take them through the marshes of fenland. Travelling from the north or midlands to Crowland they would walk on to Thorney, or if from the south from Ely and Chatteris, to arrive at Doddington where the Bishop of Ely had a palace and where close by there was a church that contained the relics of a woman who was renowned for her miracles.

This woman was St Wendreda, who is said to have been one of the daughters of King Anna and sister to Etheldreda the founder of the Abbey at Ely. Wendreda, a nun, came to March, which was then a hamlet of Doddington, to tend the sick and dying fenlanders. There is still an area in March close to the church called 'The Nunnery'. In 1814 an old messuage on that site was sold by auction, but we cannot say for certain if pilgrims ever stayed there and as there is no mention of it in the Domesday survey we must assume it was a date later than 1084 but it would have been a natural thing to do and one way for the nuns to make a living as they continued their work of growing herbs and tending the sick. The fen 'ague', a form of malaria, plague and ergotism from eating decayed corn, were common illnesses during that time.

In 1016, the Saxon army, commanded by King Ethelred's son Edmund Ironside was preparing for battle in a final effort to drive out Danish invaders. Edmund sought permission from the Abbott of Ely for the body of St. Wendreda to be carried into battle. Edmund believed that Wendreda would grant them a miracle and victory would be his. The battle was fought and lost on St. Luke's day, near the village of Ashington in Essex. The victorious Danes took the coffin to King Knut who, on hearing the St. Wendreda story, embraced the Christian faith. Her body was returned to the Saxons and enshrined at Canterbury, where it remained for 300 years. In 1343 the relics of St. Wendreda were returned to March and enclosed in a stone Sepulchre.

As well as the relics of St Wendreda the March church had other similarities to Walsingham. In the Churchwarden Records there are several entries that tell of 'Gabriel' and one entry for 'Mary'. Both were ornate statues and together with the Sepulchre had perpetual illumination by candles; the wax paid for by donations.

With colourful wall paintings and stain glass windows it was a wondrous sight for weary travellers.

Walsingham featured early in March history. The manor of Eastwood, also known as Lexhams, originated as a ⅛ fee held by the Bishop for 5s. In 1302 John de Estwode was the tenant and in 1346 Sir William de Thorpe. It came into the possession of the Lexham family in the 15th century. Margaret the widow of William Lexham and Margaret Rosse her daughter were involved in a law suit over the retention of some manorial deeds and a forged will of William Lexham. This will was produced by John Farewell and Richard Vowell, priors of Walsingham and purported to bequeath Eastwood manor to the Priory. The defendants of William Lexham were successful in their suit. The manor passed to Anthony Hansard a nephew of William Lexham, whose relict Alice passed it in 1541 to Sir John Hynde, sergeant-at-law. His son Francis was a leading freeholder of the manor of Doddington. Elizabeth Hynde relict of William, Francis's son, conveyed it in 1606 to Sir John Peyton, who later became lord of the manor of Doddington. Sir Anthony Hansart, High Sheriff for both the counties of Cambridgeshire and Huntingdonshire, married Kathren, the sister of Sir Robard Southwell the personal adviser to two kings, Henry VII and HenryVIII; the Southwell family lived at Hatchwood Manor in Knight's End, March and was probably how the ancient track got it's name.

As well as brasses to commemorate the Hansart and Southwell families, there is on the church wall a stone shield emblazoned with a swan and believed to be the emblem of the 'de Bohun' family or even that of Henry IV or V. The de Bohun family became prominent in the 12th century. Throughout the 13th and 14th centuries various members of the family claimed Earldoms in many English counties. The most powerful, which lasted 174 years from 1200 until 1343 was that of Earl's of Hereford and Constables of all England. The de Bohun badge of seal was a white or silver swan.

The swan seal of Mary de Bohun, mother of King Henry V

William de Bohun, Earl of Northamptonshire, married Elizabeth de Badlesmere, the widow of Edmund, Lord Mortimer Earl of March. Anne the granddaughter of

Edmund Mortimer and (great granddaughter of the second surviving son of Edward III) married Richard, Earl of Cambridge, (the son of the fourth surviving son of Edward III) and their son became Edward IV Earl of March. Mary de Bohun married Henry of Bolingbroke, Duke of Buckinghamshire (Edward III's grandson) and cousin of the then Earl of March (Richard II), when she was just 10 and Henry was 13. Henry became Henry IV.

Many royal visitors went to Walsingham and by the mid 13th century had become prominent as the resort of Royal and aristocratic pilgrims. It is quite feasible that they would have come to March on their way.

Henry III made substantial gifts to Walsingham including in 1246 a golden crown for the statue of Mary. Edward I is recorded as having made twelve visits and Henry VI, three. The first Edward vowed he owed his life to Our Lady of Walsingham when the roof under which he had just been sitting only a moment before collapsed during a game of chess.

In 1314 Edward II was entertained at Doddington Palace by Bishop Ketene. Could the king have been on his way to Walsingham? Isabella the wife of Edward II was crowned Queen Consort in 1308 and she was instrumental in plotting the deposition and murder of her husband. After the king's abdication in January 1327 she shared the Regency with her lover, Roger Mortimer who took the title Earl of March. Edward was murdered in September 1327 by having a red hot spit thrust into his bowels on the instructions of the Regent.

Edward III, son of Edward and Isabella, who overthrew the regents and assumed power in 1330, was also a frequent visitor to Walsingham and it was this Edward who was in favour of the Friars when they met with so much opposition from the Canons, who appealed against the establishment of the Friary at Walsingham because they thought the Friars would 'accost' the pilgrims before they arrived at the Shrine and grab any gifts they might be bringing with them. Edward II granted the Walsingham Friars the right to hold a market. Then the rents from the stallholders in the Friday market went direct to the Friary and rents from the Tuesday market stallholders went to the Priory. The Black Lion Hotel, in Walsingham is named after Edward's Queen, Philippa Hainault, who had a black lion on her coat of arms.

March Stone Cross

March had similar landmarks and buildings. Our 'Stone Cross' in The Avenue is said to stand on what was once a Saxon market. In 1343 permission was given to build a new church and legend tells us that this cross was erected on the place where the first church was being built. The project was abandoned when the stone walls kept falling down and the phenomena put down to 'devil's' work. The new church was erected where it still stands today. The Cross is said to date from about the year 1500 and would have seen the Friars preaching to the parishioners as the bells called them to worship and also encouraging the stallholders to renounce their wicked ways and take the path to the altar. Pilgrims would rest on the steps and even join in. Intriguing carvings on the top of the stonework imply an aristocratic sponsor.

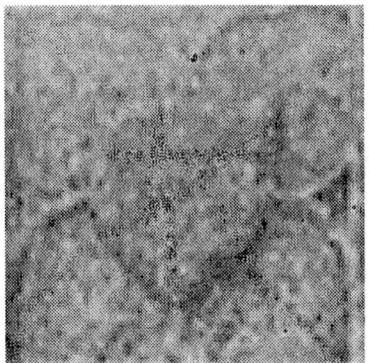

The Shield and suggestion of a Cross on March Stone Cross.

The Tudor rose with four leaves on March Stone Cross.

Investigations suggest this may have been Edward IV, the son of Richard, Duke of York, Earl of Ulster and Earl of Cambridge (who was the son of the fourth surviving son of Edward III), who was styled the Earl of March during his father's lifetime. Edward married Elizabeth Woodville at the Manor of Grafton Regis in Northants in 1464. He was declared King, after the deposition of Henry VI in 1461. Edward was deposed in favour of Henry VI in 1470 but restored to the throne in 1471.

Henry VII visited Walsingham to pray before battle and after his victory over the adherents of Lambert Simnel at Stoke sent his battle standard as an offering and subsequently made three further visits to Walsingham.

A possible connection with the Earldom is given in two ancient Inns in March, one called the White Lion and the other the White Hart. The White Lion being an emblem from the coat of arms of Edward IV and the White Hart from that of Richard II, who was also the Earl of March. Richard II succeeded his grandfather Edward III, but was deposed by Henry of Bolingbroke who usurped the throne as Henry IV when Richard abdicated. Richard was probably murdered by being starved to death whilst being held prisoner in Pontefract Castle.

Henry IV was the son of John of Gaunt the surviving son of Edward III. In 1399 when Bolingbroke made his successful coup the rightful heir was Edmund Mortimer, Earl of March, but Edmund was only 8 years old. This claim was put aside while the House of Lancaster usurped the throne. When Edmund died, in 1425, his sister's child, Richard Duke of York inherited the claim to the throne. For fifty years the House of Lancaster ruled England under Henry IV, V, and VI. Henry V executed Richard, Earl of Cambridge who was the husband of Anne Mortimer, for plotting to overthrow him.

Henry V died young and was succeeded by his son Henry VI who was a weak king and who suffered from bouts of insanity. The legitimacy of a son born to his queen, Margaret of Anjou was questioned and the royal lineage put in doubt but nevertheless the infant was created the Prince of Wales. Edmund of Langley, Duke of York and the surviving son of Edward III and father of Richard Earl of Cambridge, resented Queen Margaret's son, believing he himself was the rightful heir and proclaimed he would be the 'Champion of good government'. It was Henry's ineptitude as a ruler that precipitated the dynastic struggles that later came to be known as the Wars of the Roses.

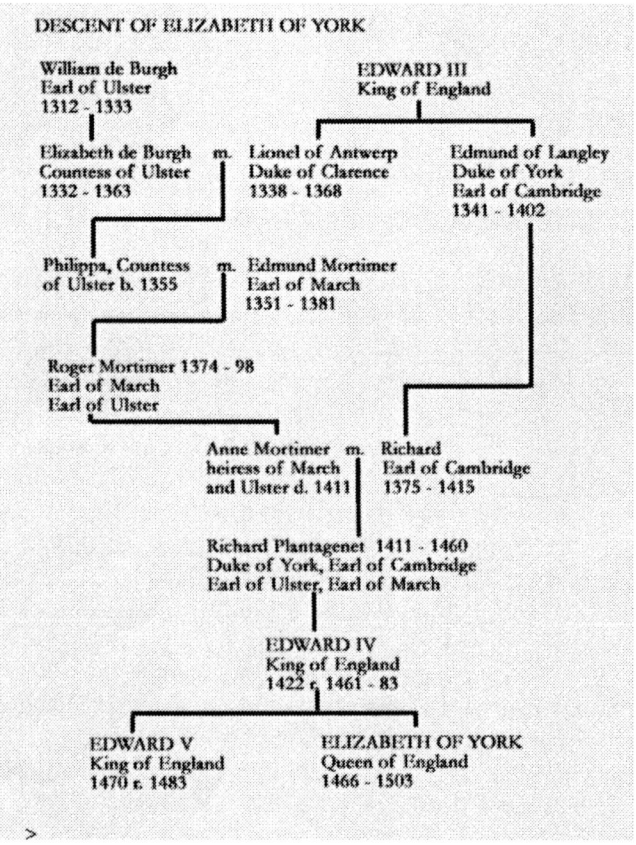

Hostilities started in 1455 and carried on intermittently for 30 years. Then in 1460, the Duke of York was killed at the Battle of Wakefield and the cause taken up by his son, Edward Earl of March, who won a decisive victory at Towton the next year. This led him to being accepted as King of England and Henry VI went into hiding but was later caught and imprisoned in the Tower. It was the tensions around which the country was governed during the madness of Henry VI, which led England down the path of civil war. However the dynastic causes of the war went right back to the usurpation of Richard I's throne in 1399. According to the rules of accession Henry IV should not have succeeded Richard II.

The Wars of the Roses is one of the few conflicts named after heraldic badges; the white rose for the county of Yorkshire and the red rose for the county of Lancashire. Elizabeth Woodville and her first husband Sir John Grey were part of the Lancastrian element of the war and Sir John was killed at the battle of Towton. Soon after securing the throne Edward IV met, and then secretly married Elizabeth Woodville, shattering the dreams of many noblemen who had hoped to arrange a marriage for Edward with a foreign princess. Elizabeth did not bring with her a dowry but is said to have brought a host of greedy relatives who sought honours, land and wealth. This attempt by the Woodvilles' to gatecrash high society was to have serious political repercussions. His younger brother, the infamous Richard III, who assumed the English throne on the death of the king in 1483. Edward IV's son, Edward V, was only 12 years old when his father died and after placing the boy king, and his brother Richard Duke of York in the Tower, their uncle Richard was crowned king. Edward V was the last Earl of March. The title lapsed after the death of the princes in the tower.

The Battle of Bosworth finally ended the Wars of the Roses. Henry VII then married Elizabeth of York, one of the daughters of Edward IV. This brought together the two warring houses and founded the Tudor dynasty.

The coat of arms carved into the stonework of the March Stone Cross may be that of Edward IV. It certainly shows a single rose with four leaves and an ancient description says fleur-de-lis could once be seen. Edward IV was born at Rouen in France in 1442. The shield seems to have a single cross – one of the earliest and noblest of the honourable ordinaries. The four leaves could denote the fourth Edward and the shield and cross his victory in battle. Could this preaching cross have been erected as a thank you for victory or a memorial to a king and March's own earl who united the country after much fighting? Or could its rich sponsors have built it as a place for pilgrims to sit and listen to the friars of Walsingham?

I strongly believe in my findings. The Marcher Earls may have existed in the wilds of Wales. But the title of Earl of March was given to princes much nearer to home. March was once a great place. I rest my case and leave the reader to decide if my case is strong enough.

Bibliography

- Walsingham – Pilgrimage and History.
- The History and Spirituality of Walsingham.
- The Victoria County Histories for March and Doddington.
- March Churchwardens Accounts.
- Britain's Royal families.
- Mercheford to March.
- Various Internet sites e.g. Heraldry Unlimited.com and tudorhistory.org.

Papers presented at the Centenary Conference1998.
Elizabeth Ruth Obbard

Alison Weir.
Edna Stacey.

The White Car
By Anne Melville

The White car flew past as she was coming back onto the motorway. She had stopped for a refresher and some petrol and was resuming her journey. Something about the car worried her ... something about the number. VVG 2865. What was it? VVG 2865. Something familiar worried at the back of her mind.

On the motorway, she could see the car ahead: not so far as she would have thought at the speed it was going. Curiosity impelled her to speed after it. She wanted another look at that number. As she drew near, it pulled out into the middle lane to pass some lorries. She signalled and followed. It kept the same distance regardless of how she drove, as though her acceleration was pushing it along ahead of her. This went on for several miles until she found herself close enough to read the number again. VVG 2865. Very, very good. Bells rang in her head.

"My God!" she said aloud. Jack's car was VVG!" She stared at the number and suddenly realised that she was closer still and eased back on the accelerator. She could see the occupant now. The back of the head ...the back of the head ... looked ... it looked ...like ...

"No!" she cried aloud. "No, it's just like him!

So like him was the man ahead, she thought, that he has the same bald patch.

'Come off, it Sarah', she thought. 'Lots of men have thin patches. Lots of men have hair curling in their necks just so, in the collar of a light brown herringbone just like that ... an old, old jacket bought in Aldershot over thirty years ago. Just like that?

"Of course", she scolded herself, "just like it."

She shook her head impatiently and eased her foot to drop back. The car eased with her. Traffic was passing in the fast lane and she had to make a decision.

"I'll pass", she decided. "It looks just like him. Lots of people have a double." She checked, signalled, pulled out and passed. Out of the corner of her eye she saw the driver and very nearly panicked.

"It is just like him!" She put her foot down and shot past, to get ahead and get away. Mixed emotions of fear and sorrow, the ache of a loss suddenly relived and sheer astonishment all fought for supremacy.

"I don't need this!" she shouted out. "I don't want it! He has no right to look like that! And in that sort of car!"

Then the number registered. VVG 2865. It was his number. No, it couldn't be. His must have been 268. It must have been ... she never would have forgotten ... would she? It was just the similarity. A sister Toyota, probably born in the same week, next on the line, registered at the same time, just a few digits different. For the life of her, she could not now recall what that number had been.

"I'll look as soon as I can", she promised herself. "I'll check as soon as I get home. I still have the old insurance slips."

Thus decided, she concentrated on the road, matching speeds, passing safely, following the rules.

In her wing mirror, she saw it. It flew up on the offside, the number flagrantly taunting her.

"It is the same ... but it can't be. It's not possible. It ... it doesn't exist anymore."

Nevertheless, it was there and a cold, horrid certainty possessed her. As the car drew up to her, still watching in the mirror she saw the face of the driver, and had to cling to her wheel. It was ... was ... just like him. No, it could not be. It could not. The cars were side by side, then he drew ahead a little and she glanced over and looked straight into his dark eyes.

It was Jack. He grinned and waved. He was wearing the old brown jacket; his hair did recede a little and curled exactly. As he passed, he gesticulated, the meaning plain. She was to follow him. As in a dream she signalled and swung behind him as he sped away.

There followed a strange, dreamy ride. The impossibility of it made her breathless. She drove automatically, following every move the white car made as though on a string. It was monstrous. This was not happening. But there was Jack in his Toyota, VVG 2865, as large and solid as life itself. She realised they were moving faster, in the outside lane, on and on and never slacking, seventy, eighty, ninety. She could no more break the invisible chain than stop breathing. They flew past the other traffic, cars, lorries, all travelling almost as swiftly as they.

"How much longer?" she breathed. "I don't think I can keep this up much longer." They had passed a great cluster of cars and lorries on a long, long bending run to the left. Jack went even faster. She did not dare look at the speedometer and she could not break away.

He was signalling left. Automatically, she followed, checking mirrors. A sign flashed by but she did not see the name. He still signalled, slipping across the lanes and she followed. He left the motorway and she followed. He swung around the roundabout at the top and left it on the third exit and she followed. It was still a dual carriageway and he led her, dazed, past traffic that seemed to be at a standstill.

Another signal, right this time, round a roundabout; a small road just before the next major road. In her eyes was the number, just the number. She could not seem to see the car. She followed the number through a small town and took a country road. They rode through winding lanes, the number slipping in and out of vision around the bends ahead, but always at exactly the same distance.

Another village. It was getting dark and she automatically put on side lights. The brake lights ahead shone red and a signal spoke. The car, seen whole again for a moment, slowed and turned into an entrance, almost still. As she pulled up behind on the street she saw him in the gloaming. He looked round at her and mouthed, "Good girl!" She could almost but not quite hear the words. She eased right back for the turn. The white car ahead slipped through an arch and swung to the right, disappearing from view.

She followed in her turn, numb with apprehension now that they were stopping. Now she would find out who this stranger was, this uncanny twin of Jack. It could only be a twin. There was no other way ... but how did he know her? Jack had never told her of a twin. No other explanation would come to her tired mind.

She drove through the arch and into the car park. As she pulled in she looked to see where VVG 2865 was parked, but it was not there. Further on, perhaps, but there was no further on. The yard had no other exit. The white car was gone. She sat staring round, shivering with new apprehension. There was one space left and she manoeuvred into it; she was shaking so much she could hardly control her car. At last, safely parked, she sat staring at the red brick wall in front of her. She was afraid to turn around in case he was there, and more afraid in case he was not.

She gave herself a smart mental slap.

"There must be another way out, or a garage."

She switched off her lights, climbed out of her car stiffly and turned. She walked slowly round the park looking at each car. Four black, two red, a green and three white, but no VVG 2865, not even a Toyota. She returned to her own car and for the first time realised that she was in a pub car park. The door spilled light across the yard, golden, inviting, and for the first time she heard voices inside and the sounds from the bar.

She took her overnight bag from the boot and locked up. Perhaps they would have a room. She could only ask. At least she could get a drink and a bar meal. She realised then that she had no idea where she was.

She was aching, stiff, and weary; the effect of the concentration needed for the nightmare drive. As she walked towards the door she began to pull herself together. No wild-eyed questions, she warned herself. Just say you took the wrong road and have they a room ... and have they seen: No! No, I don't think so.

A man came out through the door and nearly bumped into her.

"Sorry miss! Are you alright?" He looked keenly at her face. "You look very pale."

"I took the wrong road. I thought I'd rest and look at the map to get straight. I must have misread a sign in the town."

"Yeah, they're not very good. Lots of people go wrong. Where were you heading for?"

"Bournemouth."

"Cor! You *are* off track. You should have taken the motorway."

"I was on it. I came off for a rest and a meal. I was looking for somewhere likely."

"You'll get a decent meal here, love."

"That's good, I'm hungry."

She moved on into the pub. It was old and had not been tarted up. She didn't like pubs that had been tarted up. She saw a woman behind the bar and leaned across.

"Excuse me; do you have a room by any chance?"

The woman looked thoughtful.

"We don't usually, but ..."

"I've got myself lost. Stupid. I feel too tired to drive on tonight. Please, or do you know of anyone?"

"I'll see." The woman went through a door and after a few minutes came back. "We can put you up for just one night. As I said, we don't usually, but seeing as you're in need, we will. Would you come this way?"

Sarah followed her through a door marked 'Private' and up a winding flight of stairs. A remembered voice spoke in her mind, almost tangible. 'Will you come into my parlour ...?' She shuddered, but had to go up. The woman showed her into a chintzy bedroom under the eaves and the voice and presence slipped away.

"Will this do?"

"Oh, marvellous! Thank you so much."

"Would you like something to eat up here? You look exhausted, my dear."

Sarah swallowed a huge lump in her throat and managed to say, "Thank you, I'd love that."

"I'll pop the menu up in a little while. Why don't you freshen up? The bathroom's just to the left."

She went out and Sarah heard her soft footsteps going away down the stairs. She opened her case, found her washing kit, bathed her face and arms and put on a fresh sweater.

Presently, her hostess brought a menu, from which Sarah chose a chicken salad, ordered a double brandy and dry ginger, and then laid on the bed until the landlady brought up the meal.

* * *

After she had eaten she laid on the bed again, her mind a blank. She could not think and extreme weariness seemed to have invaded the very marrow of her bones. At last she summoned up enough energy to get undressed and roll into bed, to fall into a deep, dreamless sleep.

* * *

Brilliant sunshine woke her. The window was wide open and the scent of country flowers and the songs of birds filled the room. She was completely relaxed and totally content for the first time in more than two years. For a space of time, she lay exulting. Then invasive little thoughts came drifting through the sunlit spaces. She looked around the room doubtfully. This landfall was most strange and secret to her.

Slowly, she remembered. The long, wild drive into the darkness, the roar of the motorway, the winding road, and last (reluctantly) the white car. It could not exist and nor could he; and where had he gone?

She sat up. This must end. She got out of bed and briskly went about the business of getting washed, dressed and ready to face the unknown world downstairs. She looked at the time. 7:00 o'clock in the morning! Too early! But she could hear movement in the inn.

She leaned out of the window and looked across a lane winding between flowery hedges and tall trees. To her right the lane opened onto a village green so picture-book it caught her throat, with a pond and ducks and willows and little thatched cottages around it. The roof below her window was thatched and a sign swung in the gentle breeze. She craned to see.

'The White Horse', it said. A beautiful stallion raced over green hills on the board, painted by an unknown artist who would've graced any gallery. Below was the entrance off the road. She seemed to be in a typical, untouched, old world, such as has not survived in many places. It had a healing feel about it and she sensed that here, nothing mattered very much. Even the thought that she could have sworn she had driven through a small country town last night.

She turned from the window and went downstairs. The landlady was in the bar and smiled at her pleasantly.

"Did you sleep well? There's some cereal if you like, and egg and bacon. Sit down in the kitchen and I'll cook you some."

The kitchen was like the rest of the house and spotlessly welcoming. As she sat down the landlady said, "Would you like to hear the news?"

"Yes please. Although in this lovely place, it seems a shame to let the world break in."

"Ah, well, that's progress isn't it? I understand there was trouble on the big road last night. There might be something about it this morning."

"The road?" Sarah felt cold.

"The motorway."

The woman switched on a small portable radio and a voice filled the room.

"... casualties. Many of the dead have not yet been removed form their cars. Fire started in the tanker ..."

The world spun. Sarah found herself on the floor, the anxious landlady leaning over her.

"Oh dear, oh dear. What is it? Do let me ..."

Sarah struggled to her feet and clung to the table.

"I was on the last night ... I ...when did it happen?

"Towards evening. We'd been open about a half-hour when we heard the first reports. About half-past six I suppose."

"Half-past six?"

"That's right. There was a big pile up of lorries and such. Not far past our exit."

"Your exit? Which way?"

"Towards London way, I believe. Both sides. A lorry went right over the middle."

"How long does it take from here? To your exit?"

"Oh, half to three-quarters of an hour, I suppose."

"I got here just after seven."

The woman stared, turning pale.

"You must have just come off. No wonder it upset you. Sit down dear. Let me get you a good strong cup of tea."

Sarah sat down, shaking uncontrollably. She must have escaped certain death. A vision of Jack came into her mind. He made her follow him! He saved her – he led her off the road and brought her here to safety. Another question persisted. Why? Why here? What was here that was special? It could not only have been the crash. She tried to concentrate her thoughts, sipping the hot tea the woman had brought.

"Thank you, that's lovely. Excuse me asking … what's your name? and where is this place? I didn't see in the dark."

"I'm Mrs Gregory, and this is Cloudhaven." She smiled and Sarah felt warm, accepted and belonging.

"Thank you, Mrs Gregory. You're very kind."

The door opened and an older man came in.

"Morning lassie. How are you?"

"Oh, alright thank you." He seemed fatherly, concerned.

Mrs Gregory turned form the sink.

"This lass has had a proper fright. That crash must have happened just after she left the motorway last night, judging by the time she got here."

"Good grief." He paused. "You didn't see anything."

"See anything?" Sarah gasped. "What do you mean … see …?"

"I mean any smoke or owt." The man looked at her, puzzled. "It was a tanker that blew up caused it. Carrying something illegal that exploded spontaneously. That's what they think from what was seen."

"I don't remember anything. I passed a load of lorries, then I thought it was my exit and crossed over."

A hand flew to her mouth. "Oh God! You don't think crossing over …?"

"No, lass, I shouldn't think so. Folk are used to lane changing." He looked hard at her. "You seem so awful worried."

"I don't think I got in anyone's way", she said helplessly.

"Not as long as you had a good gap", he said.

"I think so."

"Well, that's alright then. Anyway, it happened back of the exit, about two miles."

Relief flooded her. "It couldn't have been me then." A strange, light-headed feeling came over her. "About two miles back?"

"Yes."

She nodded slowly. About two miles or thereabouts, Jack had passed her and waved her on, taking her at high speed away down the road. She did not normally drive so fast. They had passed a huge cluster of lorries on that bend. She visualised it. A long, long, left-hand, downhill sweep. A lorry going out there would go straight across the carriageways onto the other side. An explosion, throwing debris, cars and people across the road. At her normal speed she would have been in the middle of it. He took her out and brought her here. But why here? She puzzled over it all through breakfast. It was delicious and after her last cup of coffee, she sighed, replete.

"That was superb, Mrs Gregory. I shall have to walk it off. Is there a shop on the green?"

"Yes dear. Up the lane, across by the cottage with the roses."

Mrs Gregory's smile was enigmatic. Sarah blinked. Something was nagging again, about the village. Why had she thought it was a town? She went out of the pub and walked across the green and past the cottage with its fragrant pink roses round the door. It was so chocolate box it was not true. The shop bell clanged satisfyingly and a counter full of papers and sweets confronted her. She bought two papers and a chocolate. Leaving the shop, she wandered down the lane in the perfect morning until she came to a little church half-hidden in flowering trees. The churchyard, with its old, leaning stones, full of cow parsley and all kinds of rare and desirable flowering weeds. She was bewildered by the incongruous scene. It was a glorious, shining, summer day, but it ought not to be. It was out of season. Summer in early spring. She walked round the church and found a seat placed where the slow reach of a small river slid past grassy banks, with thick woods on the other side. It was idyllic. She could not credit her own senses, but sat down and looked at the papers.

The date was right, at least. Even if nothing else was right in this timeless place. She opened the paper and found the news about the accident. It had happened on that corner. The exploding tanker had thundered across the lanes and hit another lorry laden with something equally appalling coming the other way. At quarter to seven, said the paper. Many cars and lorries had piled up helplessly and an enormous fire had compounded the damage. A thick night fog and smoke had added to the confusion and the loss of life was horrendous. Many cars had been burned out and would probably never be identified, nor would their occupants except by inference or recourse to dental records.

Sarah put the paper down and sat looking at the dimpling water flowing by. She knew that Jack was behind her. She could feel his presence as warm as the sun on her back and she felt she could sit here forever.

She realised slowly that she had a choice to make. She could turn round, take his hand and go with him, or she could return to the world and complete her life. He had saved her from the road to make her choice and knowing him, she knew what the choice must be and that in her heart, she had already made the choice.

She felt his approval and the faintest brush of fingers on her cheek. She knew then that he had gone back, to await her at the proper time.

She sat for a while, and then got up and walked slowly back to the inn. She went up to her room and packed her bag, then found Mrs Gregory in the dining room.

"I must go now."

Mrs Gregory made out a bill and rang it up on the till.

"Have a safe journey, dear."

"I shall. Which road should I take? The motorway will be closed, won't it?"

"I think that you'll find it's alright now, dear."

Sarah stared at her, amazed. She opened her mouth and closed it again. I'll find out, she thought.

After she emerged from the car park, she was not really surprised to find that she was in a small country town. She drove back to the motorway and sure enough it was clear, with no evidence of accident or mayhem.

She joined the road and presently, she was absorbed into the flow of traffic and the strange incident she had lived through faded out of her mind. What had happened back there? If she had gone with Jack, would the whole horrific incident have been real? Could taking one person out to live, who would have died, make such a difference to so many lives? One little difference in detail that made such an enormous difference in reality.

Sarah was not a philosopher, nor even a deep thinker, but her life became easier to manage. The certainty that she would find Jack again coloured her future a happier place.

Occasionally, she would give heartfelt thanks that the accident had never happened in this particular world at this particular time. Eventually, the experience faded in her memory until it was only a strange dream.

*

Wincey
By Helen Stevens

Wincey sat on the low wall around the flowerbed in the town square. The sun was warm on her face, highlighting the many wrinkles and the grime trapped there. Her hair, which straggled down her back, was a strange colour, streaked red and orange. It was obviously dyed, with the plentiful white turned orange. She was seventy-seven years old, and looked about ninety. She'd been a "lady of the road" for nearly twenty years now, since shortly after her husband Fred and son Edward were both killed in a car accident. When they died, the light went out of her life. She stayed on in their house, but because she could never afford to pay the rent, and didn't know how to play the system, she was eventually evicted. She'd sold all her furniture, piece by piece, just to get enough to live on, and to buy the gin that she craved. Drinking gin took the edge off the pain she felt at losing her husband of nearly forty years, and her only child.

When she was evicted, she was placed in a hostel for the homeless, but they frowned on her drinking, and after she'd burned the bed-covers smoking in bed, she walked out, and had lived rough ever since. It wasn't such a bad life; there was close companionship amongst the others in her position, the older ones, that is. She had no time for the young ones, layabouts, she called them, work shy layabouts. There was always somewhere to sleep, if you knew where to look. Old, abandoned cars became her hotels. Last night she had slept in what she called Hotel Toyota, an abandoned car on the outskirts of town.

She liked sitting in the town square in summer. There were always plenty of tourists about, and she particularly liked the Americans. Of course, they were a bit loud, but they seldom smoked their cigarettes down to the filter, so threw them away with a good inch and a half left. Wincey would pounce on these, and sit, with eyes screwed up, inhaling the smoke into her ancient polluted lungs.

Wincey carried a large crochet bag, which contained all her possessions. She had got this one from a jumble sale. She had picked the bag from the heaped up jumble, dropped it on the floor, and kept one foot on it while she carried on turning over the musty garments. Then she bent down, picked up the bag, and walked out. She obtained all her clothes the same way, stealing from jumble sales. Her bag held several of the little containers that films came in, and she used these to drink her gin from. Of course, she usually had the odd quarter bottle in the bag as well. She liked the little film cases, because she could flip the lid off and daintily sip from them as she sat in the square. It would not do to be seen drinking from a bottle, as some of the other road-people did. Wincey had standards. She would never beg. She would take her old hat off, and lay it, crown down, on the wall beside her, and if some kind people put a little money in the hat, well, that was good. But she would never openly beg; it was not her way.

Today on her travels, she'd passed a block of flats, and noticed that at the back there was a storeroom where the dustbins were kept. This meant she could rummage without being seen, and Wincey liked to be discreet. She'd found half a loaf of bread, still in its plastic bag, a little stale, but quite clean. There were several wine bottles, and on checking them, she found that one was nearly half full of red wine. She quickly swallowed this, grimacing as the sour liquid hit her throat. Then she found a packet of unused hair-dye. She squinted at the label, "Vibrant Auburn". Well, it sounded interesting. She put it in her bag, and, finding nothing more that she wanted, left. She headed for the public toilets in the corner of the park. She knew that these were seldom used, as the floor was always covered in water, and the place was none too salubrious. Wincey, however, used these toilets now and again, as on the occasions when she washed it was here that she went. She decided to use the dye. After all, she was going grey now. Well, white, to be honest, although there was still a little of her original dark brown hair amongst the white. She hadn't started to go grey until she was nearly seventy. When she was young, she had a lovely head of thick, dark brown wavy hair. Now it was unkempt and stringy. It hadn't been washed for a few months, so colouring it would give her a boost. Sitting on a park bench, she looked at the packet again, and read that she would have to wash her hair, then rub in the dye, leave it for twenty minutes, then rinse it out. Couldn't be easier.

She went into the toilets, which were, as usual empty. Hanging her bag on a door handle so that it wouldn't get wet, she filled a basin with water. She used the soap provided to wash her hair. It took several washes to get it clean. Not having anything to mop her hair with, she lifted up her skirt, and used that. The skirt would soon dry in the sun, anyway. She rubbed in the dye, and, piling her hair onto her head, went back to the park bench. Twenty minutes it said on the packet. She sat down, and took the bread out of her bag. Breaking off little pieces, she slowly munched. The bread was dry, so she took out one of her film cases, and sipped the gin, which helped the bread go down.

A young woman with a baby in a pushchair and a little girl walked past. "Look at the funny lady," said the little girl. "What's she done with her hair?"

"Don't stare, it's rude," said the mother, noting Wincey glaring at the child. "Come on now, we have to get home."

Wincey sat on the bench for some time, content with her meal of bread and gin. After a while, she guessed that twenty minutes must have passed. She had no watch, and the drink made her lose all conception of time. She went back into the toilets, hung up her bag again, and rinsed off the dye. Her hair looked quite dark now, no white in sight. Of course, it might look a little different when it dried. She rubbed it with her skirt, and combed it with her fingers. Her fingernails and the cracked skin of her hands were stained with the dye. Half an hour on the bench would dry her hair, and then she would be off to the town square, to see what she could find there.

She had quite a good day in the square; and collected enough money to buy a half-bottle of gin. She couldn't buy the best stuff, it was too expensive, but what she bought did the job, taking the rough edges off life. Going into an alley, she carefully filled up her empty film cases, and after a quick swig from the bottle, walked unsteadily back to the square. She had a sick feeling in the pit of her stomach. It must have been the wine, she thought, I'm not used to it. I should stick to the gin; it's better for me. She sat down on the wall once more, and looked around her. The crowds were thinning out a little, and some of the shops were closing. Yet the sun was still warm, and people were going in and out of the pubs, and they were usually mellow enough to drop a few coins in her hat.

"My Gawd! Look at Wincey! Have we been to a posh hairdresser, dear?"

Wincey glared at the woman who spoke.

"Mind your own business, Clara. What I do has got nothing to do with you."

"Ooh, hoity-toity. You always thought you were better than us, didn't yer? Is this real, or is it a wig?" Saying this, Clara grabbed hold of Wincey's hair and tugged.

Wincey struck out, and caught Clara a blow on the side of her head, which knocked her off her feet.

"Help" Help!" she screamed; "I'm hurt! I'm injured!"

"Now what's going on here, ladies?" It was the police constable who occasionally patrolled the square. "What are you fighting about? Stop it now, or I'll have you taken to the station to sort it out."

The two women ignored the constable. He called for help on his radio, a van arrived, and the women were taken into custody.

* * *

Wincey lay on the bed in the police cell. Well, this saved having to look for somewhere to sleep. It wasn't the first time she had spent the night in a cell. It was all right, as long as the blasted social worker didn't try to put her in a hostel again.

She pulled her hair forward over one shoulder, and stroked it, admiring the colour. Maybe red didn't really suit her; it made her look a little too fiery. It certainly set Clara off! Next time I'll dye my hair blonde, she thought.

* * *

The sun shone brightly on the morning that Wincey was discharged from the police cell. The Custody Sergeant gave her five pounds as she left. He was a kind man who had a soft spot for old women like Wincey, who seemed to be always down on their luck. He thought it was likely that she would spend the money on gin, but handed her the money all the same.

"Thanks, Sarge," she said. "I'm off to the cemetery this morning. It's been twenty years since I lost Fred and Eddie, and I'll buy them some flowers."

Wincey didn't buy any flowers, but went straight to the cemetery. Maybe, she thought, I can find some flowers on the way that will do. She was, however, empty handed when she arrived at the grave, which bore no memorial stone, but instead had a small metal marker, showing that it was grave number nineteen in row number seventy-three. The grass had been clipped, no doubt by some cemetery worker, but it still looked untidy compared to the others, with their neat kerbs and headstones, coloured granite chippings and vases of flowers. There was scarcely a bump in the grass to show where the two coffins had been buried; time had almost smoothed out the last resting place of her husband and son. She sat on a hard bench under a small leafy tree near the grave, her chin sunk into her chest, with her red and orange hair hanging round her grimy wrinkled face, lost in her memories. When she heard footsteps on the gravel path, she looked up, and was startled to see Clara coming towards her, carrying a newspaper-wrapped bundle.

"I don't want no trouble from you Clara," she began.

"Stow it, Wincey. I guessed you'd come here today. I've brought yer some flowers, look." Clara opened the newspaper package and handed Wincey a bunch of only slightly crushed yellow chrysanthemums. Wincey buried her nose in the flowers and inhaled their spicy scent.

"Thanks, Clara. These must have cost you a bomb."

"Not if you know where to pick 'em up," laughed Clara. "That Custody Sergeant gave me a fiver, but I didn't spend any of it on the flowers."

"You crafty old cow, you're a woman after my own heart. He's a nice man, the sergeant; he gave me a fiver as well. I said I'd spend it on flowers, but thought I might be able to nick some instead. I'll have to get a jar or something to put them in. It's been twenty years, you know, since I lost them. Twenty years, that's a hell of a long time to be alone."

"I know, Wincey, I agree that it's a hell of a long time. But at least you had them; I never had no-one. I've been on me own since I was just a girl. Probably that's why I took to the road. I never had friends before, but I have made some good 'uns on the road. Like you, Wincey."

"But we always fight, Clara."

"I know, perhaps that's because we're really friends. You can't fight properly with someone you're not friends with, now can you?"

Wincey pondered on Clara's logic while she looked around for a container for the flowers. She walked over to the tap, and found an old cracked jar, added water, stuffed the flowers into it, and placed it carefully onto the grave.

"There you are, lads. Some flowers for your grave, so that people will know that even if you don't have a fancy stone, someone misses you."

She looked up at Clara, who had made a funny strangled sound, and saw her blow her nose on a dirty piece of rag, and then dash her hand across her eyes.

"You'll be the death of me, Wincey gal," she said. "You're making me come over all sentimental. Now, how's about spending some of our money on a good blow-out of fish and chips, and then we can go and sit in the square again and see what turns up. One thing, Wincey, you'll have to do something about that bloody hair. You make us look conspicuous, that you do."

"I was thinking about going blonde," Wincey replied.

Laughing, arm in arm, the two old women walked away in the direction of the fish and chip shop.

* * *

Wincey and Clara sat on their usual perch on the wall around the flower bed in the town square, eating their fish and chips.

"This is what dreams are made of," remarked Clara.

"Dreams! If all you dream about is fish and chips, you have low expectations, my friend."

"You know what I mean, Wincey. Good food, a good friend, and a sunny day. What more could you want?"

"Well, right now," said Wincey, screwing up the greasy chip paper and lobbing it into a nearby bin, "is a nice cup of tea."

"Tea, Wincey? I thought you preferred something a little stronger?"

"No, Clara. I've decided to give up the strong stuff. A cup of hot tea would be just right, and would clear the fatty taste from my mouth".

"You could be right. There's a tea van in the market square, we could go there."

"No, I feel like something a little better than that. After all, we still have some money left. Let's try the tea shop in the High Street."

"A little posh for us, ain't it? They'll never let us in."

"Why not? Our cash is as good as anyone else's. Let's go, Clara."

Clara stood up. "I'm not too sure about this Wincey…" she began.

"Good morning, ladies".

The two old women looked at the speaker who appeared in front of them. She was wearing jeans and a sweatshirt, and had shiny, long brown hair. At first glance, she didn't look much more than a schoolgirl, but the women soon realised that she was somewhat older than that.

"I wondered if I could buy you ladies a cup of tea?"

"What do you want of us?" demanded Clara.

"I want nothing. I'd just like to buy you tea, and have a chat."

"Why?"

"Clara, don't be so damned suspicious, let the lady speak."

"Look, I'll go and get some tea, then we'll sit in the sun and talk. There's nothing suspicious about that, is there? After all," she laughed. "I am paying!"

Clara and Wincey looked at one another. "All right," said Wincey. "We'll go along with that."

The young woman walked off, and a few minutes later came back carrying three lidded paper cups, with tea bag tags swinging from each.

"I've sugared them; I guessed you might take sugar."

"Too right," said Clara, taking the cover off her cup, and sipping the hot liquid. "Lovely!"

"Look, I'd better introduce myself. My name is Julia, and I am a nun."

Wincey let go a blast of raucous laughter. "A nun! Pull the other one, dearie."

"Yes, I really am a nun. Not all nuns dress like penguins and go around in twos these days; I'm in what we call an open order, and I wear ordinary clothes, and have money to spend."

"Well, strike me, Wincey. A nun in girl's clothing!"

The two women doubled over with laughter, almost spilling their tea.

"Seriously, though," Julia went on, "I am a sort of social worker. No, no," she said, seeing the wariness creep over the faces of the two old women, "not the usual sort of social worker that you know. We run a housing scheme for women who...well, who sleep rough, and I think that I might be able to help you."

"I was in a hostel once," Wincey told her. "Didn't stay there long, too many rules for my liking."

"We don't run hostels, we provide self-contained flats at a nominal rent, and furnish them. Then we help you get assistance, such as pensions and so on."

"Pensions?" We don't get no pensions! Likes of me and Wincey are forgotten people, out of all that, I can tell yer!"

"But you are entitled to an old age pension, everyone is. Haven't you claimed yours?"

"No, I haven't, and I don't suppose Wincey has either. We never knew we could have a pension, just thought it was for, well, regular sort of people, if you know what I mean. And as for paying rent! We never have any money for rent. It's hard enough finding a bit of cash to get a meal. We got fish and chips today because we spent the night in the police cells, and the sergeant took pity on us, gave us each a fiver." This was a long speech for Clara, and she huffed and puffed a bit as she finished.

"Look, you wouldn't be obliged to do anything that you don't want to do. We have a two-bedroom flat vacant right now; it's furnished; nothing very special I do admit, but it's clean, and I think you might like it. You'll have your own front door keys, come and go as you please. I can help you claim your pension, and any top-up that you are entitled to. So how about it, ladies?"

Wincey looked at Clara, who looked back at her friend, with hope written all over her face. "Let's give it a go, Wincey. After all, it'll soon be autumn and getting colder. A proper bed every night would be great, don't you think?"

Wincey nodded. "All right, Julia. We'll have a look at this flat, and see what we think. We don't have to go to church or anything like that, seeing as you are a nun?"

"No, we don't make you go to church; like everything else in life, it's an option, entirely up to you what you do."

"Well, options is a new one for me. How about you Clara?"

* * *

Wincey and Clara sat comfortably in armchairs in their flat.

"This is lovely, Wincey. Our own home, no one to tell us to move on; we don't have to hustle for money. Just sit back and enjoy life."

"Right, Clara. It's been a hell of a long time since I sat back in a chair in my own home. I'd forgotten just how good it could be."

"That Julia has been a good friend to us, Wincey. She's such a nice girl, just like a dau...."

"Like a what, Clara? What were you going to say?"

"Nothing." Clara picked up the local free newspaper and buried her head between its pages.

"Clara, it's me, Wincey. Come on old girl, what were you going to say? I don't know much about you, apart from your living rough, like me."

"O.K. Wincey, I'll tell yer. But you're not to say anything to anyone else, it's very private, my story."

* * *

I was fifteen when I fell pregnant. Didn't really know what was going on, and that's the truth. Fifty years ago girls were innocent, and I was about as innocent as they come. I even wore ankle socks, for Gawd's sake, not at all like these little tarts you see today. With all their make up, you can hardly tell if they are thirteen or twenty three.

The man lived next door; asked me to call him "Uncle Ernie". He used to give me treats, you know the sort of thing: chocolates, money to go to the pictures. Then he started putting his arm around me and telling me how pretty I was. And I was pretty in those days – weren't we all!

He got more and more friendly, asked me into his house when his wife was away, and in the end he did it to me. You know what I mean. He seemed to like it, but I didn't, not one bit. I knew it was wrong, but I didn't know how to make him stop. And I couldn't tell my mum; she would never believe me, that's for sure.

Of course the inevitable happened, and I realised I was going to have a baby. He didn't want to know me then. Said if I told my mum he did it he would deny it, and she would believe him. After all, he was a respectable married man, worked for the Council and attended church every Sunday.

I tried to keep it secret as long as I could, but of course Mum found out. She was livid, called me all sorts of names. Then she told Dad, you can have no idea how angry he was. I was afraid that he has going to hit me, but Mum stopped that short. Mum arranged for me to be sent away to have the baby, so she and Dad would not have the shame in their home.

When the baby was born, she was such a pretty little thing. But I had to give her up to be adopted, that's how things were done then. There wasn't the tiniest chance that I could have kept her. I see all these girls today having babies without being married; they have two or three, all with different fathers. How they manage, I don't know. I couldn't have kept my baby, not with no money.

Do you know, I think of her every day. I look at women, and wonder…what does my girl look like? Is she happy? Were her parents good to her? I wonder all the time about her. She'd be fifty now, probably a grandmother, I hope she didn't have to give away her baby.

I went back to my mum and dad after I gave the baby away, and got a job in a shop. I hated it. I hated all the women who came in wearing their maternity smocks, and I hated all the women pushing babies in prams. I was angry. Why should they be so happy? Why did that awful thing happen to me? What that man did to me made me hate men as well.

When I was seventeen I left home, and tried to start a new life. I had a whole lot of rotten jobs, mostly living in as maid of all work. I walked out of so many, once the man of the house started making moves towards me. I wasn't going to let them get near me. What was it about me that made these bloody men go for me? I didn't want them near me, not after what happened.

After a few years, I found that jobs were harder to get, after all, if you just push off you don't get a reference, and with no reference you can't get another job. I just drifted into living rough. I've moved around a lot, from town to town, never settling anywhere for long. Never had no friends, either, until I met you, Wincey.

* * *

For a long while Wincey said nothing, she sat with her chin sunk into her chest, with her dyed hair showing white roots where the colour had grown out.

She looked up at Clara. "Thanks for telling me that, my friend. It couldn't have been easy for you. I did hear that these days you can find the babies you gave away. Wasn't there something about some woman in the government who had a son that she met up with?"

Clara shook her head. "No, Wincey. I don't think I want to find out, but I do wonder, you know, all the time."

"Why don't you talk to Julia about it? After all, she is a nun, and I suppose she wouldn't be shocked at anything, these nuns seem to know a lot about life, considering that they are supposed to be so religious and all that."

"I don't know. I never spoke about it to anyone before. You're the first person I've told. I've never been back to where it happened; I don't even know what happened to mum and dad. They must have died without my knowing. I had no brothers or sisters, so they had no one either. "

For a long time the two women sat, each lost in her own thoughts. Wincey was thinking about her Fred and their son Edward, both torn from her in one horrible moment. At least she had known the true love of a man, and had held her baby, cuddled him, loved him, and seen him grow into manhood. Poor Clara, she thought. Poor old gal. What a rotten life she's had.

Clara's only memory of her daughter was that of a tiny baby, and she'd no idea where she had been brought up. She had tried for fifty years to put the memory from her mind, but it was always there, the image of that tiny little girl.

"Tell you what Clara. Let's go out and have a meal. After all, we are respectable tenants of our own home now. We've not been out since we got here four months back. What do you say? Where shall we go?"

Clara grinned. "You always know how to get me cheered up, Wincey. How about a fish and chip supper."

"Great, followed by plenty of hot sweet tea!"

*

To Love and to Hold
By Herta Davey

Sharon and I were having a tête-à-tête in the Silver Kettle in the High Street during our lunch break.

"Simon's proposed to me", I burst out, unable to contain myself, "but I've turned him down."

Sharon was aghast.

"Why, Liz? Why did you turn him down? I thought you were so keen on him. You practically lived in each other's pockets for the last two years. Simon's a smashing guy", she went on ruefully, and "you don't know how lucky you are. I wish someone would propose to me, but I should be so lucky."

"I'm not ready for marriage. My hairdressing salon's just getting off the ground and honestly, Sharon, I haven't got time for anything else. Least of all, a huge commitment like marriage. Simon understands. He'll wait."

"I hope you're right, Liz, but I wouldn't bank on it if I were you."

"I have to go now. Denise will want her lunch break. See you next week."

I left rather abruptly. Sharon's last remarks filled me with unease. What if she was right? Simon is a very attractive man. He might well get tired of waiting.

I remembered the first time we met. It was at the local railway station. I was late that morning and the train was about to pull out.

Someone shouted, "Hurry up, you can make it", and held the carriage door open. I leapt aboard with a deftness I didn't know I possessed, especially at that time of the day, and slumped onto the nearest seat.

"Thanks", I gasped.

"You're welcome", replied this pleasant male voice. "The name's Simon."

Glancing at him for the first time, I thought, 'Mmm, nice name, nice looking, too.'

Oh, mine's Liz", I said, after I regained my composure. He sat down next to me and we chatted like old friends during the half-hour journey to the City. He told me he was a partner in a law firm. We also discovered that his offices were in the same building as mine, where I worked as a secretary for a firm of accountants. We arranged to meet for lunch that day and every day after.

Two years had gone by since then and during that time our love for each other grew steadily. I gave up my job in the City to follow a lifelong dream and opened my very own hairdressing salon in Beckham, where I'd lived all my life. A lot of time, effort and not to mention money had gone into this dream. While I loved Simon deeply, marriage was not on my agenda. Not for the time being anyway.

Simon's proposal came as a complete surprise. That Saturday morning he popped his head round the door of the salon.

"Pick you up at seven, darling", he said. "I've booked a table at Luigi's for eight o'clock."

"Lucky you", quipped Denise, my hair stylist. It had crossed my mind, why Luigi's, as we go there only on very special occasions. I managed to put it out of my mind for the rest of the day, as we were extremely busy.

At the stroke of seven by the town clock, Simon arrived on my doorstep looking very handsome and immaculately dressed.

"Ready, darling", he said, handing me a beautiful bouquet of freesias, my favourite flowers. I nodded, bewildered by this VIP treatment.

The meal was excellent and we enjoyed each other's company, as always. It was over coffee that Simon became rather serious. He reached across the candlelit table, took my hands in his, gazed deep into my eyes and said, "Marry me, Liz. Please say you will."

For a while, I was lost for words.

"I can't, Simon", I managed to say at last, "it's not that I don't love you; you know I do. I'm just not sure if I'm ready to settle down yet."

Disappointment swept across his face. Slowly, he released my hands.

Suddenly, I wished my answer had been different. I hated hurting him. We finished our coffee in silence. He paid the bill and took me home, but declined my offer of a nightcap.

"I shall wait, Liz, for as long as it takes", he whispered, and then he was gone.

The shrill sound of the telephone jolted me out of my restless sleep the next morning.

"Hallo", I grunted irritably.

"Good morning, darling. You sound like a bear with a sore head. Must be the wine you indulged in last night." How could Simon be so cheerful this morning? There was I thinking he was broken-hearted and miserable.

"Listen, darling, I'm going to Eastbourne for a few days to visit mother. I might stay for the whole week or even longer. Why don't you join me at the weekend?"

"Oh, I don't know, Simon. I had thought of giving the salon a spring clean and rearranging things a little, while it's closed."

Silence at the other end. He knew it was an excuse.

"OK, Liz, see you when I get back then. Bye, love you."

After all that I couldn't go back to sleep if I tried. What I needed right then was a mug of strong coffee and a couple of aspirins. Simon was right; I definitely drank too much wine last night.

Sharon came round later in the day and gave me another lecture.

"You'll never see him again", she carried on, "I told you so." Sometimes she could really get on my nerves and this was certainly one of those times.

Monday didn't come quickly enough. Thankfully, the weekend ahead was fully booked. It seemed like everyone wanted their hair done for the weekend as it was the August Bank Holiday. By the time I got home in the evening, I was ready to drop.

Simon hadn't rung since Sunday morning. This was Thursday and I was seriously beginning to fret. I missed him like hell. My imagination was running wild. Had he found someone else? He may even have looked up one of his old flames. They're probably strolling along the promenade right now, hand in hand in the moonlight.

After a sleepless night of tossing and turning in my bed, I decided to surprise him and drive down to Eastbourne on Saturday evening.

"Catch him red-handed", I told myself.

However, when Saturday arrived at last, true to bank holiday tradition, it poured with rain. A long drive down to Eastbourne in that foul whether somehow lost its appeal. So I opted for a long, relaxing soak in the bath, wrapped myself in a huge, soft bath towel and curled up in front of the television. If the weather improved by the morning, I would go then. As the evening wore on, there was still no word from Simon. I kept watching the telephone, willing it to ring.

Then at nine o'clock, the doorbell rang.

"Please don't let it be Sharon", I prayed. "I've had enough of her lectures." I opened the door slightly, as I wasn't dressed for visitors, and found Simon standing there looking wet and bedraggled. My heart must have missed a dozen beats. My legs turned to jelly.

"Hallo, Liz. Well, are you going to ask me in or are you planning to leave me standing out here in the rain all night?"

"Sorry", I muttered, and widened the gap in the doorway to let him in. "It's just that I wasn't expecting you. I imagined you living it up in Eastbourne with ….. er…."

His eyebrows shot up and for an instant he looked angry.

"Living it up? With whom? I thought you knew me better than that."

"I'm sorry, Simon. It's just that I missed you so much I was going out of my mind."

His face softened and the anger that was there a moment ago melted away.

"Come here", he said, as he drew me gently into his arms. "You're the only one I'll ever love. I want you to remember that forever."

It was heavenly to be back in his arms and as our lips met, nothing else mattered. The bath towel slipped to the ground, but I didn't care. I knew I would soon be Mrs Simon Sauntere.

*

The Market Howard Twenties Club
By Jean P Miller

Miss Ranby Scott-Jones' hats were the talking point in the village of Market Howard every spring and autumn.

"I wonder what colour it'll be this year", Mrs Witcham would ask the assembled ladies of the Twenties Committee.

"Last spring it was cyclamen", piped up Miss Arbuthnot.

"And last autumn it was chestnut brown feathers", added Mrs Todhunter.

"The one I liked best of all was a wide brimmed hat like our old Panamas we used to wear at school, but bigger, of course, and it had a little navy-blue crown. Very smart, I thought it was." Mrs Buckle wasn't given to hyperbole and this was praise indeed.

"*My*self", said Mrs Witcham, emphasising the first syllable, "I thought the shocking pink with navy ribbons was the crème de la crème of all her hats. Though where she gets the money from for such creations, Heaven only knows." Mrs Witcham's mouth twitched as it always did when she was trying hard to suppress the unpleasant twinges of envy which Miss Ranby Scott-Jones' hats always caused her.

"Well, we'll just have to wait and see", Mrs Buckle said dismissively and the subject was dropped.

But the good ladies of the Twenties Committee, which did much to help the less well off in the village, were in for a surprise. For the first time since she came to live in Market Howard eight years ago, Miss Ranby Scott-Jones did not appear in the village wearing a new creation to greet the English Spring.

At their fortnightly meeting in the village hall tongues wagged.

"Haven't seen Miss Jones' new hat yet, have you?"

"No, and I haven't seen much of her, either."

"Wonder what's the matter?"

They were soon to be edified, for a few weeks later a tall dark stranger was seen alighting from the only taxi the village boasted and making his way to Miss Ranby Scott-Jones' front door.

"And he didn't leave that evening, so Edie Smith next door says."

"She's got herself a man then." This from Mrs Witcham.

"Looks like it", Miss Arbuthnot joined in.

All the ladies in market Howard were really looking forward to seeing Miss Ranby Scott-Jones' gentleman friend, but apart from a glimpse here and there, he remained a shadowy figure.

However, even though Miss Jones worked in the nearest town about fifteen miles away, she still did some of her shopping in the village and used the post office regularly. Soon it was observed that now she was hatless, so to speak, her hair was really very attractive. Before, it has always been overshadowed by her hat, but now it could be seen to have auburn tints and it was decidedly wavy. The ladies discussed the reason for the absence of hats. Mrs Witch had the last word: "I'm sure her man friend prefers to see her hair and not have it hidden under a hat."

One morning in May, as Miss Jones waited to the served in the village shop-cum-post-office, Mrs Buckle found herself standing behind her in the queue. Now Mrs Buckle was a no-nonsense sort of woman, given to speaking her mind. She dressed in a practical fashion; no skirt too long or heels too high; no colours that would not stand the test of everyday spillages in the kitchen, should they arise. She prided herself on being observant and apart from noticing Miss Jones' hair, she spotted immediately her pretty pin-tucked, high-necked blouse and pale blue suit.

"Very smart", she would tell the Twenties Committee later, "very smart but not very practical."

Mrs Buckle edged herself half behind and half sideways towards Miss Jones so she was in a position to speak.

Miss Jones half turned around.

"Haven't seen anything of you for such a long time", Mrs Buckle began. "Now you won't forget our Bring and Buy on the 20th, will you? The proceeds are to help towards our pensioners' summer outing."

"Er, sorry, what did you say?" Miss Jones had not been listening.

"Our Bring and Buy. On the 20th. You usually make two lovely sponges."

"Oh, yes, yes, I'll try to remember." And Miss Jones attended to her business at the post office counter and walked out.

Mrs Buckle was full of importance at the next meeting of the Twenties Committee.

"I was lucky to be standing right behind her. First thing I noticed was no hat. You know how I used to look forward to seeing her new hats. Then, would you believe it, she was wearing a pale blue suit and white pin-tucked blouse and heels that high, well, it's a wonder she didn't fall over."

"It's the man, that's what it is", Mrs Todhunter chimed in. "Changes people, it does, and I should know."

It was well known in the village the Mrs Todhunter suffered a lot from Mr Todhunter's nightly visitations to the "Pig and Whistle", so everyone clucked in sympathy.

"I'd like to see him properly", Mrs Witcham spoke. "Must be something odd about him to flit about so no-one notices him clearly."

"Well, I said straight out to her, don't forget our Bring and Buy on the 20th. She always makes us two nice sponges." She paused dramatically. "And do you know what she said? 'I'll *try* to remember', and off she went."

"Has more important things on her mind, no doubt."

* * *

Well, the Bring and Buy came and went, but this year there were no chocolate and coffee sponges from Miss Ranby Scott-Jones. The committee felt aggrieved.

The next news of the elusive gentleman was in The Daily Telegraph, where the engagement was announced between Marguerite Ranby Scott-Jones, only daughter of the late Mr and Mrs Scott-Jones of Aberdeen, Scotland and Aloysius Michael Ballantyne, only son of Colonel and Mrs Ballantyne of Banff, Scotland. Miss Arbuthnot had spotted it in the Saturday 'Telegraph and copied it to all out in the library where she often kept up with the news.

Within days, Mrs Hayes at the village shop had to order more copies of the 'Telegraph, but as nothing else of interest appeared, this practice was soon discontinued.

The good ladies of the Twenties committee were looking forward to the coming wedding.

"It's sure to be at St Michael's, especially as her parents are dead."

"I'm going to Leicester to buy a new outfit and a hat", Mrs Witcham announced.

As it was going to be a special occasion, all the ladies chattered happily about what they would be buying to wear at the wedding.

"And we must give her a present", Mr Buckle said at a later meeting. "It would be sensible for us to club together and get her something really nice, especially as none of us knows her really well."

Everyone agreed and two meetings later the merits of a crystal bowl over a table lamp were still being hotly debated.

It was, therefore, a shock when it was rumoured that the wedding was to take place in Cambridge in Great St Mary Church, as Miss Jones' fiancé was apparently a graduate of Cambridge University. It was finally confirmed when once more Mrs Buckle found herself next to Miss Ranby Scott-Jones in the queue for the post office counter; she was bold enough to ask her outright.

"She looked me straight in the eye, didn't blink and said they were getting married in the Great St Mary Church in Cambridge. Then I said casually, you know when it will be and she said on September 1st, nothing else. Quite abrupt she was."

The ladies of the committee digested all this quietly until Mrs Witcham took charge as usual.

"Well, there's no reason why we can't go and see her being married. It's only forty miles away. We could hire a minibus and all go together." Mrs Witcham was obviously reluctant to give up the opportunity of buying a new outfit.

There was a silence, which little Miss Arbuthnot broke first.

"I'd like to go."

"So would I", Mrs Todhunter agreed. To have a whole day away from Mr Todhunter would be a real treat.

"Yes, and I don't mind finding out how much the minibus would cost. My Henry knows Syd Smith. He might reduce the cost, seeing as they went to school together", added Mrs Buckle.

There was an excited buzz as everyone cheered up and began talking about buying new outfits for the wedding.

September 1st dawned fine and bright. The crystal bowl was duly wrapped in wedding paper and Mrs Witcham had volunteered to look after it and find a suitable moment to present it. This was awkward, as no-one had been invited to the reception and there had been no chance of giving it to her as she had quietly left Market Howard a few weeks earlier.

Everyone was in high spirits as the minibus left Market Howard. One stop for lunch on the way was made, where gin and tonics and Sherries put the ladies in convivial mood. Parking the minibus proved to be a problem, but the little group dressed in their best slipped in at the back of the church just in time. Mrs Witcham was in deep purple with a large hat to match. Mrs Todhunter wore a floral two piece and a small cloche hat. Mrs Buckle wore a grey dress with red flowers and no hat. Little Miss Arbuthnot was in pale lilac with a tiny hat of the same colour.

The bride entered the church on the arm of an older man. Probably an uncle of the bridegroom, Mrs Buckle decided. The bride's dress was the palest of pale yellow, like buttermilk, with a high neck and long sleeves, and her bouquet was composed of all different coloured yellow flowers.

"Beautiful, she looked", Miss Arbuthnot said later.

The little group from Market Howard had all eyes on the groom, the shadowy figure they had longed to see. Now here he was, tall, dark-haired and distinguished looking and with eyes only for his bride as she slowly walked up the aisle.

Soon it was all over and the photographer was at work. Mrs Witcham did manage to give the bride her present by sneaking round behind her after one of the photographs had been taken.

"She thanked me and passed it on to her bridesmaid and that was that", Mrs Witcham told the ladies later.

Everyone spent an hour looking around the shops and after tea, scones, jam and cream at Auntie's Café, they set off for Market Howard.

Now it was all over an apathy descended on the fortnightly meetings. A pretty thank you card arrived for the committee with the postmark 'Los Angeles', but no address. Miss Arbuthnot asked if she might keep it and no-one objected.

Then, about two month's after this, a flushed and excited Miss Arbuthnot announced, "Mr Ballantyne's a film director in America. There was a picture of the two of them attending a premiere of one of his films. I saw it in this month's copy of 'Flair'. She looked lovely, just like a film star herself."

She paused to take a breath and rushed on, "When I saw it in the library I went and bought a copy myself. I'm keeping a record of everything I read about them."

And so over the years, Miss Arbuthnot remained the main source of information. The couple looked happy and Mr Ballantyne went on directing highly successful films. The Twenties Committee continued to do good works for the less well-off villagers of Market Howard. Gradually, the memory of the former Miss Ranby Scott-Jones faded, until one evening ten years after the wedding. Miss Arbuthnot was late for the meeting, something that had never happened before.

"I hope she's not ill", Mrs Todhunter said, "You never know when someone lives on their own."

"She never forgets a meeting", Mrs Buckle added.

"It's probably something quite simple like an unexpected 'phone call", Mrs Witcham offered.

Thirty minutes after the meeting should have begun, a dishevelled little figure was seen making her way towards the village hall.

"She looks ill", Mrs Witcham observed.

"Or drunk!" This from Mrs Todhunter.

"Everyone isn't like Mr Todhunter. I'd swear she never touches a drop."

The door opened and Miss Arbuthnot stumbled in.

"You're late", said Mrs Buckle and Miss Arbuthnot promptly burst into tears.

"They're dead", she cried, "both of them. Killed in a plane crash."

"Who? Who's dead?" Mrs Witcham asked. "Pull yourself together and tell us."

"Mr and Mrs Ballantyne."

There was a silence and then everyone began talking at the same time.

"They can't be."

"How did you hear?"

"It doesn't seem possible."

Bit by bit, Miss Arbuthnot told the ladies how she had heard. She had a cousin in Broadstairs who 'phoned occasionally. She had told her all about the wedding and how Mr Ballantyne was a film director.

"She rang tonight just as I was getting ready to come to the meeting. Her brother works in Los Angeles; he's a doctor and he told her. They were flying to one of the film locations and there was some fault in the plane. It came down in a remote mountainous area. There were no survivors."

The meeting limped along. Nobody felt like discussing the Summer Fayre in aid of the Playing Field Fund, so the meeting finished an hour earlier than usual.

Three months later Mrs Witcham was asked to get in touch with Sibson & Sibson, solicitors, in London. She was surprised to learn that Mrs Ballantyne had left the Twenties Committee £2,000 to build a new village hall of extent the old one, so the will stated.

"The ladies of the Twenties committee can drink their tea and gossip in comfort", it went on. "To Mrs Witcham, I leave all my hats and to Miss Arbuthnot my butterfly brooch that she always admired."

Naturally, the debate that followed was heated.

"Called us gossips", said one.

"Still, £2,000 is a lot of money. Seems a shame not to use it."

"Let's build an extension and the Over Sixties can have a room all to themselves."

Mrs Witcham was very undecided about the hats. In the end she kept two — one for autumn and one for spring. She gave the rest to 'Help the Aged'. When she tried them on in the privacy of her own home, she realised they'd never look as good on her as they had done on Miss Ranby Scott-Jones.

Little Miss Arbuthnot was delighted. She went up in the estimation of the others and wore the brooch proudly in the lapel of her best suit.

The extension was duly built and a plaque in memory of Mrs Ballantyne nee Marguerite Ranby Scott-Jones was placed underneath the clock. Mrs Witcham, wearing her autumn hat, declared the extension open.

And so the years passed and as one then another of the ladies sometimes glimpsed a shadowy figure passing down the village street wearing a new hat to greet the spring, no-one ever mentioned it. It was a secret each kept to herself, believing she was the only one to have seen it.

*

Voyage to Ceylon
By Joan Barnett

Eddie, my husband, was a regular serviceman in the R.A.F. and in April 1953 he was sent to Ceylon. Our two daughters, then aged 6 and 3 years, and I followed in August. We were told to make our own way to Southampton by rail, on our arrival, we were met by soldiers and they carried our luggage and guided us through the Customs sheds, where we identified our three packing crates, which had been sent on ahead.

It was there that we met other women and children on their way to join their husbands and fathers in Ceylon or Singapore. All of us boarded the troopship Empire Orwell, the R.A.F. wives and children being allocated cabins on the three upper decks, while an Army division was quartered below.

The first week of the voyage was uneventful, even the Bay of Biscay was calm. We went ashore for a couple of hours at Gibraltar, then sailed eastward through the Mediterranean Sea, and the ship dropped anchor off shore from Alexandria. At that time relations between the British and the Egyptians were rather less than cordial, and the captain warned us women that armed Egyptian police would board the ship and we should neither say nor do anything to upset them. At the same time, the 'Gully-gully Man' would come aboard to entertain us. He was a conjurer who performed various tricks such as producing chicks from eggs then showing that the egg was unbroken, or borrowing rings and other jewellery from trusting women, throwing it out to sea then returning it undamaged and dry and similar illusions, all the time distracting his sceptical audience with a fast patter in broken English.

The fierce looking policeman standing beside me noticed that I could only lift one of my daughters to watch the fun, and smiling, he said, "Missy can't see," as he lifted her up on to his shoulder. So much for the enmity of the Egyptian people – its just politicians who make mistakes and cause trouble, isn't it? Linda had a perfect view of the Gully-gully man thanks to a fierce looking armed Egyptian policeman.

Later, the Empire Orwell carried us on to the Suez Canal, where the ship had to be piloted through the shallow water. For a great deal of the way there were separate channels, and it was amazing to see huge ocean-going ships standing so high above the surface that they seemed to be moving slowly across the dry desert. The southern part of the canal is made up of channels joining up a string of salty lakes, and the ship waited on the Great Bitter Lake under the night sky before going south to Suez.

Emerging from the Gulf of Suez we continued to voyage southward down the Red Sea, past sandy desert, which seemed to go on forever. One day we saw a nomad riding a donkey laden with his folded tent and chattels, two of his chattels being his heavily veiled wives, following on foot in the pitiless heat. It was so hot that some of the passengers, especially the children, suffered from heat exhaustion, and had to be issued with salt tablets. Luckily for our little group of three, we did not suffer in this way.

On reaching Aden the ship docked, and we were allowed to go ashore. The captain gave us our second lecture of the voyage, to the effect that we should not venture beyond the rather uninteresting row of shops on the sea front. I was, as they say in the services, green as grass, and a group of soldiers heard me mutter, "But I want to see the real country."

They offered to escort the two girls and me and with three of them on either side of us we walked into the dustiest place I had ever seen. I had never been outside the British Isles before, and this was a real eye-opener. There were a good many men about but no women, only about a dozen or so little girls; I thought that they looked about eight years old. They were not playing or even walking together; they were just little girls, each one separate and alone, heavily made up and with the palms of their hands stained red, and a red mark on their foreheads. Innocently I asked one of the soldiers who they were, and was deeply shocked to learn that these poor little children were prostitutes. How could these people be so wickedly cruel?

Heading back towards the harbour, we came across an old Arab with a couple of kids. (Goat kids, not human.) Linda, the older girl, loved animals, and immediately wanted to pet them. They weren't too clean, but…Anyway, the old man saw his chance, and began to bargain with me, to Linda's delight and my flat refusal. I dragged my weeping daughter back to the ship with the curses of the would-be vendor following us and our grinning escorts.

On rejoining the ship, one of the soldiers discovered that his expensive Conway Stuart had gone, and in its place was a battered old broken pen. It seemed that the pickpockets never actually stole anything; they simply exchanged them. That was their code of honour.

That evening we were served a superb meal of duck á l'orange with all the trimmings to mark the half-way point of the voyage to Singapore, where most of the families were bound. The children always had their evening meal about an hour and a half before the adults, and we settled them into bed. In our absence each cabin was guarded by two crew members. After dinner was over the ship left Aden and headed east across the Arabian Sea, where we ran into a storm and what a storm it was! The storm to end all storms! I who had boasted that I would never be seasick, the daughter of a sailor, was pathetic!

I staggered up on to the deck hoping the fresh air would improve matters and two stewardesses, experienced in dealing with passengers stupid enough to go on deck in such weather, advised me to go to my cabin.

The two crewmen had stayed with my children who were as sick as I was and had comforted and looked after them as well as any nurse. Of course as soon as I arrived they had to return to their own quarters; it was strictly forbidden for the crew to stay when the women were in the cabins. The porthole had been closed but not before the sea had come in and carried our shoes across the cabin.

After a miserable night I thought it would be advisable for us to have a little food, so we went up for breakfast and what a mistake that was! The steward was delighted to see us; we were his only would-be diners.

All the tables and chairs were chained down and as he placed our bowls of cereal before us the ship rolled and our breakfast slid along the table, finally crashing to the floor. The three of us were sick in unison. I apologised, the steward said it was so funny he didn't mind clearing up and then directed us to the sick bay. All the other wives and children and even several of the crew joined the queue, I don't know what pills the doctor gave us, but they were a real miracle cure.

The storm continued unabated for three days and nights and when we finally reached Colombo we were a day late after being blown off course. It was wonderful to see Eddie, who met us when we disembarked. He had bought a lovely little Ford Popular and he drove with us to our first Sinhalese home, in Kurana, thirty miles inland from Colombo.

We spent three happy years in Ceylon, now known by its ancient name of Sri Lanka, and made many good friends among the R.A.F. personnel and Sinhalese people, but that is another story.

*

Down Came The Rain
By Mary Wise

When George and I were first married we didn't give a thought to holidays. For one thing we were too occupied earning a living and for another, money was something other people had – ours was always spoken for! However, after three years had slog we decided we deserved a break, and George suggested a trip to the Lake District.

"We'll take that old tent and sleep under the stars," he enthused "You'll love it – might even get a spot of inspiration," he threw in for good measure. "Wordsworth did!"

Flattered by the comparison, I reluctantly agreed to give it a try, and started to make the necessary preparation for the trip.

"You can leave all the camping equipment to me," said George, "I'll see to all that."

The following day we set off in high spirits in Lucy, our ancient Morris Minor, and the journey to Keswick was most enjoyable. It was mid-August but everything was fresh and verdant, Roses galore and the cottage gardens ablaze with colour. Even Lucy behaved impeccably, except for one slight hiccough; she was often a bit erratic suffering from some mysterious internal complaint.

As we had bought her for twenty-five pounds and she had given us yeoman service for several years we couldn't really grumble.

We took our time through all that spectacular scenery, through Kendal, Bowness, Windermere, and Ambleside, enjoying every twist and turn, and arrived at the campsite in Keswick in the early evening.

George, full of enthusiasm started to erect our 6'x4' tent without delay when a giant of a man strode across to, "Give us a hand."

Now George is the kind of chap who likes to do things 'his way' like Frank Sinatra, so he was not overjoyed at this turn of events. Very politely he informed his would-be-helper that he could manage, "Very nicely thank you!" but the giant was adamant.

He was a most efficient looking German with a most determined glint in his eye and a flare for organisation. In vain did George try to explain his point of view, but alas ignorance of the German language did not help, and eventually, for the sake of Anglo-German relations he gave in and they erected the thing together.

Our next concern was a meal and George, with the panache of a conjurer producing a rabbit out of a hat, uncovered an ancient primus stove, a battered kettle, a dented frying pan and a saucepan which had definitely seen better days – obviously relics of his scouting days.

I gazed at this formidable collection aghast....

"If you think for one moment that I am going to cook with those you've got another think coming!" I told him firmly.

"I don't want you to," he replied, "I've been looking forward to this, you just sit down and watch – you might even learn a thing or two."

I smiled to myself. As far as I knew George's sole culinary accomplishment was the breakfast toast, which he invariably burned anyway. However, one lives and learns and hunger is a sharp spur to most things so before very long we were sitting down to a tasty meal of bangers, eggs and beans washed down with scalding hot tea in ex-Government enamel mugs.

I must admit I have seldom enjoyed a meal more! Afterwards we sat outside our tent getting to know our neighbours who were a very friendly lot and discussed our plans for the morrow.

"Only hope it keeps fine," said someone, "It looks a bit stormy over there," but George declared the weather forecast had been good so no need to worry on that account.

Eventually we decided to turn-in to be ready to greet the dawn in style, so we said 'goodnight' to our new friends erected our camp beds and turned out the light.

George stripped down to his pants, but firmly believing that discretion really is the better part of valour, I covered myself with an army blanket and hoped for the best.

I suppose I must have been very tired because I fell asleep almost immediately and was in the middle of a marvellous dream (I was being acclaimed Poet Laureate) when I was rudely awakened. George was shaking my shoulder and a violent storm was shaking the tent.

"Wake up luv; I think we've had it!" He cried.

"Whatever do you mean you think we've had it?" I demanded.

"The tent's coming down; we shall have to spend the rest of the night in, Lucy."

Everything squelched, our belongings were afloat and we only just surfaced before the tent collapsed completely. Meanwhile the storm raged, the thunder roared overhead and lightning tore the sky apart, breathtaking in its splendour.

Fortunately we had a flask of coffee so we watched the magnificent spectacle of an electrified sky lighting up the environment and huddled together in Lucy and waited for the dawn.

As soon as it was light the camp sprung into action. At long last it had stopped raining and the campers were inspecting their tents for storm damage, fetching water and generally preparing for another day.

Our neighbours were most concerned about our disaster and solicitous for our welfare. They insisted on our going into their luxurious tent, provided us with breakfast, and helped us to salvage and dry our possessions. The German, too, came over to commiserate, shaking his head sadly somehow managing to convey the impression that we were not 'of the stuff of which hardened campaigners were made'. However, he wished us well and saying 'goodbye' to our newly made friends we drove into Keswick. By now it had started to rain again and I have never seen so much rainwear in my life, everyone appeared to be prepared for the weather but us. "What now?" I asked, as we were sitting enjoying a cup of coffee in a pleasant little lakeside café.

"Well it seems a pity to let the weather beat us," said George, "We haven't seen anything yet and we can't go home without seeing Dove Cottage and Rydal Mount where Wordsworth lived and wrote those beautiful poems so I think the next step is to get fixed up for bed and breakfast, we mustn't leave that too late. I'm afraid the tent will not be dry enough to use for a while.

"Thank Heavens for that!" I exclaimed, "Let's get going."

Now I don't know if you have ever tried to get bed and breakfast accommodation in the Lake District at the height of the season, but believe me It must be easier to get lodgings in Buckingham Palace.

We called on various small boarding houses without success as everyone was fully booked, and we were getting desperate when a kindly soul offered us a spark of hope.

"Afraid I can't take you in myself," she admitted, "but it is just possible my daughter-in-law can put you up, the only snag is that she lives way up in the hills and you would never find your way there."

"We could always try," said George, "I've got a compass and a nose for direction."

Then the good lady had a brainwave, "I could get Charlie to guide you there," she exclaimed, "I'm sure he would do that – come inside and we will hear what he has to say."

In actual fact Charlie turned out to be a man of few words, who shuffled his feet a bit, but eventually agreed to pilot us on his motorbike.

"Off you go then", said Charlie's aunt, for this was apparently their relationship. "I'll ring my daughter-in-law and let her know you are on your way. I know you will be comfortable there."

"Great!" we said, "We can't thank you enough!"

We started off gleefully, but by now it was getting dusk and we had a little difficulty keeping up with Charlie who seemed to progress by fits and starts or at least his motorcycle did. Eventually we left the road and Charlie dismounted to open a field gate, giving us strict instructions to close it again once we were through.

"Must be nearly there now," said George a born optimist, but how wrong can you be?

We came to another field, another gate, another and then another, climbing all the time and stifling an hysterical urge to burst into 'Excelsior."

Then when almost lost in the clouds, Charlie dismounted.

"That's it!" he announced pointing to a large stone farmhouse, and disappeared in a puff of smoke.

Left to our own devices, we knocked on the sturdy oak door, and a pleasant, plumpish lady appeared.

"Come along in you poor things," she said, "You must be dying for a cup of tea." Smiling she ushered us into a comfortable lounge with a cheerful log fire burning in the grate.

"It's always cool up here", she said "and a fire is always welcoming."

It had been a long day but we felt we had fallen on our feet at last, the evening meal, taken with the family, was delicious and the company stimulating, everything was done to make us feel thoroughly at home.

Farmer Jones, our host, was 'hale-fellow-well-met', with a crippling handshake and a dry sense of humour. He was the third generation of sheep farmers and his two sturdy sons would follow in his footsteps in due course.

"It's a hard life at times," he told us, "but if you marry the right lass it helps a lot, and of course I couldn't manage without Bess and Raleigh (his wonderful intelligent Welsh Collies) We can't have everything, and we feel we have more than a lot of folk," a sentiment with which we heartily agreed.

When we awoke the next morning, after an excellent night, the sun was shining and we were on top of the world. The view was truly magnificent we could see for miles around, sheep grazed on the hills and peace prevailed, what was more the mouth-watering aroma of home cured bacon assailed our nostrils. After breakfast we were shown round the farm by Mrs Jones before saying a reluctant 'goodbye' truly grateful for the marvellous lakeside hospitality we had received for the princely sum of 17s and 6d. (87½) This of course was several years ago!

We stayed a further three days in the Lake District fascinated by the beauty that surrounded us. We visited Dove Cottage and Tydall Mount where Wordsworth had made his home and written many of those inspired poems, drove through Duddon Valley where he was beguiled by the Daffodils, sailed on those picturesque lakes, explored the numerous antique and craft shops and generally soaked up the atmosphere.

Believe it or not we didn't have another spot of rain until we got back home, - it was pouring there!

*

Frank's Day
By Pamela Joyce

The sun rose over the quiet street, promising a blazing Bank Holiday.

Inside the neat little terraced houses people began to wake and think about the day ahead, some eagerly, some with apprehension.

At number thirty-two, Frank Denton had come to the conclusion that through clock on for work at the same time for the past twenty odd years, he had irrevocably punched into his own body clock that he must wake up at this time of the morning. His body had wrestled with its inner timing mechanism, his heart argued with his stubborn brain, protesting that the day was a Bank Holiday. He wanted a lay-in; he deserved a lay-in and most of all he needed a lay-in! Frank sighed in defeat, resigning himself to the fact that he was not going to get back to sleep. He glanced over to see if Maggie looked anywhere near surfacing from the deep slumber she managed to sink into each night. Not a sign!

Maggie does not have a body clock, he mused, for there was no way her tiny frame could hold it. She would need a clock with a bell the size of 'Big Ben' to wake her before she was ready!

He smiled to himself, recalling how the family often teased about her sleeping habits and how he always boasted that he never needed an alarm clock. It was at times like this he wished that he did need some mechanical device to rouse him. At least he could have turned it off!

Gently pulling back the covers, Frank reluctantly got out of bed. Pulling on dressing gown and slippers, he padded softly downstairs.

As a young man, Frank never earned the acclaim of being handsome or dashing, just a pleasant looking, thoroughly nice guy. His most appealing feature being his rich velvet brown eyes that displayed a myriad of emotions. They revealed his warm nature, his smouldering passion, the fire for adventure and the sparkle of an impish sense of humour.

Those magnificent eyes had seen their prey from across the dance floor. They swooped and held a young Maggie in a smitten trance, their bodies swayed as the Platters crooned 'Only You'.

From that first moment of captivation Frank and Maggie launched their dream boat and a year later, set sail for a life together. Maggie, happy for a future of being a wife and mother. Frank, hoping to satisfy his boyhood desires, to make his mark on the world and provide well for his wife and future family. To be rich. To be somebody!

Years of hard work, responsibilities of a family and the constant struggle to keep their heads above the financial waterline had taken their toll. The tides of time had washed over Frank. His hopes had been tossed and scattered like flotsam on a sea of reality, each wave robbing his eyes of that youthful splendour. Now the shaving mirror reflected two muddy pools, stagnating day by day.

Frank was in desperate need of a holiday, a proper two-week break away from it all. But for the past several years, this simple wish had regularly managed to evade him, no matter how hard he aimed for it. First off, his works had suffered a trade slump and although they recovered, it had meant reduced hours, resulting in low wages for a few months. Then the next year, the car had needed replacing, along with some badly needed house repairs.

After this was the cost of his eldest daughter's wedding. Sharon deserved a day to remember and Frank made certain she had one.

The following year, Sharon became pregnant, albeit it much sooner than she and her husband Paul intentionally planned. Adorable twin boys were the outcome; however, this meant having to leave their unsuitable flat. So, Sharon, Paul and the babies, Mark and Matthew, moved in to number thirty-two. This situation had put a strain on everyone and that year's holiday money went towards a deposit on a house for the young family.

Last year, Frank's youngest child, twelve year old Richard, had begged to go on the skiing holiday organised through his school. All his friends were going, he had pleaded. By the time Frank paid the cost plus new clothes and spending money, another holiday for himself and Maggie was kissed goodbye.

As for this year, there was no chance. Melanie, his other daughter, had another year to go at college and although she earned a little with weekend jobs, money soon gets swallowed up in the quicksand of expenses surrounding a teenage girl!

Holidays from work had been spent working for his brother-in-law, not only to help him out but also for the extra income. Even this small amount was quickly consumed by numerous household expenses.

Christmas had seen him cleaning up his elderly parents' house, after a burst pipe had flooded them out. Easter came and went while he helped Bob and Angie from next door, knock a pantry wall out, resurface the kitchen floor and generally help them sort out the muddle of 'easy-assemble' kitchen units! On May Day, they had all gone to Sharon and Paul's house and between wearing himself out playing with the twins, Frank had helped Paul fix their car. As for the weekends, these were usually spent helping a local charity organisation, of which he was a very active member.

Frank hardly had any time for himself, but he never complained about these infringements, he would willingly help anyone. There is only so much that a body can take.

His inability to recharge his inner batteries had dimmed his sense of humour and his patience. Frank was not fully aware of this gradual corrosion of his body and spirit. Life can be corrosive, but our minds and bodies tend not to face reality head on, regardless of whether realism brings sadness or joy.

Running on low power means the defences are down, allowing infiltration of the mind by personal failings, doubts and insecurities. Frank felt he had not achieved the ambitions of his youth. He had not made it big in the world of commerce, travelled the world or provided for his wife and family in the way he would have liked. He was a nobody. These realisations surfaced to haunt him from time to time. The lower his spirit sank, the harder it was to keep smiling and to find the strength needed to push these destructive thoughts back into the depths of his mind.

While shaving, Frank reviewed the schedule for the day ahead. This was Spring Bank Holiday and although the first stage of his well laid plans had been destroyed through failure to lay-in, he was not going to let that minor set back deter him. This was his day, a day of solitude and rest. Weeks earlier he had decided against battling through the traffic queues to reach the coast. The rest of the family agreed and subsequently made alternative plans, which left Frank with a day free, to relax and pamper his own pleasure for a change.

Sunlight splashed into his eyes when he released the roller blind, letting it spring back to its daily position over the bathroom window. Blinking, he smiled at the prospect of the day.

Maggie sat up in bed, sipping from the cup of tea Frank had recently brought her. He had pulled the curtains back a little, allowing her to see the glorious sunshine. What a day this was going to be. It was difficult to contain her excitement and act normal, so as not to arouse Frank's suspicions. Maggie wanted nothing to go wrong with her own detailed plans for this special day.

After a large nourishing breakfast, Frank sat and allowed himself the pleasure of reading the morning paper from front to back, while it was still nearly intact. This small luxury was an impossible achievement most days. By the time he got home from work, his 'daily' normally looked like it had spent the night wrapped around a bag of chips!

While he was quietly reading, the rest of the family made ready for the execution of their respective day's plans. Maggie was off to her sister's. Melanie and the current boyfriend of the month were off out somewhere. Richard and his friend were taking a picnic and going on a bike ride to find some good spots for the approaching fishing season.

Frank settled in the back garden. The sun was warm enough to allow the wearing of just a pair of shorts. With the recline of the sun bed, he closed his eyes, then began to relax and soak up the energy giving sunshine.

Maggie bent and kissed him on the forehead, after explaining about his lunch. She fussed about risks of falling asleep in the sun and eventually succeeded in smothering him in sun shield lotion. She said goodbye and left for, as Frank thought, her sister's.

As he watched her walk back into the house, thoughts passed through his mind, leaving an impression for only a second. His thoughts moved on before he had chance to study them, as his personal projectionist was in a hurry to reach the end of the slide show. Did Maggie look a little younger of late? Was her step lighter, her smile broader, concealing an inner happiness she had chosen not to share with him? No! It may only appear that way because he had been a little low recently. Then again, had she realised Frank's own fears, that he had failed her? Could she have found someone else? Someone who would fulfil his promises, instead of surrounding her with only broken remains, as he had done. Frank floundered in the dark room of his mind, trying to capture the fleeting images.

Bob's voice switched on the light, ending the crazy film show.

Getting off the lounger, Frank went to the fence in answer to his neighbour's request. Frank liked Bob. Working for the same company as well as living side by side at home could have been a dangerous combination, but not in Bob's case. He was a terrific bloke. This admiration had prompted Frank to name Bob as 'the nicest person to work with'.

This year, the company celebrates its fiftieth anniversary and to mark the occasion, the directors planned to hold different events and competitions throughout the year. A few weeks earlier, all the employees had to submit the person's name who they thought deserved the honoured title. The votes were confidential and even the prize will not be revealed until the results are announced. It was all good fun and a nice gesture by the Board of Directors.

The two men chatted about the garden and what events the rest of the day would be filled with. Angie interrupted with a cheery greeting to Frank and a reminder to Bob that she was almost ready. They were off to spend the day with Angie's parents.

During his chat with Bob, Frank noticed the weeds infesting the border that edged the lawn. He was tempted to launch a full-scale attack on the invaders, but declared aloud, "No, this is my day of rest!" He let them be and flopped back onto the sun bed.

Apart from a few minor interruptions, Frank's day in the garden had been quite restful. Now, with a cup of tea and a plate of biscuits, he sat down to watch the evening news. The telephone rang. Trying to swallow a mouthful of biscuit, he answered it and listened to his daughter Melanie explain that her boyfriend's car would not start, and they were stranded in the town. Could he possibly go and help? She also asked how he was dressed. Managing to get a word in, he enquired what his dress had to do with it. She went on to tell him that they were outside the Gladstone Meeting Hall and on display inside was memorabilia from the fifties – his era! Melanie convinced him he'd like it and as he was coming out anyway, if he popped on a clean shirt and trousers, he would do. After adding hastily that she would meet him inside the hall, she was gone.

Frank looked at the dead receiver in his hand. His weak protests had been in vain. How did he always manage to get talked into these things?

Thirty minutes later, he pulled up outside the hall. He saw John's car with the bonnet still up, but no sign of him or Melanie. Crossing the porch, he pushed open the swing doors to enter the hall.

Frank's senses reeled and his heart nearly stopped with shock when the deafening cry of "SURPRISE" hit him like a tidal wave. A mass of smiling, cheering faces rushed forward, surging around him like a sea of love and friendship.

Still in a state of shock, but his vision clearing, he recognised the faces of his family, friends, neighbours and workmates. Everybody!

A familiar hand squeezed his and looking around he saw his dear, sweet Maggie at his side, laughing and crying simultaneously, her eyes brimming over with tears of love and happiness.

Like a man struck dumb, Frank gaped in amazement, trying to let what was happening sink in and then maybe it would become clear. It was not his birthday or wedding anniversary, so what was all this in aid of? He had tried to ask, but when he opened his mouth the words would not come.

The whistle of a microphone silenced the throng and a voice appealed for their attention. Family and friends moved aside, revealing the speaker. It was Gordon Fleming, Managing Director of the company Frank worked for. As he spoke of pride and admiration for Frank, the reasons for the celebration became known.

Occasionally, Maggie and her friend went out for a game of bingo. Earlier in the year, Lady Luck had smiled on her, bestowing a jackpot win of £400. It was on the journey home that Maggie had made a decision. If she told Frank about the money, it would have been swallowed up on household bills or the children. Not this time! This year she was taking Frank on a holiday; a proper holiday abroad. She knew he needed one desperately. They had always fancied one of the Canary Islands and although the win was not enough on its own, it was a good start. She would take in extra dressmaking and try to save a little on the housekeeping; maybe manage to get another cleaning job. Her mind was made up by the time she arrived home. Letting the rest of the family in on her plan made it snowball. They all wanted to help, even Richard willingly volunteered to chip in a little of his pocket money toward Dad's secret holiday fund.

Gordon Fleming praised the efforts of Frank's devoted family, then went on to explain how last week he'd known the result of the poll to find 'The Nicest Person to Work With'. Frank had won with an overwhelming number of votes. The Board of Directors had previously decided that the reward for such a privileged employee would be a holiday for two in Tenerife, plus a cheque for £500. Gordon had contacted Maggie, entrusting her with the result of the poll in secrecy, in order to acquire some details and get the holiday booked. It was during this conversation that Maggie excitedly poured out her own plans and how this was like a dream come true. Together, they formed the idea of a surprise party, financed by some of Maggie's winnings. Gordon cleared it with the Board that he could announce the poll result and present Frank with the prize at the party. They would still have the official announcement on Tuesday during work hours, but by all accounts virtually all of company were going to be at the party anyway. With her own family and Bob's help, the surprise party was hurriedly organised and everyone knew Frank was invited. Gordon also pointed out the mountain of gifts in the corner. They had not been a necessary part of the party, but friends and family had wanted the opportunity to give Frank a token of their love and friendship. Small reward, they had said, for all the help and support he had given freely to them over the years.

Apart from a scattering of gasps, sighs, cheers and applause, Gordon's speech had been received in silence.

The party eventually ended with a chorus of "For He's a Jolly Good Fellow …". In the midst of it all stood Frank. Deeply moved, not only by the emotional atmosphere of the crowded hall, but also by the revelation of Gordon's speech. He could no longer evade reality, it stared him straight in the face, diving into his eyes and down into his soul. Gushing back up, realisation poured from his eyes, washing away the inner fears that he had been a failure, and restoring some of their youthful magic.

Later, holding Maggie close as they danced to "Only You", Frank concluded in his own mind that he had only failed himself. He had not come to terms with the realisation of his worth to society and that riches are not only counted in pounds. For he, Frank Denton, *was* a success. He was rich with a treasure of family and friends. He had provided himself and all he was able to give to wife and children. No man could do more. He was, indeed, "the nicest person to work with", as well as a wonderful husband, father and granddad.

HE WAS SOMEBODY!

*

Heartbeats
By Phyllis Gall

Tom sat at the plastic table in McDonalds ignoring the food he had just bought, as he stared through the window. He was surrounded by noise and chatter, but felt completely alone.

On his next birthday Tom would be fifty-one years old, and on advice from his doctor after his last heart attack had retired from work. He had been told to 'take things easy', 'slow down and enjoy life', but instead he felt useless and redundant. His illness, and the resultant stress, had caused his thick, black hair to turn grey and had chiselled deep lines into his face from nose to chin. His once lean and muscular frame was now unfit and decidedly stout. Often there were times when he felt he had made the wrong choice; that he should have chosen a short life and a merry one, not the careful, slow, afraid-to-do-anything life he now lived. Had he done so he would not now be suffering the different kind of heartache that filled him with anguish as he sat gazing through the window.

Across Cathedral Square, sitting close together on a bench were two people: a slim, pretty titian-haired woman and a much younger good-looking man. They sat with their heads bent towards each other, their arms linked, oblivious to the world around them. Even from this distance, Tom could see the pleasure and affection in the woman's face.

There was no animosity in Tom as he watched his wife and her companion. After all, the contrast between himself and the young man could hardly be wider. But the pain in his heart and the misery in his soul were deep and black as if a knife had been plunged into him. He couldn't believe he had lost his beloved Margaret.

When she had married him just five short years ago he had been the happiest, proudest man in the world. He had been content and altogether a different man. Colleagues had remarked that marriage suited Tom, the one man they had seen as a confirmed bachelor. But ill health and retirement had changed him. Would Margaret still want a sick man, or would she see him as a burden and look for happiness elsewhere?

He came out of his reverie as he saw them stand and walk towards the main street. He quickly stood up and hurried out intending to follow. Keeping them in sight along the busy main shopping area was easy and he was sure they wouldn't spot him amongst all the shoppers and chatting crowds.

They came to an underpass which led to a car park by the river and as Tom was about to follow he realised that if they turned around now he would be easily spotted. He was in a dilemma. Follow them and risk being seen, wait and he would probably lose them when he reached the other side of the underpass. He couldn't bear the thought that Margaret might see him and despise him for spying on her. With a jolt he realised that was what he was doing: spying. He was ashamed of his actions but knew he would continue, for he couldn't help himself.

Tom started through the underpass, fearful that he would meet Margaret coming back, and as he walked he tried to formulate in his mind what he would say to her if he met her now. He walked with his head lowered, hugging the wall, feeling furtive and as if he was walking through alien territory. He was blind to his immediate surroundings; all he could see in his mind's eye was a couple, a man and a woman, a young man and Margaret.

He looked up suddenly as noise impinged on his reverie. Coming towards him was a group of youths. They wore thick-soled boots, torn jeans and painted leather jackets decorated copiously with bright, metal studs. To Tom, they filled the passageway as they strutted arrogantly, their shouts echoing along the walls. The young men made a formidable group, full of the confidence of youth, chattering and laughing together. One of the youths was kicking an empty beer can which clattered against the tarmac. Tom could feel his heart thumping in his fear, and the dampness of perspiration on his brow and upper lip, and he felt very vulnerable and alone.

One of the group, tall and muscular, his head shaved almost bald, grinned slyly. He walked in Tom's path deliberately making a collision unavoidable. There was nowhere Tom could walk without bumping into one or other of them. As the teenager shouldered Tom roughly aside another one collided into them causing all three to fall to the ground in a tangle of arms and legs. Tom felt the weight of the man upon him and the smell of beer mingled with sweat and stale tobacco. The youth swore loudly and obscenely blaming Tom for the incident, and as he got to his feet he aimed a kick at Tom's legs. The kick was vicious and deliberate and was meant to hurt. The others took it in turns to kick Tom, then they moved off, jeering and laughing, leaving Tom lying on the ground.

He lay there quietly until the tunnel was empty, not daring to move in case they came back. He got up slowly feeling very stiff. He felt the pain from the kicks, but more acutely he felt the pain of humiliation and despised himself for his cowardice. But would it have been worse if he had fought back?

As he stood up his foot knocked against something hard, which rattled on the tarmac. He picked up a flick-knife. The handle was made of carved bone, and it felt heavy and alien in his hand. He pressed the release catch and a shiny, lethal six-inch blade sprang from the handle. He weighed it thoughtfully, then refolded the blade and put the knife in his pocket, fearful that the youth had missed it and would be coming back to look for it. He hurried from the tunnel, Margaret and her young man temporarily forgotten.

Later that evening as they were eating their evening meal, everything seemed as normal. Margaret had greeted him in her usual loving fashion, smiling, and kissing him on the cheek.

"Did you meet anyone interesting today, dear?" he asked, dreading the answer.

Margaret looked at him then down at her plate. "No, no-one. Just the usual sort of shopping day."

Tom's heart sank. Why wouldn't she tell him? Why the deceit? He spent an unhappy evening pretending to watch television, and in bed he was restless and wakeful all night. The next day he felt heavy and sluggish as he watched Margaret preparing to go out.

"Will you be all right while I pop into town?" she asked, smiling at him.

"Yes, of course. But why don't I come with you? Its ages since we went shopping together. We could do some Christmas shopping and maybe have lunch somewhere."

Margaret laughed. "No way," she chuckled. "It's ages because you hate shopping, you know you do. Anyway, I'm only going to Marks and Spencers and Sainsburys and you wouldn't like that. You'll find it much too crowded, all that pushing and shoving. I'll take the car and I'll not be long." She draped a scarf over her coat, picked up her bag and car keys and kissed Tom warmly on the cheek. "Is there anything you want while I'm out?" she asked.

Tom shook his head. Only you and the truth, he thought.

After she had gone Tom quickly put on his scarf and topcoat. It was a cold, blustery day with spots of rain in the wind. As he put on his coat he felt the heaviness of the knife in his pocket. He put his hand around it and wondered whether he should throw it in the bin, but withdrew his hand leaving it there. Its weight against his leg gave him a spurious feeling of confidence after yesterday's incident, although he told himself he would never be able to use the knife.

On the short bus journey into town he argued to himself that maybe Margaret had been telling the truth. That she was only going shopping and even if she did meet the young man today, it needn't necessarily be in the same place. Although the town centre wasn't large he could easily miss them. But when the bus drew into the bus-station he hurried through the shopping centre and took the exit near MacDonald's. He approached Cathedral Square cautiously, his heart in his mouth, willing to see them and yet afraid that he would have his worst fears realised.

He saw his wife and the young man standing facing each other. The young man's hands rested lightly on Margaret's shoulders and, as Tom watched, he leaned forward and kissed her on each cheek. She smiled, said something to him and they parted, Margaret going towards the shops, the young man walking with long strides in the opposite direction. He was hunched against the keen wind, his hands deep in his duffle-coat pockets, but there was a look of happiness and contentment on his face.

Tom thrust his hands into his own coat pockets his hand automatically closing around the knife as he hurried to follow the young man, the threat to his happiness. He had to hurry to keep his quarry in sight and his heart was thumping ominously, his breath coming in short gasps as he saw him stride into the public library doorway.

Tom slowed his pace and entered the library slowly. It was a large, old-fashioned building, with high wooden book-shelves and many little alcoves for readers to sit and quietly peruse the book of their choice.

No-one took any notice of Tom as he looked around. Everyone was engrossed in their own books; they didn't take note of the stout, middle-aged man who stopped at each alcove and peered around each book shelf. Tom felt himself to be ridiculous and melodramatic and willed himself to leave, to go home, but an inner urge kept him to his quest. He finally found who he was looking for, sitting quietly in the furthest alcove from the door. The young man was entirely alone, and as Tom looked around he could see no-one, and at that moment he felt as though he and the young man were the only people there. As Tom stared at the seated figure the young man looked up at him, smiled briefly and returned to his book.

Tom stood to one side taking in the other's youth, good looks and obvious good health. He thought of the contrast between the two of them, and almost without thinking his hand withdrew the knife and in the same movement the blade sprang from the handle and Tom lunged forward.

It was as if he was an observer watching as someone else drove the knife deep into the young man's chest. Tom watched detached as he dropped his book and, just before death overcame him, looked up at Tom his face a mask of puzzled bewilderment.

Appalled at what he had done Tom walked from the library, his heart pounding and his legs almost buckling under him. He walked quickly, automatically, not really seeing where he was going, until he came to a bench where he sat heavily and buried his head in his hands. Oh my God, what have I done? What have I done?

Time ceased for him as he sat on the bench trying to gather his thoughts. He wished fervently he could turn back the clock and undo what he had done. Why hadn't he stayed at home this morning? How could he face Margaret? How could he live the rest of his life with the terrible knowledge that he had taken another man's life.

Finally the cold and exhaustion drove him home. The house was just the same as when he had left it, but nothing would be the same again.

There was no mention of the murder that took place in the library on the local television news. Margaret was concerned that Tom had no appetite for his meals.

"I'm not feeling too good," said Tom. "I think I'll go to bed."

"Shall I call the doctor?" asked Margaret, her face anxious.

"No, I'll be fine in the morning. I'm just tired."

The next morning, as Tom tried to eat some breakfast he sat listening to the local radio station. He had spent a sleepless night. Each time he closed his eyes he saw the bewildered face of the man he had murdered and it was not until the early hours of the morning, as a grey light was filtering through the curtains that he realised he didn't even know his victim's name.

Just before eight o'clock the postman delivered the day's letters and Margaret hurried to the front door the moment she heard the letter-box snap. She came into the kitchen her face all smiles, waving a white envelope.

"It's come, Tom. It's come." She turned her shining eyes to her husband. "Oh, Tom I have such exciting news to tell you. It's wonderful...."

She broke off and listened as the newsreader said ".....found stabbed in the library sometime yesterday morning. The dead man has been named as David Lawrence, a school teacher from Norwich. Police are appealing for anyone who was in the library yesterday morning to please come forward. Any information, however small, might help with their inquiries."

Tom stared at Margaret as a wail of pure agony burst from her lips. "No, no. Not my David. I've only just found him."

Tom stood rigid, rooted to the spot. He wanted to put his arms around her and comfort her but was afraid. Afraid he would blurt out 'I did it.'

He felt helpless against such raw emotion, and his lips were stiff as he said, "What do you mean?"

The radio was now playing music unheeded by either of them. Tom waited, dreading the answer and wished fervently he hadn't been the cause of her tears. She turned to him and through her sobs cried, "That was what I was trying to tell you. David was my son, my boy. I had him when I was only sixteen. My father made me put him up for adoption. I didn't want to. I wanted to keep him, but he said I wasn't to parade my shame before all the world." She sat down heavily on a chair. She looked up at Tom. "After all these years he found me. We found each other."

Tom stared at her in disbelief, unable to speak, unable to move. His chest felt heavy and the blood sang in his ears. Her voice sounded far away as she said, "This is an invitation to his wedding. I was going to tell you today, to let you meet him….. Tom"

She screamed. "What's the matter?"

But Tom heard no more. As he fell to the floor his heart stopped beating.

*

Lesson for a Libertine
By Sandra Finney

Simon Cockerill was a hunk and he knew it. He was also a married hunk—he knew that too but refused to let it blight his fun.

Penelope knew that other women couldn't keep their hands off him but, as long as he provided her with a generous allowance and came home to her, she didn't seem to mind.

"Who's a pretty boy then?" Amanda's flushed face appeared in the bathroom mirror beside his own. "When are you going to leave her, Simon? You've been promising to tell her about us for ages."

He rinsed his toothbrush under the tap and grabbed his towel. "Not that old coconut again," he sighed tiredly.

Amanda pouted, "You're going off me."

"Good God, woman," he snapped, "I get nagged enough at home without you starting. And if you think I'm stupid enough to swap one nag for another you can think again."

"I'm not a nag," she sulked.

He splashed cologne onto his tanned, exquisitely sculpted face and ran a comb through his thick, dark brown hair. "Come here, silly," he pulled her gently towards him.

Coyly, she pretended to resist but she could never resist him for long.

"You know I love you, don't you?" he placated. "I've known Penny since childhood; it was a foregone conclusion that we'd marry." He cupped her face in his hands and kissed the tip of her nose. "I will tell her but I'll choose the right time—let her down gently. You're her best friend, for goodness sake. I can't just spring this on her without warning, she doesn't deserve that."

Nestling her head against his chest, Amanda murmured, "You're too considerate sometimes, darling, but that's why I love you."

"Not for my dashing, debonair looks?" he flashed an admiring glance at the mirror.

"That goes without saying," she crooned. "Now I'll remind you why you love me." Giggling, she tugged mischievously at the towel around his waist.

Clutching at the towel, he stepped sideways and strode into the bedroom, "Come on, Mand, I've got to get home." He shrugged his shirt over muscular shoulders. "Pen thinks I'm out with the lads from work and as long as I roll up eventually, she won't suspect anything."

"See what I mean? You've never spent one whole night with me. You're always rushing back to her." She flopped heavily onto the bed.

"Don't sulk again, Mand, you knew the score from the start." Slipping his feet into Gucci loafers, he strutted across to the wardrobe and inspected himself in the mirror.

"I didn't ask to fall in love with you," she retaliated.

"Life would be easier if we didn't live on opposite sides of Sheffield. Cheer up, Mand, it's not for much longer, I promise." He kissed her tenderly, "How about a smile before I go?"

* * *

As he drove home he decided to dump Amanda. She'd become far too demanding, too clingy. His other women weren't like that; they were just flattered that such a handsome creature should find them desirable. He wasn't looking for lasting entanglements—he had that with Penny. He shoved the Lexus into first and roared away from the lights, cutting in front of a Toyota.

The young driver brandished a middle finger after him, "Cocky bastard!"

* * *

"Where've you been?" Penelope was not happy. "Your dinner's wrecked. It's in the oven. You know Mary finishes at six."

"Have you tried escaping from computer analysts when they've had a few drinks? It's a virtual impossibility—no pun intended." He placed his briefcase on the hall table casting an admiring glance in the mirror above it.

"You could just leave, you're the boss. They probably mock you anyway. You know—fraternising with the workers?"

Gliding over to his wife he slid both arms around her waist and feigned remorse, "I'm sorry, Pen, forgive me?"

Gradually a smile lit up her pretty face. He'd won again.

He nuzzled her earlobe and fondled her breasts before deftly unfastening her bra. "Sod dinner, let's go to bed," he murmured huskily.

* * *

Penny awoke with a start and flicked on the bedside lamp. Simon was groaning and thrashing about in his sleep. His body glistened with sweat and his face was ashen.

"Simon! Wake up, it's okay, darling, I'm here." His long, dark eyelashes parted abruptly revealing the fear in his striking blue eyes. His breathing came in shallow gasps, as though he'd been running. "Oh, Pen, thank God!" Trembling, he clung tightly to her.

"There, it's all right," she soothed, cradling his head against her breast, "I've got you now, shush."

"What a foul dream." He shuddered. "I dreamt I was murdered. One minute I was in my car, then I was lying in the road tied up and some man had me pinned down. A woman was in my car, revving it really hard. Then it screeched forward, he jumped off me and she ran over me. It was so real I could feel the pain; I heard them laughing and I knew I was dead."

Penny slapped his hand playfully, "Simon Cockerill! I appear to have married a chicken—no pun intended. You should feel ashamed of yourself, a grown man afraid of a dream. If I'd known you were such a wimp I'd never have married you," she teased, "and I thought I married my hero." She stroked his damp forehead.

"You can scoff," he mumbled tetchily, "but some dreams are premonitions. You remember that PR chap at work? Dreamt that his wife died; two mornings later she was dead in bed beside him. Some woman dreamt that the Titanic would sink and begged them not to sail. She was called a crank but the rest is history."

"I'm sorry, darling, but it really was just a nightmare. You won't even remember it in the morning." She scrambled out of bed. "I'll fetch you a brandy."

Now that he was fully awake, he felt foolish. He'd been prattling on like some old woman.

Penny returned with a large brandy, "Come on, down the hatch. You'll be asleep before you know it." She snuggled back in beside him.

Before falling asleep, Simon vowed to ditch Amanda the following Friday. It was probably her persistent carping that caused the nightmare. He'd enough on his plate with his other paramours.

A fortnight later his nightmare was a vague memory, as was Amanda. He'd felt vindicated in ending their affair when she started bitching at him the minute he'd walked into her house.

"Some lover you are. Why didn't you say you weren't coming till Saturday? I waited all night. You didn't even ring me."

Momentarily his resolve wavered, "Sorry, Mand, I left my mobile at work."

"You will be sorry," she shrieked, "I don't know why I bother. Just second best to you, aren't I?"

"Second best?" he exploded, "Don't flatter yourself, you're not even fourth best." The words were out before he'd realised it. "You didn't think you were my only bit on the side, did you? You didn't seriously think I'd leave Penny?"

"I'm sorry, I didn't mean it. I was just worried when you didn't turn up." Scurrying across the room she flung her arms around him. "I love you," she babbled, "I won't nag any more, I know you'll leave her when ---"

"Watch my lips, woman, it's over." He prised her arms from his neck and pulled away. "Whinging is a most unattractive quality in a woman. It'll be difficult to forget me, I know, but I'd rather finish it now than grow to hate you."

Outside, he inhaled deeply, thankful that it was over. He ran a hand through his hair. Pen would be pleased; he'd be home early next Friday.

* * *

Simon was delighted with his new Friday girl. In the car park beneath the flats where she lived, he unlocked his car and threw his briefcase onto the passenger seat. Sighing contentedly, he was about to ease himself behind the wheel, when a blonde haired youth appeared behind him, startling him.

"Lovely motor you've got there. Lexus, ain't it?"

Simon smirked proudly, "Spot on. She is impressive, isn't she?"

"You can say that again. Mind you, a good looking bloke like yourself wouldn't look right driving anything less. You've got class, I can see that just looking at you."

"And I can see you're a man who appreciates good taste," Simon fawned. "I must admit, I do pride myself on my choice of car," he agreed conceitedly.

"Bleeding hell!" The youth whistled, "Are they real leather seats? Don't they get mucky being white?"

If Simon weren't so puffed up with pride, he'd have questioned the youth's motive for initiating conversation in a deserted car park. But caution had been cast aside by flattery. It did cross his mind that the youth looked vaguely familiar.

"She's like a high speed armchair," he bragged, "I've had her up to a hundred and sixty."

"Nah, get away."

The youth was impressed, he could tell. "Would you like to sit in her for a minute?"

"Cor, yeah! You sure, mate?"

He stood back as the youth slid behind the wheel. "Cool or what?" he enthused. "What's this switch for?"

Simon leaned over to show off the electrical gadgets.

* * *

He was cold, his head hurt and he could taste blood. His hands were tied and something pressed against his chest, restricting his breathing. He must have had an accident. Opening his eyes he saw the youth, illuminated in the orange glare of a street lamp, sitting astride him.

"Well, well, awake are we?" he sneered.

They were now in some side street. An ageing Toyota was parked close by with its engine running. Relieved, Simon realised that his hands weren't tied but merely pinned beneath him. Unless he was mistaken they were at Heeley and there was a police station just around the corner. Maybe he could make a dash for it.

The air was thick with exhaust fumes as another car engine revved wildly. He turned his head towards the noise and recognised his Lexus. He was puzzled to see Amanda peering at him over the steering wheel.

"If you want the car just take it, I won't tell anybody."

"I want blood, mate, not your poxy car. Nobody messes my sister around. Bad move, dumping her like that." He leered malevolently, "Run over by your own motor, eh? And Amanda'll do the honours." The Lexus's headlights snapped on; Amanda revved the engine again.

The hairs on the back of his neck bristled as his dream came back to haunt him. A warm wetness spread across his groins making him blush with shame.

"Hey, sis, dirty bastard's pissed himself."

Simon pleaded for his life, "Allow me to die with some dignity, please, not run over by a woman driver. What if she misses and has to do it again? I'm begging you."

Seeing hesitation cloud his captor's face, he continued, "What sort of man are you, getting a woman to do it? Not got the guts to do it yourself?"

That seemed to hit a nerve and the youth glared at him. Then he shouted and beckoned Amanda, "Sis! Come here, keep your eye on this piece of shit. That's no job for a woman; I'll do it." Grabbing Simon by the collar he pulled him up until his face was level with his own. "Nothing will give me greater pleasure," he snarled. Thrusting his victim roughly back onto the road he jumped up.

It was the opportunity Simon had hardly dared to hope for. Scrambling to his feet, he made a dash for the Toyota, rammed it into gear and roared off. They could hardly chase him round to the police station.

He vowed to be less vain in future. Yet, in a way, vanity had saved him. By appealing to the youth's vanity he had escaped.

Penny smiled as she heard the front door open. Amanda had kept her promise.

*

That Was That
By Wyn Land

John Robinson threw the remaining items into his grip and went downstairs where his wife and children were watching TV.

"Well, I'm off now, Tracy and kids – I'll give you a ring as soon as I can."

He gave his wife and his daughter a peck on the cheek and, much to his annoyance, ruffled his son's hair.

It was only five minutes walk to the station. There was ample time to catch the train and he already had his ticket. John was feeling relieved that at last he was on his way. He had been feeling guilty about this trip for weeks and was glad he no longer had to hide his excitement from his wife, pretending it was a humdrum event that he was about to attend, which really was rather a bore.

He was going to an annual cricket weekend 'get-together' with a club to which he used to belong. The troubling factor was the hidden agenda, which he had not revealed to anyone. It was not in John's nature to be devious, but he had felt it necessary to be so, in order not to allow the real reason for the visit to where they used to live in Essex to be known by Tracy. He had played it correctly, had asked her if she she'd like to come on the weekend while her mother looked after the children, as had happened before. He knew full well that as his daughter Lauren was taking part in a ballet dancing display, Tracy would choose to see that. So John had managed to make his arrangements without arousing any suspicions.

Once in the train, he put the newspaper up in front of him, although he was not taking in the words he read. He was, in fact, discouraging anyone from talking to him while he thought things over. Now that he was on his way, for a moment he wondered what on earth had possessed him to undertake this scheme. Here he was in his early forties, happily married and settled with a family he thought the world of.

Was he about to wreck everything?

No; he dismissed the idea. He was about to settle the matter. Exorcise the ghost, so to speak. He wanted to rid himself of those dreams, pure fantasy, which had troubled him several times a week for the past three years, since they had moved to the Northamptonshire town where they now lived.

The train arrived on time. John took a taxi and soon reached the hotel, where he met his old mates from the cricket club. That evening was taken up exchanging news of former friends and the escapades of club events, peppered with the usual joking and banter that takes place over a drink at the bar. Tomorrow he would attend to the business for which he had planned this visit.

He was already waiting for the local library to open at 9:00 a.m.. Knowing the area, it did not take John long to locate the specific electoral roll he sought. No Belmonts, but what about Humphries? The search for Doris Humphries did not take long. He carefully wrote the down the information he needed and provided himself with a photocopy of the map of the surrounding streets. Some half an hour later, John was ringing the bell at a well-appointed, detached house. A pleasant looking, elderly lady opened the door.

"Mrs Humphries?" enquired John, thinking as he did so that there appeared to be no similarity in looks between her and Roz.

"Yes", she said.

"Do hope you'll excuse my taking the liberty of coming to your home, but I am trying to get in touch with Roz Belmont. I believe she is your niece. I was wondering if you could let me have her address?" Seeing a look of doubt flicker across her face, John gave a short, nervous laugh.

"Oh, it's alright, I used to live in the town and am here for a cricket weekend. I shall be busy for most of the weekend, but have a few hours free this morning and would like to look her up for old times' sake."

"Come in a moment and I'll let you have it; I'll just write it down."

John's heart was thumping once he had the precious addressed in his hand. He glanced at the paper, making sure it was clearly written, as Doris Humphries added, "It's only five minutes walk away. If you like, I'll draw you a map. You go out of the gate to the right and at the end of the road, right again."

Pocketing the address and map, he politely declined the offer of coffee, pleading shortage of time. He thanked her once again, smiled and waved goodbye from the garden gate.

As she shut the front door, just for a brief moment Doris questioned the wisdom in providing the address to a stranger. Fortunately for him, not only had he appeared a pleasant man, but an account of the cricket reunion had been reported in the local paper. Mention had been made that it had attracted past members from all over the country. Doris dismissed her slight concern, gathered her gardening tools and set about tackling the weeds in her garden.

John's mouth had become dry as he approached the address written on the scrap of paper. What was he going to say? He knocked on the door before he could change his mind. A woman of about the same age as him, wearing jeans and a tee shirt, opened it.

"Could I speak to Roz Belmont, please?" He faltered.

"Yes, I'm Roz."

The answer floored him! He was expecting Roz to be a quite dazzlingly, beautiful, young blond. He meant no disrespect to this woman. Nice enough as she was, she could in no way be compared to the Roz with whom he'd been obsessed for the past three years.

"Oh", he said, stumbling over his words, "there must be some mistake. Have you an aunt called Doris Humphries?"

"I certainly have. Why?"

"Well, I knew a girl named Roz Belmont some years ago, but it wasn't you. She told me she had an aunt named Doris Humphries."

"Really? Well, I have no identical twin, no sisters or cousins, and I'm my aunt's only niece. What did this Roz look like?"

"She was fair", stammered John. The woman chuckled.

"Ah, a blonde." John blushed.

"Look here, I do feel a fool. I'm so sorry to have bothered you."

"I think you need a coffee. Would you like one? Perhaps we can unravel the mystery."

John hesitated. The woman's offer was obviously a kind gesture and he badly needed to sort the matter out.

"Thanks", he replied, as he was shown into the lounge by the present Roz before she went to make coffee.

The room was modestly, but comfortably furnished. It was dominated by a large bookcase, filled with books on a variety of subjects. There, in the section that obviously housed novels, to his surprise were four that immediately grabbed his attention. The author was Roz Belmont!

'There must be a clue here somewhere', thought John. He memorized the titles and managed to seat himself on one of the chairs before the coffee arrived. Once the usual ritual of sugar and a biscuit had been performed, Roz commented, "Now, how did you find my address?"

"Well, you weren't on the electoral roll, so I found your aunt's address."

"I see. I only moved back to the town a few months ago, having been abroad for a couple of years. Where did you meet this other Roz?"

"Actually, it was a social occasion at the George", John replied vaguely, "about three years ago. It's all rather silly really. I'm here at a cricket reunion, had a few hours to spare and thought I would look Roz up – oh heavens, that's you!"

"The lady mentioned my aunt?"

"Yes, she said you were very close."

"That's true enough", she added gently. "It looks as though your Roz was pretending to be me. You see, I write novels and it sounds like she is local and has, perhaps, read about a new book in the paper. She probably knows my aunt or lives near her. I really can't think of anyone who might impersonate me. What an idea for a title – Double Identity!" Roz smiled brightly. "One of your friends couldn't have put her up to it for a lark, could they?"

"No, I'm sure they didn't. I've never had such a thing happen to me before."

The conversation turned to generalities and John was soon telling Roz all about Tracy, his children, his job and the cricket club. She was a good listener. She had the ability to make people feel comfortable. Her parting shot as he left was to call after him, "Nice to have met you, John. Have a good weekend. If you ever solve the mystery, let me know. Meanwhile, watch out for Rozes!"

Having laid his ghost to some extent, the weekend with his old friends proved to be most enjoyable. It was good to get home to Tracy and the children, feeling more relaxed than he's done in ages.

John was used to solving problems and disliked mysteries. He had never read women's magazines or books, but to establish a link between the girl he had met and Roz the author, he ordered the four novels that he had seen on the bookshelf through the inter-loan system at the library. He no longer experienced the dreams that had worried him for so long, but he did not wish to confess their previous existence to anyone. When the postcard telling him that the books had arrived was delivered, he was forced to pretend they were for a colleague at the office. In fact, he read them during his lunch hour each day.

Almost as soon as he started reading the third book, something seemed familiar. The main character was a girl named Zoe. A number of expressions used by her were similar to those used by the girl who had introduced herself as 'Roz'. If she had not written the novel, she must have read it. Reading the description of the close-fitting dress worn by Zoe, a midnight blue, he realised that it matched that worn by the mystery Roz of whom he had dreamed so frequently. Even details of the earrings and the necklace fitted exactly. The account of an unhappy childhood, a failed relationship and the possibility of a part in a TV serial, alerted John to the need to view this girl through new eyes. She was obviously seeking attention, using the storyline as her own life story.

As he made his way home from work, he relived the two hours or so he had spent with this girl. It had started innocently enough. A colleague at work had invited all the office staff to an evening celebration after her wedding. At the last moment, as their son was unwell, Tracy would not leave him but encouraged John to go nonetheless. There were many distant relatives, colleagues and friends associated with both bride and groom, many of whom had no idea who the others were. It had been an enjoyable evening, complete with a light buffet, drinks, a disco, cabaret and a short presentation together with a few speeches. The office crowd had formed their own group and became quite a merry bunch of revellers who entered into the spirit of the occasion by the end of the evening. At pre-arranged times, various friends and relations came to ferry them home. Before John could order a taxi, the lady of his obsession suddenly appeared form nowhere and seated herself beside him. She engaged him in conversation and used her eyes to good effect. She soon dragged him to his feet to dance, instigating very close body contact as they moved around the floor. Returning to the table, she made a point of listening, reacting to every word he spoke as though it was the most fascinating and original thing she had ever heard. Never having before been the object of female adoration, it was not surprising, perhaps, that she had so impressed him.

The next day, as John flipped through the remaining chapters of the book, he could almost have written them himself. Zoe's involvement with an older man, and its devastating outcome. John recalled clearly the final half-hour spent in the hotel. Roz-the-impostor had suddenly decided to go to the ladies room. He knew he must soon go home, but courtesy dictated that he should say goodbye. Having a good view of the door to the ladies' cloakroom, he felt sure she had not left. In fact, being anxious in case she was unwell, he had asked a member of staff to investigate. He was assured that nobody was in the cloakroom and had no alternative but to accept Roz had left. He took a taxi home where, fortunately, he found Tracy fast asleep. This final event kept recurring in his dreams, as it made no sense. All those months of wondering what had happened now came to a logical conclusion: the girl had either changed her clothes to disguise her appearance or had left the cloakroom by climbing out of the window. It was all part of her ploy to create a mystery around herself. John wondered if she made a habit of it. She had certainly made him realise how gullible he had been. He found himself being more understanding of several married friends with whom he'd previously had little patience, when they had become entangled in extra-marital affairs.

Thinking about his family's situation three years ago, John could now trace a clear pattern. His father had been ill in hospital before dying. Tracy's sister had had problems that had affected them all. Tracy had just returned to work, which meant that caring for the children needed more organisation, just as the new job and the subsequent move came about.

Well, all that was behind him now. He did not feel any older, just that he had 'come of age'. As regards his little obsession, *THAT WAS THAT!*

At her house in Essex, Roz Belmont had already written the draft of her new book. Under a different name, something about the main character would resemble John. She even had a suitable title in mind!

*

PA845
By Terry Schooling

The cab made good time from downtown San Francisco. Lon Rosenman found himself at the airport with plenty of time to spare. Paying off the cab driver, he gave him a sizeable tip for the trouble-free journey.

The check-in hall was the usual melee of people coming and going to who-knows-where. Tearful friends and relatives were saying their goodbyes to loved ones. The Pan Am check-in was reasonably clear as he dodged left and right in his progress toward the desk. He glanced up at the departures board, and was gratified to find Flight PA845 to Tokyo was scheduled to leave on time from G14 International.

After checking in, there didn't seem to be much sense in hanging around among the flyers and non-flyers in the check-in hall, so he went straight through to the airside lounge. He browsed around aimlessly in the bookstall, flicking through a couple of books and magazines. Finally, he settled for Time magazine. He grabbed a pack of peppermints from the checkout, and paid the sales clerk.

He headed for the cafeteria, and bought a large black coffee. Glancing around, he saw a quiet booth in the corner. He thrust the magazine in his top coat pocket, then took it off and threw it over his arm. With the coffee held in his free hand, he headed for the vacant booth.

The coffee was hot and smooth, and he felt at peace with the world. Snuggling back into the high-backed seat, he pulled the magazine out from his coat pocket. He flicked back and forward through the magazine a couple of times, and finally settled on an article with a picture of a 747 taking off.

* * *

Flight Operations was busy as usual. Dave Christie had been a 747 pilot from the time they entered service with the major airlines, so to him, this was just another day at the office. Larry Savage, his Number 1, had been qualified on Boeing 747s for around a year, and still regarded flying the big jets as an adventure. Arlyn Solberg, the senior engineer for the trip, was already in 'Operations with his second flight engineer, Jim Thompson, when the pilots arrived. After handshakes all around, they set to making their pre-flight checks. Soon afterwards, Larry Davis, the second officer joined the others.

Dave had been thinking about retirement for some time now. He and Julie were financially secure, so he surely didn't need the income any longer. She had inherited a good sum of money from her folks after they had been killed in a road accident two years ago. Dave had also inherited a business from his dad. After seeing his mom was OK, he had sold off the business and invested the remainder of the money. The income from the investments provided more than enough for him and

Julie to live on. Life had been good to them, and maybe the time was right to take up the slippers and pipe, and move up into the Rockies.

Runway 28L had been designated as the take-off strip. Larry calculated his V_1, V_R and V_2 speeds for the runway, and then passed the figures to Dave for him to check. He had to tap him lightly on the arm to bring him back from his daydreaming. The skipper cast his eyes casually over the information before him, like he had done a hundred times before, nodding his agreement. He had flown in from Honolulu late the evening before, and had slept badly, so he more or less took the figures as read. He found himself daydreaming again as he looked forward to his three days off in Tokyo, before he took over the flight from Tokyo into New York next Friday.

Their work done in 'Operations, the three men made their way to dispatch, to meet up with the rest of the crew for today's flight.

* * *

Lon checked his watch again, and then the departures board.

They would be in Tokyo early tomorrow morning local time. His first meeting in the City wasn't until Thursday, so he had time to see some of the sights. He hadn't been in Japan for over two years, so the opportunity to renew some of his experiences of the country was welcome.

Fed up by now, and getting stiff from sitting around, he decided to take a slow walk over to G14: his flight would be boarding soon. He had flown from San Francisco many times before, so he knew that the gate was a tidy walk from the lounge. He discarded the magazine on the table, and made his way to the International concourse. As he followed the sign to Gates 1-16, he noted absently that some gates were silent and empty. Others were filled with people, either seated expectantly or milling around the entrance to the air-bridge as their boarding cards were checked.

He looked up at the gate number ahead of him, G12. His eyes flicked over to a departures screen in the corner of the lounge, and saw PA845 was now flashing the "Boarding" announcement intermittently with the scheduled departure time. Lon quickened his pace – he didn't want to get involved in the pushing and shoving at the air-bridge, but he didn't want to sit around aimlessly again either.

* * *

The flight deck crew were making their pre-flight checks, while involving themselves in small talk to pass the time. Larry scanned the array of instrument before him.

"Anything planned while you're in Tokyo Dave?"

"Yes, lots of sleep! I seem to have had no sleep for days, and I'm bushed. I've got three days coming, and I might just sleep through all of them. What about you?"

"I'll probably look up Kunica; see if she wants to get together."

Dave shook his head, with a wry smile at his Number 1.

"What about Sally; what if she gets to find out?"

"How can she find out?" Larry replied, "What she doesn't know won't harm her. We have a good marriage and I think that is partly because she doesn't make me feel like I'm on a leash."

"You're a cool one. If I was fooling around, I think Julie would know – I don't know *how* she would know, but she would know."

"Well, each to his own, Dave. I guess we're all different."

They fell silent again, except for confirming with a sharp "Check" as each part of the pre-flight was verified.

* * *

The queue at G14 consisted of a single suit and a family of four. Lon breathed a sigh of relief as he stepped forward and offered his boarding card and passport to the checker. Nonetheless, he was surprised that the queue for boarding was so small. He strode out across the air-bridge, and was soon saying 'good morning' to the stewardess at the forward door to the aircraft.

He moved down the aisle, dodging the people fiddling with the overhead lockers. 'Why can't they just put their carry-on luggage in the locker and sit down', he thought. The occasional passenger glanced in his direction, momentarily curious about the new arrival. The family who had boarded ahead of him were having trouble with their two boys. They both wanted to sit at the single window seat. Meanwhile, their mother, with a slight air of exasperation, was trying to maintain her composure, while explaining how their shared wish was not practicable. Lon's uncharitable self came to the fore again and he thought 'give the little bastards a slap lady and tell them to shut up'.

A few rows down in economy, just forward of the wings, he noticed that all 5 seats in the centre were empty. He folded his coat and quickly put it in the overhead locker. As he sat down, he looked around and noticed that there were many empty seats in the plane. He smiled to himself in smug satisfaction. With any luck, he would be able to stretch out across all five seats and sleep away the flight over the Pole. He sat down in the aisle seat, and snapped shut his seat belt. Stretching out his legs, he closed his eyes and relaxed.

He was brought out of his dozing by the safety demonstration announcement. He watched the pretty stewardess standing close to him as she demonstrated the safety equipment. He found himself taken more by her figure than anything she was doing. He noticed how her full round breasts thrust at her blouse as she demonstrated how the life jacket was passed around the back. He became aware of his trousers constraining his manhood as he stared intently at the stewardess.

* * *

As they completed their final gate checks, air traffic control called the flight deck with final departure instructions.

"Flight 845! SFO tower. NOTAM advises that your designated runway two-eight-left is closed. Proceed to runway zero-one-right. NOTAM advises that the first 1,000 feet of zero-one-right is closed but this will not affect the runway distance available for a 747 take-off. You are cleared for push back."

"That's a roger – zero-one-right."

Savage gave the 'go' instruction to the cabin crew.

"Crew to doors."

Harvey Masters gave his crew the instruction to secure all doors.

"Ready when you are ground control."

"Ground control - roger that."

The chocks were pulled away from the nose wheel, and the tug took up the strain on the tow-bar. With a hardly discernable lurch, the huge plane began its slow reverse out on to the apron. The driver of the tug made a slight adjustment, and the 747 turned to face the taxiway.

The ground controller moved forward to disconnect the tow-bar. Christie watched as the tug moved away and returned to the parking area below the sky-bridge.

"You are clear to proceed captain; have a good trip."

"Roger ground control and thanks."

He waited for the ground controller to appear below. When he appeared on the port side, he turned, and gave the thumbs up to the captain. With a brief wave each to the other, the ground controller turned again and walked briskly away.

"PA845 to tower. Flight 845 ready for departure."

"Roger PA845 – follow taxiway three-five-niner out to runway zero-one-right."

"Roger tower – three-five-niner to runway zero-one-right."

The Boeing edged forward to begin its long run out to its designated runway.

★ ★ ★

As he had anticipated, nobody had chosen to sit in any of the four seats alongside him. Lon luxuriated in the prospect of being able to lay full length for much of the journey to Tokyo. He thought he might even ignore the meal calls after breakfast. He would wait until the cabin crew started to serve coffee and then ask for a blanket.

He glanced across to the left-hand side, and saw the terminal buildings disappearing behind. He picked up the magazine, and resumed skimming through it. As he felt the aircraft making the turn at the end of the runway, he couldn't resist looking up. Staring out of the right-hand windows, he saw the runway stretching out to the side of the aircraft, its lines of white lights merging to form the apex of an imaginary triangle in the distance. Then the image was gone, and the giant plane stood motionless like an athlete waiting for the starting gun.

Soon after, the engines began to roar to a crescendo, before the Boeing began to move. It quickly accelerated towards its take-off speed in its mad dash for the freedom of the skies.

* * *

The final checks were being completed as the 747 approached its turn from the taxiway. The fresh paint on the runway surface signalled the changed threshold.

"All clear to go Skip"; came the verification from Solberg.

"PA845 to tower – checks complete and ready to go."

"Roger, PA845. You are cleared for take-off. You should climb due west to angels 10,000 before you make your turn."

"Roger that tower."

"Have a good trip 845."

Dave reached for the four throttle levers, and felt Larry's hand rest firmly upon his as they pushed forward the levers together. Larry called the engine revolutions at take-off power, and the brakes were released. Their hands stayed on the throttle levers as the aircraft moved forward and started to gather speed. As the airspeed climbed, they released their joint hold on the throttles, and Dave waited for Larry to call V_1 – the point of no return and the aircraft committed to take off.

The aircraft was still accelerating to take-off speed and everything was running sweetly. Dave found himself urging Larry mentally to call V_1. 'Must be getting old', he mused, 'but we do seem to be a long way down the runway'.

"V_1!"

At the long awaited call, Dave glanced at the airspeed indicator, but the aircraft was still well short of V_R. Dave could now see the approach light gantries clearly ahead. He had a momentary thought that he hadn't noticed that before. He really needed to quit this job – he was starting to see ghosts where none existed.

"V_R!"

Dave called back "Rotate" and hauled back on the yoke. The nose gently lifted as the forward wheels of the undercarriage left the runway. He glanced to the left as the light gantries streamed past just below the aircraft. Almost at the same instant, he felt the Boeing shudder. Then almost immediately, a violent jarring went through the airframe followed instantly by a huge bang.

'Not an explosion; not loud enough', he thought.

He called out to Larry, "What in hell's name was that?"

Larry had visibly blanched, and shrugged his shoulders as he continued to stare through the windshield ahead.

Dave glanced back at Arlyn, who was scanning the instruments. Some of them were going wild.

"We've lost some of the hydraulics, Skip", yelled Solberg as he continued to look for the problem in the instruments.

"Some malfunction in the undercarriage too. We need to turn around Skip – I just don't know what the problem is or how serious it might be. I've never seen anything like it."

"I think we hit the lighting gantries with the undercarriage Dave."

"What did you say", said Dave, even though he had heard Larry clearly.

"I think we hit ...." His speech tailed off as the full horror of what may be below their seats struck them all with ice-cold reality.

"Do we have an undercarriage fit to get us down Arlyn?"

"I just don't know Dave. It's the hydraulics that worries me most."

"Well its plain that we're still flying, so lets get back to the tower and get some space."

Dave controlled the airliner on its steady climb, while Larry called the SFO tower.

* * *

Lon was sitting back with his eyes closed at he felt the aircraft lean back gently, and start to haul itself into the afternoon sky. He felt a definite shudder, and glanced at the cabin crew for clues. Before he could draw breathe, there was a grinding bang, and chaos broke loose in the passenger cabin. A shaft of steel erupted through the floor, striking Lon in the right shoulder, and pinning him to the seat as it went straight through him, out the back of the seat and into the ceiling above. There was no sensation of pain, more one of shock. He screamed at the sight of the metal holding him fast to the seat.

When he tried to move, the pain came in searing waves of agony. It was some time before he became aware of passengers and crew gathering around him, trying to pry him loose from the metal holding him captive. He also became aware of the sound of air rushing into the cabin, and the sensation of cold affecting his feet and legs. He was certain that he was dying. He screamed again as a well meaning and muscular passenger yanked at he metal pinning him to the seat.

"No; please", he whimpered in response.

The cabin had erupted in pandemonium. People were screaming and crying. The cabin crew did their best to calm people down, while attending to the injured. Lon had been the worst affected, but several people had been struck by flying debris, and were in various stages of shock. Ethel Bernstein, the passenger in the seat immediately behind Lon had also been hit by debris coming through the floor. She was smearing blood across her face and at the same time yelling through her tears that it was a bomb, and everyone was going to die.

Two passengers, a man and a woman came forward, saying they were doctors, and another woman said she was a nurse. The cabin crew thanked them, and asked if they could attend to the worst injuries.

Meanwhile, Harvey had gone forward to the flight deck, and had established quickly that the aircraft was flying reasonably safely. He briefed Dave quickly on the situation back in the cabin. Dave said they were turning back to SFO. Harvey returned to the passenger cabin, and used the PAX to call for passengers to be quiet.

"We have experienced a problem in take-off, and the captain has decided to return to San Francisco. It is in everybody's interest that you stay as calm as you can. Will those passengers that are not injured please move to the rear compartments of the aircraft, so that we can attend to the injured people in the forward compartment?"

"The captain has asked me to emphasise that the Boeing 747 has an exceptional safety record. The aircraft is flying perfectly well, but we are returning to San Francisco so that the injured can be attended to and the problems with the aircraft can be addressed. Thank you for your co-operation."

Robert Wayne, another elderly passenger in the aft cabin had both hands clasped to his chest. Joan, his wife, panicked quietly, unsure what to do as she leaned over him. A trainee nurse who was on board and seated nearby reacted quickly to the situation, recognising the symptoms. She helped Robert out of his seat, and onto the floor of the aisle, where she gently laid him on his back. With Joan's help, she began loosening his clothing, while talking to him softly.

The smoke and fine debris that had filled the forward cabin at the moment of impact was beginning to settle, covering everything in a grey-brown mantle of dust.

* * *

The air traffic controller monitoring the departure of PA845 saw its track on his screen moving out over the bay. Suddenly, the voice of Larry Savage was on his headset.

"PA845 to tower, we have a problem and require immediate clearance for a landing."

"PA845 – this is the tower. Please repeat."

"PA845 to tower, we have struck an object on take-off, suspect it may be the ALS gantries. The aircraft is flying, but we do not know the extent of the damage. We have many warnings indicated relating to the hydraulics and the undercarriage. We have a number of injuries to passengers and crew, and will need full emergency services."

"That's affirmative PA845. You will need to dump fuel. Continue on your present heading and climb to angels 3,000 until I give you a new course."

"Roger tower. We are now dumping fuel, but I say again, we need immediate clearance to land."

"Roger that PA845."

While he was speaking, the air traffic controller was handed a message taken by the shift supervisor. He had received a call from airfield maintenance, saying one of their people had seen a Pan Am 747 destroy part of the ALS on take-off. He was unable to give any indication of the damage sustained by the Boeing, but was sure the undercarriage had taken most of the impact. He had seen smoke at the time of the collision, but there had been no sign of fire as the 747 gained altitude. He had seen debris falling from the aircraft, but was not able to say how much was from the plane and how much was from the ALS.

"PA845 – this is the tower. Please confirm your current altitude and airspeed."

"PA845 to tower – we are still climbing through angels 2,000, and our airspeed is 250 knots."

"PA845 - you are cleared to make a 90º turn to the right. Retain your height at angels 3,000; hold your present airspeed of two-five-zero knots. Stand by for further instructions."

"Roger tower – standing by for your instructions."

Meanwhile, air traffic control was on full alert. Pending departures were being held at their gates and aircraft queuing for takeoff were being returned to the terminal buildings. Controllers were instructing all aircraft on final approach to make a fly-by, and then stacking them pending further instructions. All approaching aircraft beyond the outer markers were being diverted to neighbouring airports.

"PA845 – this is the tower."

"Roger tower – PA845."

"PA845 – you are being cleared to land on runway two-eight-left which has been opened in preparation for your landing. I say again, two-eight-left."

"Roger that tower: two-eight-left."

"PA845 – what is your current status?"

"We have sustained damage to the underside of the aircraft. We have control of the aircraft, and flight controls seem to be adequate. We do not know the status of the undercarriage."

"Roger PA845. We have the emergency services in place."

As he spoke, the controller was watching the fire trucks and ambulances sprinting out to the end of runway 28R.

* * *

The flight deck crew were still struggling with the condition of the aircraft when Harvey came in to report the situation back in the passenger cabin. He told Dave about the injuries, and briefed him on the serious injuries, especially those to Lon Rosenman. He told the flight deck crew about the steel girders that had come through into the interior of the aircraft. He said the major panic that was developing had been contained by the cabin staff, although there were still a lot of very frightened people back there.

He asked if he could be told what was happening, so that he could brief the passengers. While Larry concentrated on flying the jet, Dave briefed Harvey as best as he could. He said the consensus view was that they had hit the approach light gantries, and had sustained damage to the hydraulics and the landing gear. He added that they could not be certain of the scale of the damage, nor predict the effect that the damage might have brought about when they attempted to land. He instructed Larry and Jim to go back into the cabin with Harvey to assess the damage for themselves.

"You had better prepare them for the worst, Harv, and anticipate an emergency landing. I'll keep you informed through the intercom."

"May God be with us", was Harvey's whispered prayer.

He had been through the drill so many times. He hoped he knew it off by heart. Even though the drill was repeated over and over as part of every training programme, nobody really expected that it would ever happen to them.

Harvey told the captain how he had distributed the passengers, so that the injured could be given whatever aid was possible in the circumstances.

"Good job, Harvey! Now you'd better get back there, brief the other guys then prepare for the bumpiest landing you are ever likely to experience."

"Good luck captain."

* * *

The momentary increase in the sense of foreboding among the passengers, caused by Harvey's announcement of the pending return to San Francisco, had subsided. The wailing and the tears had given way to an uneasy silence brought about by resignation to death or serious injury.

By now, the forward part of the passenger cabin was becoming very cold. The inrush of air was taking its toll. The cabin was filled with shrill whistling sounds from the multiple breaches in the floor. The flight attendants were continuing to keep the lid on the latent panic among many of the passengers. They went from seat to seat, issuing blankets and pillows, hot drinks and any other comforts they were able to provide. They knew, above all, that worse may be yet to come. The landing on a suspect undercarriage and using damaged hydraulics to control the aircraft was likely to be hazardous at best. The possibility of catastrophic failure of any of the systems was too bad to contemplate. They welcomed the fact that the need to attend to so many frightened people kept them from dwelling on the possibilities.

By now, the aircraft was on its final approach to its rendezvous with whatever awaited it. It was time for Harvey to make the announcements that every air traveller dreads.

"This is Harvey Masters, your chief fight attendant ladies and gentlemen. As you know, the aircraft has sustained damage during take-off. We will shortly be landing at San Francisco International Airport. The captain has alerted the airport to our situation, and they have made the arrangements necessary for our arrival on the ground."

"We are now going to give you instructions for your safety on landing. Firstly, you should remove your shoes and push them under the seat in front of you."

"After we have landed and the aircraft has come to a stop, the cabin attendants will open all the doors to the aircraft, including the emergency exits. We will be asking passengers currently occupying seats by these doors to move once again, in order that the exits can be made ready for our landing. All of the exits are equipped with emergency slides, which will be deployed as soon as the doors have been opened. You will leave by the exit closest to your seat. The cabin attendants will be there to help you, so please remain calm and follow their instructions."

"As the aircraft approaches touchdown the captain will issue the instruction 'Brace'. The cabin staff in the aisles will now demonstrate what you must do in response to this instruction. Firstly, sit well back in your seat. Place your hands at the back of your head and lock your fingers together. Then lean forward from the waist, so that you are facing downwards to the floor, and your head is touching the seat ahead of you. For passengers who are unable to assume this position, for instance passengers with medical conditions and mothers with small children, the cabin attendants will provide special instructions."

"The captain has asked me to assure you that the Boeing 747 is an excellent aircraft, and has safety systems installed for just the sort of situation we are faced with. The instructions I have just given you are for your added protection. Emergency evacuation is standard procedure. It is designed to get you clear of the aircraft as quickly as possible, so that ground staff can get aboard. Thank you for your attention."

For several moments after Harvey finished speaking, the silence on board the aircraft was palpable, broken only by the whistling of the air from the holes in the floor, and the sound of passengers crying softly. The brief lull was broken by an outburst of questions from the passengers; an outburst that swelled to an incomprehensible howling.

"Ladies and gentlemen", Harvey held up his hand as though trying to stem the flood of questions, "as the cabin attendants and myself come around, we will endeavour to answer all your questions. In the meantime, for the safety of everyone, please try to remain calm. Thank you."

* * *

The white lights of the runway could be seen clearly some miles ahead of the aircraft, even though the ground was bathed in afternoon sunshine.

In every way, but for the arrays of warning indicators flashing urgently in front of them, the flight deck crew was preparing for another landing like every landing they had experienced. The initial frantic concerns for the state of the aircraft and its control systems had subsided. The plane was holding its own, and behaving perfectly, needing only an occasional adjustment to the trim.

Dave Christie and Larry Savage had been in continuous contact with the SFO tower, but the to-and-froing had subsided to the level of occasional checks on the status of the aircraft. Thanks to the dumping over the ocean, the fuel on board was now down to the level required for landing.

The ILS would normally be used for the final approach, but this was not the time to rely on potentially corrupted systems. Dave and his colleagues stuck with the well-rehearsed drills for just such an occurrence as this. Even so, emergency approaches on a simulator and this – the real thing – were worlds apart.

"Well guys, here goes nothing. Lets get this baby down on the ground, and then I'll buy you a large, stiff drink." Dave's comment was a good deal more sanguine that he felt.

"Roger that, captain", was echoed in quick succession by Larry and Arlyn.

"Five degree flaps."

"Five degree flaps", echoed Larry.

The engine speed rose in response to the drag caused by the extension of the ailerons on the wings. The aircraft jigged slightly left and right as it was maintained in alignment with the runway ahead. The whine of the flaps being extended further and further was audible on the flight deck as the Boeing continued its progress toward the airport.

The undercarriage, never having been retracted after the abortive takeoff, remained extended. Some of the legs of the system were missing. Others hung loose and swayed in the slipstream, like broken legs on a giant bird anticipating touchdown on mother Earth.

Anxious eyes on the ground were shaded from the sun, as they looked eastward at the approach of the distant outline of the stricken 747. One of the fire crew reached for a cross around his neck, and kissed it with a silent prayer, his gaze never shifting from the distant spot in the sky.

"Full flaps", Larry called in response to Dave's instruction.

The airbrakes flicked up and down on the surface of the wings, slowing the aircraft to the desired airspeed for landing. Although there was nothing abnormal about the approach itself, Dave was impatient to get the aircraft on the ground, so that any other, long-anticipated failure would cease to matter.

He could see the bright red blobs of the fire trucks aligned on either side of the threshold of 28L, together with the whites and creams of the ambulances. Red and blue lights atop each vehicle could be seen, twinkling like stars.

Then the aircraft was roaring over the threshold and for the briefest moment, Larry was aware of the emergency fleet to his right moving in behind the landing aircraft, to follow it down the runway. The plane seemed to slew and rock violently as the wheels felt for the concrete below them. The Boeing jumped into the air again, before returning to the runway. The wrecked undercarriage began to disintegrate beneath the plane. Fortunately, nobody on board could hear tyres exploding above the sound of reverse thrust being applied to the engines. As it slowed and the undercarriage faltered, the Boeing began to slew to the right and off the runway.

The trembling from the corrupted undercarriage grew in intensity. Then the shaking that threatened to destroy it began to reduce as the aircraft slowed further, and then ground to a stop. Dave glanced up, but the wrecked and misshapen remains of the gantries that had brought them to their demise were too far away to be seen.

"Finish with engines. Let's get out of here!"

The emergency fleet was already alongside, the fire trucks covering the smouldering undercarriage with a blanket of foam, quickly stifling the small flames that would otherwise engulf the plane. Exit doors were tumbling to the ground, as the emergency slides exploded out into the warm air and descended quickly to the concrete. Ground staff ran forward into position at the foot of each slide. Passengers appeared in the doorways, their arms crossed in front of them like corpses, as one by one they jumped onto the slides and descended to the waiting arms below.

* * *

The passengers looked anxiously to each side in turn as the Boeing banked right and left on its final approach. Some were saying silent prayers to themselves. Others were passing rosaries urgently through their fingers in an attempt to complete their prayers before meeting their maker. Some of the people in the window seats were transfixed, with their noses pressed against the glass as the ground came closer and closer.

As the high rise buildings of San Francisco appeared on each side of the aircraft, Harvey reminded the passengers of the command to brace that they would hear from the captain. The cabin attendants were making final checks before they, too, strapped themselves in ready for the landing.

The command "Brace" caught many passengers unawares and involuntary cries came from several of them. Most of the people adopted the position that had been demonstrated by members of the cabin crew. A few stragglers looked around anxiously for some sort of guidance, before they, too, assumed their version of the brace position, looking anxiously to the people alongside them to see if they were sitting correctly.

The surprise was universal as the wheels were felt to touch down. Even the vibration was attributed in people's minds to the reverse thrust they had experienced so many times before. Some of the passengers sat upright as soon as they felt the wheels touch, as though in some misguided way the danger was over. When they saw their fellow passengers were still in the brace position, they quickly leaned forward again, like the child caught at the cookie jar.

The aircraft was slowing noticeably, and then shuddering to a standstill. Harvey was among the first on his feet, calling the cabin staff to the emergency doors, and instructing the passengers to stand up, but remain by their seats.

"Move quietly and calmly to the exit nearest your seat", came Harvey's authoritative voice. After that, the aircraft rang with voices shouting to passengers at the head of the slides.

"Go!" "Go!" "Go!"

There was a simple humility on the part of the passengers, as each obeyed the instruction shouted loudly in their ear and the rough handling of their arms as they were forcibly crossed over their chest. Then the equally humble act of faith as they jumped into the flapping white material, down which they were being transported quickly to the ground below. Ground staff at the foot of each slide jerked each passenger upright as they arrived and pushed them unceremoniously away from the aircraft.

One slide was being forced aside, as steps were placed at a doorway, now vacated by escaping passengers. Emergency staff were running up the steps as they were driven into place. Meanwhile, the passengers on the ground were being shepherded aboard buses brought close to the Boeing, to be whisked away to the terminal buildings and a health check and debriefing. Some tried to ask questions, or explain they needed to retrieve something from the overhead locker, to be told without any thought for the finer courtesies to shut up and get aboard the waiting bus.

As the buses drove away, the former passengers looked back at the stricken aircraft, seemingly floating on a sea of foam, while the chutes hanging from each of the open emergency exits swayed back and forth like some absurd decoration.

Aboard the plane, the injured passengers were being given first aid, fixing them up temporarily for their move to the terminal buildings, then on to the San Francisco's General Hospital. As each left the airliner, they were guided gently down the stairs now placed at the forward door, or carried out through the same route on stretchers and other appliances for the non-walking wounded. They were ferried away aboard the fleet of ambulances waiting by the stairway.

As the last of the injured passengers was led away, they glanced over at Lon Rosenman, whose cries had now been silenced through the mercy of anaesthesia. Some winced as they watched the fire crews use cutting gear to extricate the man from the airframe to which he had been inextricably united, and then from the blooded seat itself. Then he, too, was carried away, lying on his side on a stretcher, with the shape of the remains of the metal spar still in his body, forming its obscene projection from under the blanket.

Epitaph

Remarkably, due to the wonders of modern surgery, Lon Rosenman recovered completely from his injuries. Aside from a wide scar on his chest, and a similar scar and indentation in his back, nobody would suspect the ordeal he had encountered on that day in July 1971. Today, he lives quietly in San Diego. He has a new job; one that doesn't require him to travel. He speaks very little about the incident, preferring to leave his nightmares behind in San Francisco.

Captain Dave Christie suffered a stroke six months after landing PA845 successfully at SFO, which left him partially paralysed. He now lives quietly with Julie in the suburbs of San Francisco and ignores the occasional roar from an aircraft passing overhead, in-bound to SFO. He retains no interest in flying or planes. Julie is the ever-dutiful wife at his side, stalling every attempt to get him to talk to other pilots about his experiences.

Larry Savage continued with his flying career. He moved to American Airlines, an upcoming carrier at the time, and is now a captain qualified to command the Boeing 747 and all other wide-bodied jets in service with the airline. Arlyn Solberg inherited his father's company in real estate, and moved to his home town of

Tucson, Arizona to continue the business. Today, he is a success by most measures and sees the risks inherent in real estate as being infinitely more manageable than those in aviation.

Harvey Masters is the only member of the cabin staff that remains in the airline business. He now teaches aviation safety to new cabin crew recruits; he says jokingly that he feels uniquely qualified for his new career. All the other flight attendants from PA845 decided the glamour of flying was illusory at best, and that there were equally well paid (and safer) jobs that allowed them to keep their feet firmly on the ground.

As for the main player in the drama, the Boeing 747 labelled temporarily as PA845 underwent extensive repair and refurbishment. The review of the incident later judged it to be due to pilot error. It was found that the $V_1/V_R/V_2$ calculations were inadequate for the change of runway and should have been revised accordingly. The senior pilots were held to be at fault, because neither had taken action to revise the (now) faulty calculations. The ground operations procedures were criticised, in that it was known that runway 01R had been substituted for the closed 28L, but the information given to the aircrew had not advised them of the change until it was too late. The judgement was that the aircraft took off too far down the runway and as a result, had struck the ALS at the seaward end of the runway. As steel members of the gantries ripped their way through the underbelly of the Boeing, three of the four parallel hydraulic systems providing control of the flying surfaces were destroyed.

Nonetheless, the airliner was returned to service with Pan American and clocked up an additional forty thousand hours after the near-terminal events of that day in SFO. Boeing has received lavish praise for the design of the aircraft that by all design standards should have crashed into the ocean. It is the rare events like those in San Francisco in July 1971 that have seen the big Boeing jets set the standard for all other wide-bodied jets flying today.

*

I'm Getting Another Dog
By Danny MacCullough

When our Border Collie, Lass, died at the age of fifteen, my wife and I decided it was time to see if we could live without the company of a dog. For her, I knew it would be difficult. In twenty-five years of marriage there wasn't a day when she was apart from our dogs. First, Gilly and Meg, then Pip, finally Lass. For me though, because much of my working life was spent away from home, it was different. Although I loved the dogs I knew I could handle being "dogless".

I booked the holiday; it was to be a week in Magaluf. With all the arrangements in place, including renewing passports, we headed from our home in Cambridgeshire along the M11 to Stansted Airport. Part of the arrangement I made was to stay overnight at the Stansted Hilton Hotel. To me, that was a sensible thing to do – we wouldn't have to get up at some ungodly hour to catch the early morning flight. It was when we arrived at the hotel that things began to go wrong.

"Sir", said the receptionist, when I gave her my name, "you should have checked in yesterday – your flight left this morning".

I could sense my wife's embarrassment and anger. How could I make such a mistake? Did I not check the departure date in the travel documents? My response to that was I thought I had – not at all a satisfactory answer.

"Don't worry", the receptionist said reassuringly, "I'll get you on a flight in the morning but it will mean a surcharge as well as a payment for a room tonight".

I was so relieved. I would have willingly paid double the going rate.

"Now you pop along to the Lounge and have a coffee and I'll get back to you shortly" – the comforting words of the receptionist, comforting to my ears though I'm not sure if her words registered with my wife.

We sat in the lounge in total silence, the coffee untouched. I wanted to speak but dared not. It was my wife who broke the uncomfortable silence. Her earlier embarrassment and anger erupted like a sleeping volcano.

"How could you make such a hash of everything? You are hopeless – you always have been".

She was right of course. Metaphorically I threw up my hands in a show of undeniable guilt.

"Right", she exclaimed after what seemed like a never-ending pause – "we're going home!"

Going home! I was engulfed in total panic. Everyone knew we were going abroad on holiday – family, friends, everyone. I had even cancelled the daily papers at the Newsagent's. Fortunately for me the helpful receptionist came to my rescue. I'm sure that as she entered the Lounge she was proudly riding a white charger, not a knight in shining armour, more like a Joan of Arc, though the cause in this case was not as historically dramatic.

"Good news", she announced. "Your flight is booked for tomorrow morning and the hotel has kept your reservation".

I'M GETTING ANOTHER DOG

The week in Magaluf went well. The weather was sunny and warm, the hotel pool invitingly cool. On the return flight I felt relaxed. The trauma of the past week behind me, I began to think about the next holiday. "Where abroad would you like to go next?" I asked my wife.

"Abroad?" I didn't like the questioning tone in her voice. "Abroad?" she repeated. "I'm not going abroad – you can if you like". I knew why of course and her next words came as no surprise –

"I'm getting another dog".

*

Printed in the United Kingdom
by Lightning Source UK Ltd.
116554UKS00001B/4-51